DE ORE DOMINI

Preacher and Word in the Middle Ages

DE ORE

| Western
| Michigan
| University

DOMINI

Preacher and Word in the Middle Ages

Thomas L. Amos
Eugene A. Green
Beverly Mayne Kienzle

EDITORS

SMC XXVII
Medieval
Institute
Publications

Kalamazoo
Michigan

1989

© Copyright 1989 by the Board of the Medieval Institute
Kalamazoo, Michigan 49008-3851

Library of Congress Cataloging-in-Publication Data

De ore Domini : preacher and word in the Middle Ages / edited by
  Thomas L. Amos, Eugene A. Green, Beverly Mayne Kienzle.
       p.   cm. -- (SMC ; 27)
    ISBN 0-918720-28-1. -- ISBN 0-918720-27-3 (pbk.)
    1. Preaching--History--Middle Ages, 600-1500. I. Amos, Thomas
Leslie. II. Green, Eugene, 1944- . III. Kienzle, Beverly Mayne.
IV. Series: Studies in medieval culture ; 27.
BV4207.D42   1989
251'.009'02--dc20   89-38714
                                                                  CIP

Cover Design by Cynthia Tyler

Printed in the United States of America

Dedication

De Ore Domini is dedicated to Father Eugene A. Green, colleague and dear friend, whose ideas helped to initiate both this project and the Medieval Sermon Studies sessions at the International Congress on Medieval Studies. His careful and gracious suggestions shaped the quality of the articles here. After a five month struggle, he died of cancer on February 8, 1989. He contributed to the book as long as he was able to work, revising his own paper and editing others. From his hospital bed he dictated ideas for the preface, and in his last days made notes for the subject index. His essay, "Enoch, Lent and the Ascension of Christ," nearly completed, was finished by the editors and is placed at the beginning of this volume in his memory.

Thomas L. Amos
Beverly Mayne Kienzle

Contents

Editors' Preface	ix
Introduction: Medieval Preaching *John W. O'Malley, S.J.*	1
Enoch, Lent, and the Ascension of Christ *† Eugene A. Green*	13
The Two Worlds in Bede's Homilies: The Biblical Event and the Listener's Experience *Lawrence T. Martin*	27
Preaching and the Sermon in the Carolingian World *Thomas L. Amos*	41
Aelfric the Catechist *† Eugene A. Green*	61
Archbishop Stephen Langton and His Preaching on Thomas Becket in 1220 *Phyllis B. Roberts*	75
Maternal Imagery in the Sermons of Hélinand of Froidmont *Beverly Mayne Kienzle*	93
Humbert of Romans's Material for Preachers *Simon Tugwell, OP*	105

The *Rethorica nova* of Ramon Llull:
An *Ars praedicandi* as Devotional Literature   119
   Mark D. Johnston

Preaching the Passion:
Late Medieval "Lives of Christ" as Sermon Vehicles   147
   Lawrence F. Hundersmarck

New Sermon Evidence for the Spread of Wycliffism   169
   Simon Forde

From Treatise to Sermon:
Johannes Herolt on the *novem peccata aliena*   185
   Richard Newhauser

Pyres of Vanities: Mendicant Preaching on the
Vanity of Women and Its Lay Audience   211
   Thomas M. Izbicki

Egidio da Viterbo's Defense of
Pope Julius II, 1509 and 1511   235
   Ingrid D. Rowland

Subject Index   261

Editors' Preface

The idea for *De Ore Domini: Preacher and Word in the Middle Ages* grew from the Medieval Sermon Studies sessions at the International Congresses on Medieval Studies held at Western Michigan University. Since 1984, the Kalamazoo sessions have provided an annual forum that complements the work of the Medieval Sermon Studies Symposium, held at Oxford from 1979-86. This volume's development has been aided by the growing cooperation and communication among scholars in the field, made possible by the two conferences and by the *Medieval Sermon Studies Newsletter* begun by Gloria Cigman of the University of Warwick. The 1988 Symposium, held at Dijon, approved the inauguration of the International Medieval Sermon Studies Society, and the 1989 Kalamazoo session was the first sponsored by the Society. *De Ore Domini* presents the combined efforts of scholars from both sides of the Atlantic and thereby strengthens this increasing international collaboration.

This volume consists of thirteen essays, constituting a series of chapters in the history of preaching, and an introduction by John W. O'Malley, S.J., which surveys the development of methodology in sermon studies and provides a broad historical analysis of medieval preaching to serve as a background for the essays. The thirteen chapters present a diversity of historical periods, audiences, and methodologies. Ranging in time from the 700s to 1511, they cover a space that stretches from Johannes Herolt's Germany to Ramon Llull's Mallorca, from Bede's England to the Italy of Bernardino of Siena and Egidio da Viterbo. As our title suggests, the mouth of the Lord spoke with many voices, and the contributors to this volume provide important examinations of individual preachers, genres, and sources of sermons. Commentary and analyses are made of materials from the symbolical and allegorical to the practical and dogmatic, even

Preface

the educational. Further, the essays discuss how sermons were used at different periods and how they addressed the different audiences which their preachers faced. The studies illustrate new methods and concerns in the field of sermon studies, and, collectively, they point to a central problem in the historiography of sermons and preaching.

The origins of preaching and the sermon within Christianity can be traced rather exactly. Jesus entered the synagogue in Nazareth, read from Isaiah 61:1-2, and began to describe his mission as a fulfillment of that prophecy. This account from Luke 4:16-30 demonstrates how the early Church borrowed the long-existing practice of exegetical explications of portions of Scripture made during synagogue services and adapted it into its own patterns of worship. A second example can be seen in the "sermon" which Peter preached to the people of Jerusalem at Pentecost, as described in Acts 2:14-40. Taking as an impromptu "text" the prophecy of Joel 2:28-32, Peter explained the Pentecostal gift and preached one of the first surviving Christian missionary sermons.

The sermon developed and flourished as part of the liturgy during the Patristic Age. In the hands of such masters as Origen in the East and Augustine in the West, it became a vehicle for expounding doctrine and practices and for educating new and old Christians about correct patterns of moral behavior and spiritual life. These patristic sermons served as a treasure-chest of materials from which medieval preachers drew heavily in creating their own works. The studies in this volume point to the influence of Augustine, Caesarius of Arles, and Gregory the Great which stretched over the nine centuries that our authors cover. Our volume contains no studies of preaching in the eastern churches, an omission which we hope specialists in that literature will correct for a general audience.

During the Middle Ages, sermons and preaching took on a number of new roles, reflecting the changing nature and interests of clerics and the needs which sermons tried to answer. One of the reasons that the sermon spoke with many voices is the great change in the number of forms and styles of medieval preaching. To the sermons preached at mass of the patristic age

Preface

were added missionary sermons of the early Middle Ages. As structures within the Church--and within medieval life and thought generally--grew more complex, so did the styles of sermons and preaching. No one single thread runs through our thirteen papers. Taken together, however, they testify to the variety of medieval preachers and preaching materials and methods as the sermon was adapted over time to meet changing conditions.

In the early Middle Ages, roughly 600-1000, the sermon became a tool used in the conversion and education of new Christians. It also became an instrument of reformers who worked within the regional churches of the early medieval world to improve the conditions of both the institutional Church and the spiritual lives of the people they served. Lawrence T. Martin examines how Bede sought to make the experience of the biblical event come to life for his Anglo-Saxon audience. At a two-hundred year remove, Eugene A. Green describes how the Anglo-Saxon cleric Aelfric used the sermon as a means of sustained catechetical education for his hearers. Thomas L. Amos explores the role established for the sermon on the Continent by the Carolingian reforms and suggests some of the purposes for which Carolingian popular sermons were used.

The period of the high Middle Ages, 1000-1300, saw numerous developments within both the Church and the framework of medieval society. Some of these developments, such as the Investiture Controversy and the Crusades, both of which had an impact on preaching, do not fall within the confines of our volume. The secular clergy of this period are represented by Archbishop Stephen Langton, whose role in helping to establish the cult of Thomas Becket is described by Phyllis B. Roberts. This period saw a new flowering of the monastic world. Beverly Mayne Kienzle's examination of the maternal imagery of Hélinand of Froidmont looks at how symbolic imagery and devotion to the Virgin are reflected in the work of a Cistercian preacher. Simon Tugwell's study of the *ars praedicandi* of Humbert of Romans shows the materials and methods which the Dominicans used to help train members of the Order of Preachers. The scholastic learning of the universities came to influence preaching as well, as demonstrated in the study of Ramon Llull's *Rethorica nova* by Mark D. Johnston.

If not exactly "a distant mirror," the late Middle Ages, 1300-1500, was a period which seems to have consisted of one crisis after another. Spiritual problems of the sermon audiences received fuller treatment by many preachers of this period. Lawrence F. Hundersmarck examines two literary sources which helped preachers to emotionalize and personalize their sermons on the Passion. Simon Forde's discussion of the sermons of Philip Repyngdon demonstrates the variety of responses made in England to the challenges presented by John Wyclif. In Germany, preachers and theologians sought more precise and effective descriptions of sins to use in sermons, as Richard Newhauser shows in his study of Johannes Herolt and the nine accessary sins. Italian towns are the scene of our final two papers. The moralistic preaching of the mendicants and their dispute with canon lawyers on the vanity of women are treated by Thomas M. Izbicki. Ingrid D. Rowland examines the humanistic preaching of Egidio da Viterbo and his role in the complicated papal politics of Julius II. These studies well convey a sense of some of the later medieval problems.

The thirteen essays in this volume illustrate questions which are being addressed in contemporary sermon studies. Most of our authors are involved in editing the sources which they employ, or have already produced editions of sermons. The number of new editions and discoveries and the excellent *Quellenkritik* being done are among the great strengths of this field. In searching for a "standard" general history of medieval preaching, one of its greatest weaknesses is uncovered. The existing modern histories of preaching provide excellent treatments of specific periods and geographical areas or of preaching techniques, but no "standard" general history can be said to exist. The lack of such a work becomes more apparent as we learn more about medieval preachers and sermons.

For general information or a synthetic view, it is still necessary to turn to histories written in the nineteenth century. Some of these, such as Rudolf Cruel's *Geschichte der deutschen Predigt im Mittelalter* (Detmold, 1879; rpt. Darmstadt, 1966), have a regional focus but contain material on preachers and sources that still has value. More recent attempts at a synthesis for the Middle Ages as a period have not proved altogether successful. In almost all such works, the authors achieve their greatest success only in the periods of their own specializations.

For English-language works, the situation is worse. Our nineteenth-century histories tend to jump from Augustine to Gregory to the friars with few or no stops in between. Such is the case, for example, with Edwin C. Dargan, *A History of Preaching,* 2 vols. (New York, 1905-12; rpt. New York, 1968). Most modern English-language works on preaching are general works intended for seminary students of homiletics. Perhaps the best single-volume history of preaching in English is Karl Mattson's translation of Yngve Brilioth's *A Brief History of Preaching* (1945; rpt. Philadelphia, 1965). Its only faults are its brevity and the fact that work done since 1945 has tended to put it, also, out of date.

If our collection of studies has highlighted this weakness, it may also suggest a solution. It is clear from the work done and ongoing in the field of sermon studies that a single specialist in one area may no longer be able to write a good general history of medieval preaching. Our studies demonstrate the strengths of individual work in the various areas our authors cover. Perhaps the next comprehensive history of medieval preaching will be written by a team of scholars able to take advantage of the new discoveries of sources and studies of preachers to provide us all with a new single-volume or multi-volume history of medieval preaching. In the meantime, our volume takes a step forward to fill this gap in the religious and intellectual history of the Middle Ages.

In addition to the work done by the individual contributors to this volume and the Medieval Institute Publications staff, a number of other people played important roles in helping bring it about. The editors would like to thank Dr. Jonathan Black of the Hill Monastic Manuscript Library for writing computer programs that helped in the editorial process, and Margaret Studier and especially Sara Hazel of the Harvard Divinity School who

Preface

cheerfully and skillfully assisted with typing and processing nearly one quarter of the manuscript.

Thomas L. Amos
† Eugene A. Green
Beverly Mayne Kienzle

Introduction: Medieval Preaching

John W. O'Malley, S.J.

Preaching is at the center of the public ministry of the Christian church. When Christianity is at the center of a civilization, as it surely was in the Middle Ages, we can take it as axiomatic that study of preaching can contribute greatly to our understanding of that civilization. The articles presented in this volume are proof positive of how operative this axiom is today among scholars, who are not only exploiting the immense mass of materials relating to preaching that have come down to us but are doing so with a comprehensiveness and sophistication never before applied to them.

The complexity of this task is suggested even by reading the titles of the studies contained in this volume. The titles span almost a millenium and range over a wide variety of authors and genres. They indicate a major shift in the past several decades in how the history of preaching is done. Until just a few years ago, the history of preaching was a handmaid to the history of dogma or theology, for scholars searched sermon materials almost exclusively to discover the "doctrine" they taught.

Assessments of these materials tended to be based on the orthodoxy or "truly evangelical" nature of the doctrine, and the norms for the assessments of that doctrine derived rather obviously from the confessional bias of the scholar dealing with them. In other words, preaching was studied not *qua* preaching, but as a source for discovering and vindicating theological positions. Doctrinal content was its centerpiece. Typical questions concerned how St. Augustine presented his anti-Pelagian stance in his sermons, or how the theology in Calvin's sermons, for instance, correlated with the doctrine found in the *Institutes*.

Valid though such questions might be, they are extremely limited, and they fail to take into account all the other questions that might be asked of these materials. Most important, they fail to take into account the most distinctive feature of preaching, that is, it is a *speech-act*. The greatest challenge to its interpreters is to overcome the written and static nature of the evidence we possess in order to try to arrive at a better understanding of a reality that was oral and fleeting. Even as we concede that a full reconstruction of such a reality is by definition impossible, the admission of the reality begins to restructure the considerations with which we approach the written texts. In a word, that is what has been happening in the past few decades, as scholars try to take into account such features as audience, liturgical (or non-liturgical) setting, the variety of sermon forms, the vast variety of purposes that might animate a preacher, the political, ecclesiastical, and cultural pressures that might press upon him, the specific homiletical tradition in which he might stand, the use he might make of different "aids" to the preacher, differing understandings of the nature and function of scriptural exegesis, and even the maternal or paternal understanding he might have of the Godhead.

The complexity of the task is daunting. The scholar must draw upon the findings and methodology of exegesis, liturgy, theology, social history, cultural history, literary criticism, textual criticism, and many other disciplines, as he or she at the same time contributes to them. The studies contained in this volume do precisely that, and they stand as emblematic of where we have arrived in recent years.

We now see more clearly than ever before that the history of preaching is not an undifferentiated *continuum*, nor is it the story of the rise and fall of "true doctrine." In its various expressions, preaching is part and parcel of general culture, and we understand it best by studying it in that way. Thus a phenomenon that has been continuous in the history of Christianity and that has always prided itself on that continuity is seen to fall into various periods that correspond to larger shifts in culture.

We can therefore speak of "medieval preaching" as something that was notably different from what both preceded and followed it and that had distinctive characteristics. We must at the same time be acutely aware of the almost infinite variety that obtained during this long period. Even within a determined and quite circumscribed span of years, preaching was different in different settings and as done by different preachers. Generalizations are risky business.

Nonetheless, as medieval culture changed, so did preaching. The decline of the monasteries and the concomitant rise of the cities, universities, and mendicant orders had, for instance, an immense impact on how preaching was conceived and executed. A new corps of preachers entered the field, animated by a new vision of the preaching enterprise. A new style of culture came into being that radically transformed understanding of what truth was, whence and how it was derived, and how it was to be presented. A new set of spiritual needs began to be expressed and, if all went well, met.

We can, in fact, easily justify dividing the history of medieval preaching into at least two stages, with the line of demarcation somewhere around the twelfth and thirteenth centuries, as might be expected. The earlier stage was characterized by sermon forms and preaching practices that were obviously modeled on such Fathers of the Church as Augustine and Gregory the Great. Whether the sermons were delivered in a monastery or in a parish church (or its equivalent), the "sermon" tended to be dependent on the paraphrastic form of the so-called homily popularized in the West by Augustine and his followers.

In this form, the preacher generally followed the text of the pertinent pericope of the Bible in something like a line-by-line, or even word-by-word, exegesis. Even when he departed somewhat from this form in favor of a more topical treatment, he was still obviously dependent on the text, to which he frequently referred. We thus see how form influences content, for the interpretation of the scriptural text obviously had to provide a fair amount of the content in this form of preaching. Perhaps one of the most striking advances that preaching scholarship has made in recent decades is this attention to form as indicating the purpose and ethos of any given preachment and as shaping content. It is considerations along these lines, in fact, that give us our first basis for dividing the history of preaching into distinctive periods.

When we are dealing with the homily properly so-called, our attention is immediately directed to the style of exegesis that is applied to the sacred text, as I just pointed out, and we are thus led into another set of fascinating problems. Typological exegesis retained a firmer hold on the historical character of biblical texts, for instance, whereas the more poetic interpretation of the Cistercians and others in the twelfth century moved into a more transhistorical understanding. The Cistercians showed a decided preference, accordingly, for the sapiential literature of the Bible, especially the Song of Solomon. The center of interest of the preacher had moved into a more inward and intimate sphere. By comparing these two styles of exegesis what we see is a shift in spiritual values, even differing understandings of the nature of the Bible and of where one locates "the canon within the canon"--and, hence, differing understandings of Christianity and its message.

In this early period we also see clear continuities with the catechizing interests of Augustine and other Fathers. This indicates for us again the complexity of the phenomena that we often in undifferentiated manner gather under the heading of "preaching." The Jesuits would, in the sixteenth century, speak of their primary task as "ministry of the Word of God," in which they gave primacy of place to preaching in the usual sense of that word, but also included catechesis, public lectures ("adult education") on Scripture, and even private conversations, which they called a "kind of personalized sermon." The Jesuits' designation could well be applied to the medieval period, for the term "preaching" does not do full justice to the reality with which we are concerned.

Despite their obvious continuities with the patristic period, the sermon materials from the earlier Middle Ages strike us, when they are studied in their full context, with how different they are from what the Fathers produced. They come from a society, first and foremost, that was largely illiterate, and they address an audience that in many instances was imbued with the values of the barbarian tribes. As preachers and preaching theorists tried to respond to this new situation, they reconceived their task. Some preachers, moreover, were still supervised by their bishops, but many others by abbots and by agents of the emperor or some other lay magnate. Later on, with foundations like Cluny, preaching was almost completely displaced by other forms of liturgy, a development unknown in the patristic period. Moreover, as bishops became more enmeshed in the feudal system, they tended to abandon their traditional roles as the principal preachers to the Christian community.

With the Gregorian Reform, the new enthusiasm for the *vita apostolica* of the eleventh and twelfth centuries, and the first emergence of "the schools," preaching stood at the threshhold of a distinctively new phase. A renewed enthusiasm for its importance gradually took hold. This enthusiasm manifested itself in some members of the episcopacy, but eventually even monks such as the Cistercians began to be pressed into service. We also read of charismatic lay persons such as Peter the Hermit and Henry of Lausanne engaging in it, sometimes with disastrous results.

By the end of the twelfth century, the form of the sermon had begun to change. In its transitional phase, it fell midway between the more conversational and paraphrastic homily and the highly structured "thematic sermon" of the next few centuries. Whereas the homily relied upon persuading its listeners by touching the emotions through rhetorical devices, the newer form employed techniques of instruction--clearer organization, fuller documentation, and even some *distinctiones*. Yet it at first retained much of the informal sequence from one idea to another, usually by word association. At the end of the century, Alan of Lille defined preaching as an "instruction in faith and morals," a definition that would be accepted and repeated by preaching theorists throughout the rest of the Middle Ages. The maturation of the universities and the founding of the Dominicans and Franciscans in the early thirteenth century would bring these developments to fulfillment. The changes are so many that they are difficult even to enumerate.

The Gregorian Reform had strengthened the episcopate and set it on a path that would culminate in the massive efforts at

Trent to transform the bishops from "feudatories to pastors," as Hubert Jedin observed in this regard. The Council tried to reinstate preaching as the *praecipuum munus* of all bishops and, correlatively, of all parish priests. While in the intervening centuries many bishops did preach and preach effectively, the most active and respected body of preachers, however, would have been the friars, who with their canonical exemptions from episcopal authority over their preaching and their liberty to preach outside parochial settings went about the task in quite distinctive ways.

The friars were imbued with enthusiasm for the *vita apostolica*, which meant that they resurrected the ideal of itinerant preaching found in the gospels, Acts, and the Pauline epistles. Not Augustine the bishop but Paul the wandering evangelist became their implicit model. This model would lead even St. Francis far afield to preach to the infidel, the Sultan of Egypt. In later centuries, it would contribute to the friars' enthusiasm for accompanying the discoverers to the various "Indies."

Partly by reason of the itinerant nature of much of their ministry, the friars tended to detach preaching from a Eucharistic setting. While such detachment was not entirely new, it was a factor in encouraging a certain amount of "preaching" by lay persons in the later Middle Ages, especially in confraternities and similar associations. Women who were superiors of convents sometimes addressed their subjects on religious themes.

Meanwhile, the friars preached to large audiences in the public squares of the cities of Europe, outside churches and convents altogether. Theirs was an urban ministry--in a newly urban society, beset with new moral questions. While moralizing had long been part of the heritage of preaching, it received a powerful confirmation and impetus in the ninth chapter of the Rule of St. Francis, where the friars were instructed to preach "vice and virtue, punishment and glory."

That chapter is one of the most influential statements ever made about Christian preaching, and the history of its impact would be enlightening to trace in detail. Some indication of its importance can be gleaned from the fact, however, that many centuries later it is paraphrased in the decree on preaching of the

Council of Trent as if it did not require explanation or justification. I here call attention to that chapter of the Franciscan Rule because it illustrates a major problem in doing research in this field: one of the most extraordinarily influential statements regarding preaching was made in a document that at first glance would seem to have nothing to do with preaching. Where does the student of preaching draw a line about what is pertinent to the task?

Especially beginning with the thirteenth century, there is in fact so much that is *obviously* pertinent that we are almost overwhelmed by these materials alone. The monastic *scriptoria* continued their output, albeit with diminished importance. Now more significant would be the publishing industries that grew up around the universities, as scribes raced to produce the texts demanded by this new enterprise.

We tend to forget that the scholastic masters counted preaching as one of the three major duties incumbent upon them--*legere, disputare, praedicare*. They were "masters of the sacred page," and as such devoted much of their energy to the elucidation of the Bible, a task immediately relevant to the proclamation of the biblical message in sermons. Even their *summae* and *quaestiones* could not be completely divorced from their preaching concerns.

The scholastics left us, furthermore, not only a huge corpus of sermons, but an even larger corpus of materials to "aid" the preacher. In keeping with their peculiar style of learning, these materials took the form, *inter alia*, of compilations of data and handy *florilegia* of patristic and other texts that were organized on an entirely new basis. This means that the interpretation of the texts of sermons must take these factors into account and that critical editions of texts are almost a prerequisite if we are to know what is borrowed and what is new. Otherwise we do not realize that the most burning excoriation of the vices of the papal court in a fifteenth-century sermon, for instance, is in fact an unacknowledged borrowing from Bernard's *De consideratione* in the twelfth.

Of all the new genres pertinent to preaching that the scholastics produced, none was more important than their *artes prae-*

dicandi. These were handbooks on how to preach. For all the concern of the Fathers of the Church with preaching, only one work from the patristic era received from subsequent centuries consistent and frequent recognition as dealing with that subject, the *De doctrina christiana* of St. Augustine. Augustine's treatise was basically a work on invention--how to discover what to preach--and therefore had more direct import for theories of exegesis than for other aspects of the art of preaching. Nonetheless, in the fourth book, Augustine justified for the preacher the use of certain principles of classical rhetoric, while he at the same time vindicated a distinctively Christian rhetoric based on Scripture.

The *artes* surely manifest some continuity with Augustine's treatise, but they are remarkably different in their scope, style, and organization. They were a new genre. They held up a faithful mirror to the scholastic culture of which they were so integral a part. For all their limitations, they provided clear, pithy, and comprehensive directives concerning every aspect of the preaching task--the religious qualities requisite in the preacher; ways to adapt the material to diverse listeners; suggestions for appropriate dress, setting, posture, and gesture; suggestions as to how to modulate and vary one's delivery; listings of the topics about which one might preach; and, finally, directives as to where to find materials for the sermon and how to organize them.

As might be expected from the scholastics, the organization or structure of the sermon was an absolutely crucial consideration. Just as expectedly, the scholastics dealt with this problem in their own unique way. First of all, they characteristically insisted that there *be* a structure, and in that they emphatically departed from the "formless form" of the Fathers and of the monks, that is, the homily, which had no structure except the course of the scriptural passage upon which one was preaching. Second, for that structure they did not employ the "parts" that classical rhetoric prescribed for a speech--exordium, narration, confirmation, etc.--but devised a new set of parts, a new structure. This structure came to be known as "thematic," because of the critical role played in these sermons by the *thema* or quotation from Scripture with which they inevitably began.

The *artes* thus described and promoted a new style of preaching that, while adumbrated in the twelfth century, came into its own only with the full flowering of the universities. This thematic style was characterized by its highly developed structure of theme, pro-theme, prayer for divine aid, repetition of theme, division, and (usually) three clearly delimited and often unrelated parts. This structure, we must note, almost in and of itself reshaped the practice of exegesis, as the text of Scripture no longer determined the course of the sermon but became its jumping-off point. Thematic sermons were in many ways mini-*quaestiones*. Their tense, dialectical, and staccato energy contrasted mightily with the leisurely ramblings of the homily.

Just how frequently the rigid formulae of the *artes* was actually reduced to practice is still a matter of dispute, but most sermons as we have them in published form from the later Middle Ages at least show their influence. We are certain, however, that the written sermons in many instances do not correspond very closely to what was delivered. This is especially clear when we have Latin texts for sermons that were preached in the vernacular, as a comparison between the Latin and vernacular texts of the sermons of St. Bernardino of Siena evinces. Although by this time most sermons were preached in the language of the people, the Latin texts are what has principally survived--which presents another immense methodological problem.

The *artes* must be viewed by and large in a university setting, and, indeed, the thematic sermon is sometimes referred to in its purest form as the "university sermon." The friars had a university education, or at least an education based on scholastic principles, yet they were generally called upon to preach to popular audiences, which would be impatient with both the form and much of the content that the thematic sermon prescribed. Popular preaching surely deviated from the *artes* in important respects, and it focused not so directly on Scripture and doctrine as it did on "vice and virtue, punishment and glory." It was characterized not so much by loving ruminations on the scriptural text or by the resolution of abstruse doctrinal questions as it was by stories, legends, and popular *exempla*. This preaching, with its emphasis on "punishment and glory" is sometimes referred to as "penitential," for it called for conversion of life--conversion away from the sins and vanities supposedly rampant in the culture of merchants, artisans, day-laborers, and brokers in local and regional politics. When used with due caution, sermons in this style can be made to reveal something of that culture.

By the end of the Middle Ages, therefore, at least three distinctive styles of preaching were being practiced. There was the "university sermon," delivered to those who could be expected to appreciate it. There was the popular preaching of the mendicants, practiced on a wide scale throughout the cities of Europe. There was the homily, which was still known and admired, it seems, in certain restricted circles. There were, moreover, various admixtures and adaptations of all three forms. The first two of them were coming under increasing criticism as being either too abstract and academic, on the one hand, or too vulgar and sensational on the other. They were both criticized for being too far removed from the text of Scripture.

By the beginning of the fifteenth century, the classical revival had begun to take hold in Italy and affect in notable ways the elite strata of its culture. Central to the revival of the study of the classics was the study of rhetoric, that is, the art of oratory. It was inevitable that this phenomenon would have an impact on how preaching was conceived and done. It was inevitable that the principles of classical rhetoric would be applied to preaching and begin to tear down the sturdy edifice the Middle Ages had erected.

As best we now know, the first person to have made this application in any consistent way was Pier Paolo Vergerio the Elder. In Padua, around the turn of the century, he applied principles of classical panegyric to funeral oratory and to the praise of the saints. As the decades passed, Vergerio's method began to be applied to Christ and to the mysteries of the Christian faith, so that by the end of the century we have another new style of preaching operative in refined circles in Italy such as the papal court--with all the correlative changes this implies for exegesis, for response to the new aesthetic and religious sensibilities of the audience, for the education of the preacher, and even for the understanding of what the sermon is all about and is supposed to accomplish. A renewed appreciation for the historical character of the Bible ensued; it was considered more a book of the *magnalia Dei* than, as for the scholastics, the Creed writ large. We begin to move from *sermo* to *oratio*, from *praedicare* to *concionare*.

Part and parcel of the revival of antiquity that the Renaissance sought, however, was also a revival of the Fathers. In somebody like St. Leo the Great, as well as in the oratory of some of the Greek Fathers, preachers in the Renaissance found some models for their new classicizing structures and style. But in Augustine, Gregory, and Origen they found the simpler homiletical form, for which they soon began to express a new admiration. It was this style that Erasmus came to admire both in Origen and in his own contemporary, the Franciscan, Jacques Vitrier.

Even had the Reformation not happened, therefore, it is certain that preaching--"ministry of the Word"--was entering into a new period, one that would be quite different from the Middle Ages. When Erasmus published in 1535 his great treatise on preaching, the *Ecclesiastes sive de arte concionandi*, he dealt the death-blow to the *artes praedicandi*. Replacing the *artes* would eventually be the new "ecclesiastical rhetorics."

The Reformation, however, accelerated and drastically modified changes that had long been in the making. Even as Catholics resisted the Reformation and tried to contain its impact, they were thereby affected by it in innumerable ways, including the content and style of their preaching. Once again, preaching would be a faithful mirror of the profound changes taking place in culture and religion and an important vehicle for promoting them.

Enoch, Lent, and the Ascension of Christ

† *Eugene A. Green*

>This essay was delivered by Eugene A. Green at the Twenty-second International Congress on Medieval Studies in 1987 and was completed for this volume by Beverly Mayne Kienzle and Thomas L. Amos. To investigate why Aelfric included Enoch in a Lenten sermon, the essay examines Aelfric's Lenten and Ascension preaching as well as biblical commentary, liturgical practice, other sermons, Old English poetry, and iconography. Eugene A. Green's summary of Aelfric's life and work is found in the note preceding his "Aelfric the Catechist" in this volume.

Enoch, the seventh descendant from Adam, appears numerous times in Old English literature: in homilies, saints' lives, letters, biblical commentary, and poetry. The Anglo-Saxon homilist Aelfric (ca. 950-ca. 1010) called upon Enoch frequently and in a way that leads us to discover a powerful association between the translation of Enoch and the Ascension of Christ. Starting from his sermon for the first Sunday of Lent (Second Series), this essay will investigate why Aelfric departed from his source to mention Enoch, who was not generally associated with Lent. We will examine biblical commentary, liturgical practice, Ascension sermons, Old English poetry, and iconography to observe the development of a tradition linking Enoch, Elias, and Christ, as well as striking parallels between the representations of Enoch's translation and Christ's Ascension. Considering these various appearances of Enoch will permit us to reflect on the literary and theological purposes served by the invocation of his name.

Near the beginning of his sermon for the First Sunday of

Enoch, Lent, and the Ascension of Christ

Lent (Second Series), Aelfric praises the values and virtues of the Lenten discipline and observes that Christ's forty-day fast was foreshadowed by the fasts of both Moses and Elias. But while he is speaking about Elias, Aelfric says: ". . . and afterwards he was transported bodily in a celestial chariot to the life above, and will come again, he and Enoch, against Antichrist, that they may overpower the Devil's lies with God's truth."[1]

Aelfric had two chief sources for this homily. The body of the sermon devolves from the pseudo-Augustinian sermon No. 310, *De Misericordia*.[2] The introductory section of Aelfric's homily, less than one-quarter of the total, includes the reference to Enoch and is sprung from Gregory the Great's Homily 16 for the First Sunday in Lent, a sermon found in Paul the Deacon's Homiliary for the first Sunday of Lent.[3] Gregory, however, speaks only of Moses, Elias, and Christ and does so, it seems, simply to point up their fast of forty days as model for the Church's Lenten discipline.

Tradition does not generally associate Enoch with the forty-day Lenten fast, and Aelfric does not try to create or force such an association. Why, then, does Enoch appear in Aelfric's sermon? Why does Aelfric break momentarily from his Gregorian train of thought and build into his homily this almost parenthetical but seemingly important reference to Enoch? One approach to these questions lies in biblical commentary and liturgical practice; another is grounded in some relevant Anglo-Saxon art.

In the literature of biblical commentaries, Enoch is linked with Elias on several occasions. There are three principal locations where one might expect to find discussions linking Enoch and Elias: Genesis, Kings, and Apocalypse.[4] The *locus classicus* for the most traditional association between Enoch and Elias is Apoc 11:3: "And I have two witnesses whom I will appoint to prophesy."[5] The weight of a long and heavy tradition makes these two witnesses Enoch and Elias. Among traditional commentators close to Aelfric's time we find Enoch and Elias identified as the two witnesses in Bede, in Pseudo-Bede, and in Ambrosius Autpertus.[6] Beyond Aelfric's day, the tradition continues through the *Glossa ordinaria*, Hugh of St. Cher, and the *Bible Moralisée* (with its wonderful depiction of the translation of Enoch: long frizzy hair, hands in *orans* position, looking a bit befuddled, carried aloft by four angels holding him in a blanket).[7] Typically, therefore, and over the course of a long tradition with which Aelfric was familiar, commentaries on the Apocalypse speak of both Enoch and Elias when the "two witnesses" are mentioned.[8]

One might expect to discover an association of Enoch with Elias and a note on their parallel destinies in biblical commentaries on the second chapter of second Kings: the rapture of Elias (2 K 2:11-13). Rabanus Maurus, drawing some of his material from a sermon by Gregory, establishes extended comparisons and distinctions between Patriarch Enoch and Prophet Elias.[9] In general, however, Kings' commentaries on the translation of Elias do not automatically, not even generally, mention Enoch.[10]

In Genesis commentaries, on the other hand, a quite different state of affairs is found. From the patristic age to the Carolingians, Genesis commentators on Enoch regularly described his translation in vague terms which linked it to the Last Judgment.[11] Bede, drawing upon Ambrose's *Enarratio in Psalmum XLV*, gives what seems to be the first instance of an Anglo-Saxon exegetical tradition for Genesis associating Enoch and Elias with the apocalyptic battle against the Antichrist:

> The universal faith of the Church believes that Enoch, before the day of judgment, with the coming of Antichrist imminent, will come again with Elias in order to convert this age, insofar as, by the persuasion and wisdom of such distinguished teachers, the hearts of men can be instructed and strengthened to endure and to prevail against the onslaughts of the Son of Perdition.[12]

Proof texts could be multiplied; in fact, this association can be found throughout Bede's writings: even, as his editor noted, in the grammatical work *De schematibus et tropiis*. The conclusion to which the evidence points is that Bede originated a tradition which links Enoch and Elias in an almost reflexive kind of association in later Anglo-Saxon biblical commentaries on the relevant passages in Genesis and Apocalypse. This tradition also influenced literary and artistic works.

It is worth noting a special emphasis given to Genesis commentaries by monasteries with which Aelfric's name and influence are associated. Aelfric wrote a liturgical guide commonly called the "Letter to the Monks of Eynsham," of whose monastery he was made abbot in 1005. The letter was edited in the late nineteenth century by Mary Bateson, neither flawlessly nor completely.[13] Generally known as "Aelfric's Letter to the Monks of Eynsham" by literary historians and "The Eynsham Customary" by liturgists, this document is divided into three sections: (1) the letter proper in which Aelfric explains to his brother monks why he is writing to them; (2) the *consuetudo* proper, based largely on the *Regularis Concordia*; and (3) a concluding section in which Aelfric adds details of monastic observance, dealing especially with the lectionary and the *responsiones* for the Night Office. This last section supplements the *Regularis Concordia* and gives important witness to late tenth- to early eleventh-century English monastic usage.[14]

The Eynsham Customary is based upon the *Ordo Romanus* XIIIA, which dates to the first half of the eighth century.[15] The Eynsham Customary stipulates that the whole of scripture be read in the Night Office during the course of each liturgical year. During Lent, for instance, from Septuagesima until the fourth week of Lent, the Pentateuch plus Joshua and Judges would be read; from Passion Sunday till the eve of Easter, Jeremiah would be read. The Eynsham Customary deviates from the *Ordo Romanus* arrangement, however. It concentrates its attention during Septuagesima and the first weeks of Lent on Genesis alone, followed at mid-Lent by Exodus. In the words of Aelfric:

> Because you have asked, brothers, that [I] write about how you ought to read or sing during the course of the ecclesiastical year, I shall explain to you in accordance with the authority of the church and in accordance with the custom with which we have been versed thus far, that we ought to read Genesis from Septuagesima until mid-Lent.... In mid-Lent we read Exodus.[16]

On Sundays and major feasts, the Office recited or sung during the night had three Nocturns; each Nocturn included four lessons. The lessons of the first two Nocturns were scriptural (from Genesis, for example, in the early weeks of Lent); lessons for the third Nocturn included the gospel incipit and a homily or sermon upon it or a biblical commentary. It bears repeating at this point that the chief source for Aelfric's sermons was the homiliary, which provided the readings for the third Nocturn on Sundays and feasts.

To return to Enoch, several observations can be made. Enoch, of course, first appears in the book of Genesis, and it is Genesis which, according to Aelfric's directions, is meant to receive such focused attention during the first half of Lent. Genesis commentaries, it seems likely, provided some of the materials needed for Lenten reflection during the Divine Office.[17] And so the book itself and commentaries upon it were likely receiving greatest attention at the liturgical season for which Aelfric's sermon was designed.[18]

Furthermore, Aelfric's habits of composition can also help us to understand the appearance of Enoch in this Lenten homily. At the start of this sermon, it appears that Aelfric wanted to establish parallels to Christ's forty-day fast. Inspired by his Gregorian source, Moses and Elias sprang to mind. In his sermon for the Lord's Ascension,[19] Aelfric faced the same problem: seeking parallels to Christ's Ascension, Elias again came to mind, but so too did Enoch, again inspired by the Gregorian source. Aelfric's Second Series, in which the Lenten sermon appears, was completed no later than 995, just a few years after he had completed the First Series, in which the Ascension sermon appears. Aelfric's memory was such that mention of Christ's rising (*a Easterlican maersunge Cristes aeristes*) and mention of Elias (*se maera witega Elias*) brought clearly to mind a Gregorian Ascension homily about Christ's rising and Elias, in which Enoch also features.[20] Recent scholarship has shown us the power of recall and association from memory in Aelfric's homiletic method.[21] In a situation where a Lenten homily by Gregory is being used, it does not seem far-fetched for a mind such as Aelfric's to draw upon another Gregorian homily, especially one used elsewhere already and appropriate to this new context.

Aelfric mentions Enoch in the second paragraph of his Lenten sermon. The opening paragraph, still unsourced and perhaps

Enoch, Lent, and the Ascension of Christ

Aelfric's own invention, presents a comprehensive liturgical picture: the movement through Lent from fasting to feasting, from repentance to forgiveness. The preacher urges prayer, abstinence, and almsgiving upon his congregation so that, as he says, "we may with boldness and spiritual joy honor the Paschal festival of Christ's ascension / resurrection."[22] Thorpe translates "*maersunge Cristes aeristes*" as "the celebration of Christ's ascension"; he is probably ill-advised to use "ascension" where context would suggest "resurrection" as a more exact translation. Even so, the age of Aelfric understood that Easter and Ascension, though separated by forty days, celebrated two inseparable halves of the same theological event. In any case, this paragraph of his Lenten sermon leads us to think about Aelfric's Ascension Day preaching. In fact, Aelfric has a homily for Ascension which, like the one for First Lent, is heavily indebted to Gregory.

Gregory's sermon for the Feast of Ascension is most regularly studied because of its extensive use by Cynewulf in *Christ II*. The sermon inspires the Cynewulfian question about why the angels of Christmas did not wear white garments at Christ's Nativity but do wear white at his Ascension.[23] Aelfric's homily raises the same question. Following Gregory's lead, Aelfric introduces the Ascension of Jesus with an elaborate description of its two Old Testament forecasters. Just as the fasting of Moses and Elias introduced the fasting of Jesus, so here the ascension of Enoch and Elias introduces the Ascension of Jesus. Aelfric says:

> We read in the old law that two men of God, Enoch and Elias, were lifted up to heaven without death. . . . They . . . continue in some secret dwelling place . . . until they shall return at the end of the world against Antichrist. . . .[24]

All three men--Enoch, Moses, and Elias--are types of Christ. But while Moses and Elias clearly embody a spirit appropriate to the initiation of the Lenten fast, Elias and Enoch embody a spirit appropriate to the conclusion of the Lenten fast: a spirit of Easter joy; a spirit of resurrection; a spirit of ultimate triumph over the forces of evil, Antichrist, and death itself. I would hasten to add that, indebted as Aelfric is to Gregory, the eventual confrontation with Antichrist is his own addition and, as noted, is a detail regularly found in Genesis commentaries on Enoch.[25]

Further connections between Enoch and the Ascension, as well as Enoch and Lent, can be considered in light of Enoch's treatment in several works of Old English poetry and art. One final piece of evidence further suggests that it was Genesis commentaries on the translation of Enoch that brought this patriarch to mind at the beginning of a season which ends in resurrection and ascension and brought him to mind as soon as Aelfric mentioned Elias, Enoch's partner in ascension.

In the *Old English Genesis*, that long biblical paraphrase traditionally associated with the name of Caedmon, Enoch features importantly. In the poem's list of patriarchs, most of them receive little more than honorable mention. Enoch, however, is given some thirty lines. In lines that at once bring Christ himself to mind, he is called "the fair first-born" of his father. After describing a life characterized by cloudless happiness and peaceful leadership, the poet says that "Enoch, while still alive, went travelling with the King of Angels out of this transitory life [and did so] in those robes which his spirit received before his mother brought him forth to men."[26]

Verbal echoes that associate Enoch with Christ (and with the victorious Christ at that) are made explicit in one of the Junius manuscript drawings.[27] Here we see the translation of Enoch, not an especially remarkable scene perhaps, until we look at a few contemporary representations of Christ's Ascension. Then we notice two things in particular about the representation of Enoch. First of all, his leave-taking is being observed by twelve men, just as the twelve apostles are inevitably depicted viewing Christ's Ascension. More interesting still, his disappearance is described in the same visual language as the disappearance of Christ at the Ascension. Represented, as it were, from the point of view of the apostles, the disappearance of Enoch emphasizes his passage into a cloud by showing just his lower body and feet as he moves from sight.

A similar iconography is deployed to represent the Ascension of Jesus. In the Bury St. Edmunds Psalter, for instance, at the very top of the composition we see what appears to be the bottom of a cloud into which Jesus is entering and through which he is disappearing from the view of the apostles.[28] As Christ disappears, we see the hem of his garment and of course his feet surrounded by a mandorla. The feet of the Bury St. Edmunds Psalter are the same as the feet of the Hereford Troper, at least in their shared emphasis on disappearance.[29] A later and more highly stylized version of the same disappearance motif appears in the twelfth-century Shaftesbury Psalter.[30] Of all three examples, the Troper depicts more of Christ's garments and includes the disappearing legs of Christ up to and including the right knee.

Two remaining artistic details from the art of the Ascension are relevant to the Enoch problem. In some representations of the Ascension, the composition includes a cloud. English tradition from Bede onwards was greatly interested in the cloud and felt compelled to comment on it.[31] In particular, the point is made that the cloud was present, not because the ascending Christ needed it to convey him to heaven, but rather because Christ the Judge would return on the same cloud at the end of time. As the Blickling Homilist puts it: "He disappeared in a cloud from their sight and ascended into heaven as a sign that from thence in like manner he will on Doomsday come again upon this earth."[32] The emphasis is eschatological. Also eschatological is the attention to place.

The Hereford Troper, for instance, on its representation of Christ's Ascension inscribes "mons Oliveti" beneath the feet of Christ and above the heads of the onlookers, although there is no similar inscription for Enoch.[33] But the Mount of Olives is an equally significant feature of the Enoch story. According to a considerable body of apocalyptic commentary typified by Adso, *mons Oliveti* will be the location for the Final Battle and the spot on which Antichrist will be killed. In the words of Adso's *De Antichristo*:

> Afterwards [Antichrist] will slay Elias and Enoch . . . until at last the ire of God descends upon him. . . . We have been taught that Antichrist will himself be killed upon the Mount of Olives--the very mount from which the Lord ascended into heaven.[34]

Even as regards the place of Christ's Ascension, then, an association between Christ and Enoch exists, and specifically at the point where suffering turns to glory.

Thus the elements common to the representation of Christ's Ascension are deployed in representations of Enoch's departure: the body disappearing into a cloud, the feet dangling out, a band of men staring up into the heavens. In addition, the tradition of apocalyptic exegesis associates Enoch with the Mount of Olives: the location of final confrontation with the Antichrist, the location of Christ's final victory, the location of Enoch's resurrection and departure into heaven.

This shared iconography of ascension or disappearance is complex. Nevertheless, several uncomplicated comments can be offered: (1) the representation of the disappearing Christ (and Enoch) is unique to England; (2) the disappearance / ascension motif appears as a significant art form in the late tenth to early eleventh centuries and, by some art historians, is regarded as precocious; (3) the disappearance / ascension motif is associated with a well-defined cult of the Ascension in England that, among other things, emphasizes the Church of the Ascension in Jerusalem and the permanent impress of the feet of Christ on the ground from which he departed: observations made in both vernacular and Latin literature.[35]

We will perhaps never know exactly why Aelfric departed from his Gregorian source in order to mention Enoch and make an eschatological observation. It is clear, however, that long before Aelfric's day, Enoch already held a secure place in Genesis and Apocalypse commentaries and enjoyed a powerful association as well with the Ascension of Christ. It is clear, too, that Old English artists, poets, and other homilists were fond of this seventh descendent from Adam, Patriarch Enoch. Perhaps, considered from a liturgical perspective, this biblical figure who lived for 365 years and "walked with God" seemed wholly appropriate company for the pilgrimage from fasting to feasting, from Lent through Easter and Ascension. Perhaps, considered from the cultural-historical perspective of an age that took the apocalypse so seriously, Enoch reminded his audience that while death must come to all of Adam's children, the triumphs of Antichrist are inevitably temporary and the reign of Christ is ultimately assured.

Notes

[1] ". . . and siððan hé wearð geferod lichamlice on heofenlicum cræte to ðam upplican lífe, and cymð eft, hé and Enóch, togeanes Antecriste, to ði þæt hí þæs deofles leasunge mid Godes soðfæstnysse oferstælan" (Aelfric, *Dominica I in Quadragesima*, Benjamin Thorpe, *The Homilies of the Anglo-Saxon Church. The First Part, containing the Sermones Catholici or Homilies of Aelfric*, 2 vols. [London, 1844-46; rpt. New York, 1971], 2:100-01).

[2] See Wolfgang Becker, "The Latin Manuscript Sources of the Old English Translations of the Sermon *Remedia Peccatorum*," *Medium Aevum*, 45 (1976):145-52; and "The Manuscript Sources of Aelfric's Catholic Homily II 7--A Supplemental Note," *Medium Aevum*, 48 (1979):105-06.

[3] Gregory the Great, *Homiliae in euangelia*, 16, *PL* 76:1135-38, and especially 1137; and Paul the Deacon, *Homiliarum*, 1.76, *PL* 95:1223-28.

[4] For a general survey of exegetical works on Enoch and Elias with reference to the Apocalypse, see R. E. Kaske, "Dante's 'DXV' and 'Veltro,'" *Traditio*, 17(1961):185-254, especially 200-24.

[5] "Et dabo duobus testibus meis et prophetabunt . . ." (Apoc 11:3).

[6] Bede, *In Apocalypsin*, *PL* 93:164; Pseudo-Bede, *Commentariorum in Apocalypsin*, 5, *PL* 100:1147C-1149C; and Ambrosius Autpertus, *Expositionis in Apocalypsin*, ed. R. Weber, *Ambrosii Autperti Opera*, pars 1, CCCM 27 (Turnhout, 1975), pp. 414-16.

[7] *Glossa Ordinaria*, *PL* 114:730 (at duobus testibus); Hugh of St. Cher, *Commentariis in totam Sacram Scripturam*, 8 vols. (Lyons, 1655-59), 7:398r; and *Bible Moralisée* (Vienna, Österreichische Nationalbibliothek, Codex vindobonensis palatinus 2554), fol. 3a (see Reiner Haussher, ed., *Bible Moralisée--Faksimile Ausgabe*, Codices Selecti, 40, 2 vols. [Graz, 1973]).

[8] See also Richard Kenneth Emmerson, *Antichrist in the Middle Ages: A Study of Medieval Apocalypticism, Art and Literature* (Seattle, 1981), especially pp. 95-101.

[9]Rabanus Maurus, *Commentaria in libros IV Regum*, 4, ii, *PL* 109:222-23.

[10]See, e.g., Claudius of Turin, *Quaestiones XXX super libros Regum, IV, PL* 107:771-72; and Angelomus of Luxeuil, *Enarrationes in libros Regum*, 4, ii, *PL* 115:495-98.

[11]See, e.g., Rabanus Maurus, *Commentarius in Genesim*, 4, 7 and 5, 21 *PL* 107:507-08 and 510; and Angelomus, *Commentarius in Genesim*, 4, v, 17, *PL* 115:151.

[12]"Quem tamen fides ecclesiae universalis habet ante diem iudicii, id est imminente adventu Antichristi, rediturum cum Elia ad conversationem huius seculi, quatenus auctoritate ac doctrina tantorum virorum erudiantur et confirmentur corda hominum ad tolerandam et superandam persecutionem eiusdem filii perditionis . . ." (Bede, *In Genesim*, II, v. 23-24, *PL* 91:80; and ed. C. W. Jones, CCSL 118A [Turnhout, 1967], p. 96; see Jones's analysis of the sources there. One additional source for this passage may have been Gregory the Great, *Homiliarum in Ezechielum*, 1, xii, 7-10, *PL* 76:921-22).

[13]Mary Bateson, ed., *Excerpta ex institutionis monasticis Aethelwoldi episcopi Wintonensis compilata in usum fratrum Eyneshamnensium per Aelfricum Abbatem*, in G. W. Kitchin, ed., *Compotus Rolls of the Obedientiaries of St. Swithun's Priory, Winchester* (London, 1892), Appendix, pp. 171-79. (A new and complete edition is being prepared by Milton McC. Gatch.)

[14]Milton McC. Gatch, "The Office in late Anglo-Saxon Monasticism," in *Literature and Learning in Anglo-Saxon England*, ed. Michael Lapidge and Helmut Gneuss (Cambridge, 1985), pp. 341-62.

[15]For a comparison of Aelfric's Letter and the *Ordo Romanus* XIIIA, see J. R. Hall, "Some Liturgical Notes on Aelfric's Letter to the Monks at Eynsham," *Downside Review*, 93 (1975):297-303.

[16]"Quia rogastis, fratres, scribi vobis qualiter legere sive cantare per anni circulum in ecclesia debeatis, exponam vobis secundum auctoritatem ecclesiasticam et secundum consuetudinem in qua hucusque conversati sumus, ita ut in septuagessima legamus genesim usque in mediam quadragessimam. . . . Media vero quadragessima, legimus exodum" (Letter to the Monks, ed. Bateson, *Compotus Rolls*, p. 194; English translation by Beverly Kienzle).

[17]See nn. 11-12 above for examples of Genesis commentaries; and n. 3 above for Gregory's Homily for the First Sunday in Lent and its appearance in Paul the Deacon.

[18]See n. 11 above.

[19]Thorpe, *Homilies*, 2:294-310.

[20]Thorpe, *Homilies*, 2:98 and 100. For the Gregorian text, see Gregory the Great, *Hom. in Evang.* 29, *PL* 76:1216-17.

[21]See, e.g., James E. Cross, "'Legimus in ecclesiasticae historiis': A Sermon for All Saints and its Use in Old English Prose," *Traditio* 33 (1977): 128-31. Cross also discusses Aelfric's use of recall and association, rather than direct consultation of sources, elsewhere, as in "Aelfric--Mainly on Memory and Creative Method in Two Catholic Homilies," *Studia Neophilologica*, 41 (1960):135-55; and "The Literate Anglo-Saxon--On Sources and Disseminations," (Gollancz Lecture) *Proceedings of the British Academy*, 58 (1972):67-100.

[22]". . . þæt we bealdlice, mid gastlicere blisse, ða Easterlican mærsunge Cristes æristes wurðian moton . . ." (Aelfric, *Dominica I in Quadragesima*, ed. Thorpe, *Homilies*, 2:98).

[23]See, e.g., Peter Clemoes, "Cynewulf's Image of the Ascension," in *England Before the Conquest: Studies in Primary Sources Presented to Dorothy Whitelock*, ed. Peter Clemoes and Kathleen Hughes (Cambridge, 1971), pp. 293-94 and see p. 295, n. 4 for a comparison with Aelfric.

[24]"We rædað on ðære ealdan æ þæt twegen Godes men, Enoh and Helias, wæron ahafene to heofonum butan deaðe. . . . Hí . . . and drohtniað on sumum diglan earde . . . oðþæt hi eft ongean cyrron, on ende þisre worulde, togeanes Antecriste . . ." (Aelfric, *Sermo in Ascensione Domini*, ed. Thorpe, *Homilies*, 2:306-08).

[25]Compare here the treatment of Enoch in the Bedan commentary, n. 12 above, with the treatment of Enoch in the Carolingian commentaries referred to in n. 11. Aelfric seems to be drawing on an Anglo-Saxon exegetical tradition for his remarks.

[26]". . . ac he cwic gewat [caesura] mid cyning engla/ of þyssum laenan [caesura] life feran/ on þam gearwum [caesura] þe his gast onfeng/ ær hine to monnum [caesura] modor brohte" (*Genesis B*, lines 1210-13, ed. George Philip Krapp, *Genesis B. The Junius Manuscript*, The Anglo-Saxon Poetic Records, 1 [New York, 1969], p. 38).

Eugene A. Green

[27]Oxford, Bodleian Library, MS Junius 11 (S.C. 5123), p. 11. For a description of this manuscript, see Elzbieta Temple, *Anglo-Saxon Manuscripts, 900-1066*, A Survey of Manuscripts Illuminated in the British Isles, 2 (London, 1976), pp. 76-78.

[28]Bury St. Edmunds Psalter, Vatican, Bibliotheca Apostolica, MS Reginensis latinus 12, fol. 73^v. For a description of this manuscript, see Temple, *Anglo-Saxon Manuscripts*, pp. 100-02.

[29]Hereford Troper, London, British Library, MS Cotton Caligula A. XIV, fol. 18. For a description, see Temple, *Anglo-Saxon Manuscripts*, pp. 113-15.

[30]Shaftesbury Psalter, London, British Library, MS Landsdowne 383, fol. 13^v. For a description, see C. M. Kaufmann, *Romanesque Manuscripts, 1066-1190*, A Survey of Manuscripts Illuminated in the British Isles, 3 (London, 1975), pp. 82-84.

[31]See, e.g., Bede, *Expositio Actuum Apostolorum*, 1, 11, ed. M. L. W. Laistner, CCSL 121 (Turnhout, 1983), p. 9.

[32]". . . & he mid þy tacne swa on þaem wolcne from heora gesihþe gewát, & in heofenas asrag, þoet he þonne swa wile on domes daeg est on þysne middangeard cyman in wolcne . . ." (Blickling Homilies, 9, ed. R. Morris, *The Blickling Homilies of the Tenth Century*, EETS, o.s. 58, 63, 73 [London, 1874-80], 58:121).

[33]See n. 29 above.

[34]"Postquam Heliam et Enoch interfecerit . . . ad ultimum veniet iudicium Dei super eum. . . . Tradunt autem doctores quod in monte Oliveti Antichristus occidetur . . . in illo loco, contra quem unde ascendit Dominus ad celum . . ." (Adso, *De Ortu et Tempore Antichristo*, PL 40:1134; and ed. D. Verhelst, CCCM 45, [Turnhout, 1976], pp. 28-29).

[35]See Meyer Shapiro, "The Image of the Disappearing Christ: The Ascension in English Art Around the Year 1000," *Gazette des Beaux-Arts* (1943): 135-52; rpt. in Shapiro, *Late Antique, Early Christian and Medieval Art, Selected Papers*, vol. 3 (New York, 1979), pp. 267-87.

The Two Worlds in Bede's Homilies: The Biblical Event and the Listeners' Experience

Lawrence T. Martin

The Venerable Bede (c. 673-735), the great scholar-monk of early Anglo-Saxon England, is today known chiefly as the author of The Ecclesiastical History of the English People. *However, in his own time and throughout the medieval period, Bede's fame rested very much on his scriptural commentaries and on his collection of fifty* Homilies on the Gospels, *arranged in two books and covering most of the Sundays and major feasts of the liturgical year. Bede's homilies were widely circulated, especially through the incorporation of many of them in the homiliary assembled by Paul the Deacon.*

Bede's homilies are carefully-crafted pieces of literary art, designed not only to explain the gospel reading of the day but also to illuminate the connection between the world of the gospel story and the world of the audience. This concern is especially evident in passages of direct address, where Bede extends the methodology of typological exegesis to include the present experience of his audience. Bede's approach differs from the fanciful allegorical or moral exegesis found in much medieval preaching inasmuch as Bede is extremely careful to ground his interpretations on the concrete historicity of the biblical event under discussion. Finally, Bede often calls attention to the interrelatedness of the world of the gospel story and the world of his audience by such stylistic devices as syntactic parallelism and wordplay.

The task of the preacher of an exegetical homily is to relate two worlds--the past world of the biblical text and the present world of his listeners' own experience. It has been said that a good preacher has a Bible in one hand and a newspaper in the other, and you get something of a feeling of that sort of preach-

The Two Worlds in Bede's Homilies

ing in some of the sermons of Caesarius of Arles or Gregory the Great. Both of these men were bishops with pastoral concerns, and their homilies were addressed to a cross-section of people; consequently, their sermons were full of newspaper--that is, full of concrete reference to the everyday social realities of the world of their listeners. Gregory, for example, sometimes referred to the plague which in his day claimed many victims, while Caesarius's sermons are a valuable source of information for historians concerned with things like gender roles, abortion, and contraception.[1]

With Bede it is different. In his collection of fifty gospel homilies, there is almost no newspaper. It is not that Bede lacked interest in his own world and its social, political, or ecclesiastical events. The *Ecclesiastical History* and *The Lives of the Abbots* give the lie to that. In his homilies, however, Bede made almost no reference to the concrete present social realities of the world of his mostly monastic listeners (or readers). The very lack of such specific reference, in fact, made Bede's *Gospel Homilies* accessible to and immensely popular with audiences that stretched over several centuries and all of Europe.[2] In fact, the one sermon in which Bede broke his rule of silence and made considerable direct reference to the present historical experience of his Anglo-Saxon monastic audience perhaps retained its appeal to the wider audience of different places and times only because some scribes eliminated the specific references to the world of Anglo-Saxon England.[3] If there is not much newspaper in Bede's homilies, does this mean that they are all Bible? By no means. Whether his sermons were actually preached, or only written to be read in *lectio divina*, Bede realized that his task as a preacher was to illuminate the connection between the world of the biblical story and the world of his listeners' or readers' present experience.

Bede's homiles are generally structured simply as line-by-line exegetical commentaries on the gospel reading of the day. There is usually a brief introduction and also some sort of conclusion--though the conclusions vary a great deal in both length and character. Often in the conclusion to an entire homily, as well as in the last part of the explanation of many particular gospel verses, Bede addressed his listeners directly. Frequently the transition to such a passage of direct address is marked by a formula such as *fratres carissimi*, as well as by a switch to verbs of the second person plural (or more often first person plural, since Bede liked to identify with his listeners in his exhortations). This essay examines these passages of direct address with a view to determining how Bede kept the past world of the biblical story before his listeners while at the same time speaking to the world of their own experience.

I will first discuss Bede's use of an extended form of typological thinking in the direct address passages. Bede's homilies are rich in typological exegesis, which centers around the perception of a relation between an earlier, usually Old Testament, event (the *figura* or "type") and a later reality (the *veritas* or "fulfillment," which the earlier event announces). The fulfillment is generally some element of Christ's saving work, though it may be an aspect of the church or the sacraments. Unlike allegory in general, and unlike tropological or moral exegesis of the sort we find in many medieval preachers, typological exegesis takes the biblical event very seriously as an historical reality. As Eric Auerbach put it in his classic essay on the subject, in figural or typological exegesis "something real and historical . . . announces something else that is also real and historical."[4]

Typological exegesis had been well-established in the writings of the fathers and had secured a place within the liturgy itself. Bede's sermons incorporate many standard typological patterns--for example, Isaac or Moses or Elijah as types of Christ's crucifixion or resurrection, or the temple as a type of the church, or the theme of the exodus as a prefiguration of human redemption through Christ's saving passage through death, a theme which Bede wove beautifully through his homily for the Easter Vigil.[5] More original, to be sure, was Bede's practice of reading New Testament events as types or figures of events in the history of the church--for example, Herod's attempt to murder the infant Jesus was regarded as a figure of the persecutions of the early church.[6]

What concerns us in the present discussion, however, is

Bede's use of the typological style of thinking, and also of the terminology of typological exegesis, in passages of direct address, in order to bridge the gap between the world of the gospel story and the world of his listeners. Bede often found the fulfillment of a biblical type or *figura* in the immediate situation of the individual listener or reader, and sometimes these typological connections provide a structurally unifying theme as Bede's exegetical homily moves from verse to verse of the gospel reading.

One of Bede's Eastertide sermons, on the gospel story of the women at the empty tomb, begins with the announcement that the reading is clear and the preacher sees no need to explain the well-known mysteries of the faith which the reading discloses. He will therefore, he says, concern himself with "what we should be doing in imitation of this same reading" (*quae nobis sint ex eiusdem lectionis imitatione gerenda*).[7] The first verse of the gospel states that the women came to the tomb at early dawn. This, says Bede, gives us a "typological example" (*nobis typicum praebent exemplum*)[8] of how we should seek the Lord in our lives, namely by casting off the works of darkness and living in the light of the day--Bede thus works in a quotation from Romans 13.

Bede next directs his attention to the spices which the women were bringing to anoint Christ's body: "These spices are the words of our prayers" (*Aromata etenim nostra uoces sunt orationum*)--an equation developed via a quotation from the Apocalypse and some brief Latin-Greek philological exercise.[9] The preacher then closes the gap between the world of the biblical event and the listeners' world of liturgical experience:

> We therefore bring spices to the tomb of the Lord early in the morning . . . at all times, but especially must we do so when we go into church in order to pray and when we draw near to the altar in order to partake of the mysteries of the Lord's body and blood. If the women in the story sought Christ's dead body with such concern, how much greater should be our reverence when we stand in his sight as we celebrate his mysteries?[10]

As Bede then moves to the women's finding the stone rolled

back, the typological connection between the world of the story and the present world of the listeners is enriched by characteristic wordplay. "According to the historical sense," (*iuxta historiam*) says Bede, the stone was rolled back to demonstrate to the people there that Christ had risen, but

> Mystically speaking (*Mystice*), the rolling back of the stone (*reuolutio lapidis*) suggests the disclosing of divine mysteries (*sacramentorum est reuolutio diuinorum*), which were formerly hidden and closed up by the letter of the law. For the law was written on stone [tablets]. And for each of us as individuals, when we make public acknowledgment of our faith in Christ's passion and resurrection, surely the closed tomb is opened. . . . But for those, whether Jews or pagans, who mock the death of our redeemer in which they believe or who refuse to believe in the triumph of his resurrection, the tomb remains still closed with a stone.[11]

The gospel reading goes on to tell of the women's confusion at finding the tomb empty, and for us this is a reminder that we cannot find the Lord fully on this earth, and "all the more should we be confused in our minds insofar as we see that we are still far in our journey from him."[12]

Concerning the angels' coming to comfort the women, Bede says that this happens "invisibly in our situation" (*inuisibiliter nobiscum*) when we meditate on the eternal blessedness of those in heaven, in which we hope to share.[13] "We must also believe," Bede then says, that

> The angelic spirits are especially present to us when we give ourselves up in a special way to divine services, that is, when we enter the church and open our ears to sacred reading or give our attention to psalm-singing or apply ourselves to prayer or when we celebrate the solemnity of the mass.[14]

The past time of the gospel event thus becomes the present moment of the listeners in their choir stalls.

One of Bede's Christmas sermons utilizes a similar theme in a long concluding passage of direct address. Meditating on the angels' hymn "Glory to God in the highest," Bede asks his listeners first to emulate the angels in the liturgical celebration of the feast:

> Here, by their praising, the citizens of heaven teach us also how we ought to celebrate the joys of this most sacred solemnity and what great praises we ought to say to the Word of God because on this [feastday] "He was made flesh and dwelt among us" (Jn 1:14), so that he might raise us up to the vision of his glory and grant us a share in the grace and truth with which he himself was full.[15]

Bede later moves to the angels' announcement of "peace on earth to men of good will," which signifies love of God and neighbor as shown forth in action. These things ought to characterize our lives at all times, says the preacher, but especially so at the annual feast of Christmas. The preacher concludes this line of thought with the following direct appeal:

> Therefore, dearly beloved brothers, may this solemnity be shared by us--not only may this solemnity be shared by those on earth and those in heaven, but also may our whole way of life be fitting to the company of the citizens of heaven. Meanwhile, [while we are] on the way let us meditate about what we desire to have in our fatherland. Let us also be united now, insofar as we can, with that most pure life of the blessed spirits, since we hope then [in heaven] to be associated with the inner purity of their mutual love.[16]

Earlier in the same homily, Bede makes a connection between the manger where Christ lay as an infant, a place where animals came to eat, and the sacred table of the eucharist, where the faithful are to be refreshed by the mysteries of his incarnation.[17] Bede's homily may have influenced the artistic motif of an altar-shaped manger seen, for instance, in tympanum sculpture at the church of La Charité-sur-Loire and at Chartres.[18]

In a homily for Holy Thursday, Bede makes clear that Jesus's washing of his disciples' feet is "an example of great humility for us,"[19] but in addition, the fact that it was their feet which were washed has figurative meaning regarding the daily life of the listeners. For when Jesus said to Peter, "A person who has had a bath needs only to wash his feet, and he is completely clean" (Jn 13:10), this clearly indicates that:

> The washing of feet indeed designates the pardoning of sins, and not only that which is given once in baptism, but in addition that by which the daily faults of the faithful, without which no one lives in this life, are cleansed by his daily grace. For as we walk our feet touch the ground, and for this reason we are unable to keep them [as] free of contact with dirt as is the rest of our bodies. [Therefore, the feet] designate the necessary results of our living upon earth. . . . One who has been cleansed in the baptismal font and [has received] pardon for all his sins has no need of being cleansed again; moreover he cannot be cleansed again in the same way, but he still finds it necessary for the daily defilements of his life on earth to be wiped away by the daily forgiveness of his Redeemer.[20]

In another Holy Week homily, on the story from John's gospel about how Mary anointed Christ with perfume and wiped his feet with her hair (Jn 11:55-12:11), there is a particularly striking passage in which the distance between the world of the biblical event and the world of the listeners dissolves in the preacher's typology:

> We anoint his feet when we preach with due praise the mystery of the incarnation which he took upon himself; we anoint his head when we venerate the excellence of his divinity with words of worthy assent. . . . We anoint our Lord's feet when we revivify his poor by a word of consolation . . . and we wipe his feet with our hair when we distribute some of what is superfluous to us [in order to alleviate] the situation of the needy. . . . Here we are clearly shown that what Mary once did as a type [*typice*], the entire church and every perfect soul should do always.[21]

For all of its effectiveness in bridging the gap between the world of the gospel story and the world of the listener, this extension of typological thinking into the present existential situation of the Christian is a risky business, for it presents a real danger to the essential basis of typology as "something real and historical which announces something else that is also real and historical," to recall Auerbach's definition.[22] G. W. H. Lampe contrasts typological exegesis, which is solidly based in historical reality, with the sort of fanciful allegorical exegesis, especially common in preaching, which regards the Old Testament books as a collection of oracles and which disregards historical context, ultimately reducing exegesis to arbitrary reading into the biblical text of the allegorist's own pet themes. Lampe laments the contamination of typological exegesis by such allegorization because it leads to a loss of the sense of salvation history and an inclination to treat events as "ordained merely to teach moral lessons." It was a tragically easy step, says Lampe, from this sort of muddled thinking about the Old Testament to the application of the same sort of approach to the New Testament, so that "New Testament history, like that of the Old Testament, becomes parabolic . . . a symbolical description of the present existential situation of Christian believers," and the gospel then "could readily become gnostic myth."[23]

Did Bede achieve the homiletic advantage of effectively relating the gospel world to his listeners' own world without falling into the dehistoricizing trap Lampe describes? For the most part, I think he did. Even when Bede developed an extended typological theme which finds its fulfillment in the listeners' present situation, he seldom lost sight of the concrete historicity of the biblical event which is the type. For example, the sermon on the women at the tomb, which I have outlined above, ends with a long and very detailed discussion on tomb construction in Palestine, based on a pilgrim's account of a visit to the holy places.[24] In the Christmas homily discussed above, there is a passage which invites the listeners to make a moral application to their own lives derived from the fact that the occasion of Christ's being born in Bethlehem was a Roman census. Interestingly, part of Bede's moralization is based upon a discussion of the precise value and physical form of a Roman denarius, which, says Bede, was the coin given in the act of reporting in the census.[25] In the Holy Week sermon on the story of Mary's pouring of the perfume on Christ, which I quoted from briefly, Bede carefully compared the different evangelists' accounts of the event, noting ways in which Matthew and Mark[26] differ from the Johannine reading under discussion, and Bede further, following Ambrose, argued that the account in Luke 7:36-38 is, despite its differences in detail, a version of the same event.[27] Modern biblical scholars might disagree with this particular judgment, but one cannot fail to admire Bede's careful attention to the details of the literal, historical sense upon which his figurative reading is based.

The extension of typological exegesis into the present world of the listener may be considered a "figure of thought." I will conclude by briefly pointing out two "figures of style" by which Bede drew his listeners' attention to the interrelatedness of the world of the gospel story and the world of their own experience. The first of these stylistic figures is a syntactic device and the second is a form of wordplay.

It was probably from St. Augustine that Bede acquired a fondness for juxtaposing parallel constructions, often expressing some striking contrast or reversal.[28] Bede sometimes used a particular variation on this syntactic figure in order to confront his listeners with an awareness of the two worlds--that of the gospel story (what God has done), and that of their own spiritual situation (the human implications of what God has done). For example: "May *we* deserve to see him reigning on his father's throne whom *they* saw crying in a manger."[29] Or there may be a series of such paired constructions, as in this example:

> *He* put on flesh that *we* might put on the virtue of spirit; *he* descended from heaven to earth that *we* might ascend from earth to heaven; *he* paid tribute to Caesar that he might grant *us* the grace of eternal freedom.[30]

The second stylistic device which Bede used to relate the world of the gospel story to the listeners' world is a process which Philip West describes as "centonization," in which "striking and recognizable words and phrases" are taken from the exposition part of an exegetical homily (that is, the world of the biblical story) and then repeated in the exhortation addressed directly to the listeners' world.[31] This associative technique is similar to the way in which Bede, like many other monastic authors, treated biblical words and phrases--repeating them and recombining them in fugue-like patterns of allusion.[32] However, with Bede, the words so treated are the words of his own explanatory comment on the verses of the gospel reading, and the repeating of these words and phrases in the exhortation was a way of reminding the listeners subliminally of the relation between their world and the world of the biblical event. By its nature, this process is difficult to illustrate in a short space. In Bede's Palm Sunday homily, on the story of Jesus's triumphal entry into Jerusalem, a rather long exhortation begins with the customary formula, "It is therefore necessary, my brothers,"[33] and the point of the exhortation is that the listeners should persevere in their ascetic practices for the remaining final week of Lent, and that those who have been slack in this regard should at least start such practices now. Bede says:

> Let such a person by crying out "Hosanna in the highest," implore the benevolence of him who, coming in his father's name brought blessing to the world, and entreat that he be saved in the fatherland on high. Let him spread his garments on the road, that is, let him humble his body, . . . and let him cut branches from the trees and spread them on the road, that is, let him zealously call to mind the writings of the saints.[34]

This is all a tissue of allusions to Bede's preceding explanation of the significance of the cry "Hosanna" and of the peoples' spreading their cloaks and branches in Jesus's path.

To conclude, Bede's gospel homilies enjoyed tremendous popularity throughout the entire medieval period, as surviving manuscripts show. Indeed, one might argue that, in monastic circles at least, Bede was one of the most popular preachers of the entire Middle Ages. This popularity was surely based partly upon Bede's unusually careful attention paid to the historical sense (the world of the biblical event), combined with an ability to speak at the same time to universal elements of his listeners' or readers' own world of experience.

Notes

[1] See Gregory's Homilies 19 and 38 in *PL* 76, and Caesarius's Sermons 42 and 44 in *CCSL* 103.

²See, however, Alan Thacker, "Bede's Ideal of Reform," in *Ideal and Reality in Frankish and Anglo-Saxon Society,* ed. Patrick Wormald, Donald Bullough, and Roger Collins (Oxford, 1983), pp. 130-53. Thacker describes Bede's concern about a lack of effective leadership in the Anglo-Saxon church of his time and his proposed reform which would spread from the monasteries to the church and society as a whole. Thacker draws on many of Bede's works, and although he makes comparatively little use of Bede's *Homilies,* he does argue that Bede's reform ideas are reflected in the picture of church leaders, teachers, and preachers presented in *Hom.* 1.7, 1.9, 2.15, and 2.22. Nevertheless, Bede actually made no explicit reference to the Anglo-Saxon religious situation in these homilies, and the notion of the role of leadership and preaching in the church there presented would be equally appropriate to other times and places.

³Bede, *Homeliarum Evangelii Libri II,* ed. David Hurst, *CCSL* 122 (Turnholt, 1955), *Hom.* 1.13, p. 91, line 99 to the end of the homily. Subsequent references to Bede's homilies are to the *CCSL* edition.

⁴Erich Auerbach, "Figura," in *Scenes from the Drama of European Literature* (New York, 1959), p. 29.

⁵*Hom.* 2.7 *CCSL* 122:225-32; see Philip J. West, "Liturgical Style and Structure in Bede's Homily for the Easter Vigil," *American Benedictine Review,* 23 (1972):1-8.

⁶*Hom.* 1.10, *CCSL* 122:70, lines 73-78.

⁷*Hom.* 2.10, *CCSL* 122:246, lines 1-5. All translations are from the translation of Bede's homilies prepared by Lawrence T. Martin and Dom David Hurst, to be published by Cistercian Publications, Inc., Kalamazoo, MI.

⁸*Hom.* 2.10, *CCSL* 122:246, lines 17-18.

⁹*Hom.* 2.10, *CCSL* 122:247, lines 24-30.

¹⁰"Diluculo igitur aromata ad monumentum domini ferimus . . . et omnibus horis et tunc maxime fieri oportet cum ecclesiam oraturi ingredimur cum adpropiamus altari dominici corporis et sanguinis mysteria sumpturi. Si enim mulieris tanta cura corpus domini mortuum quaerebant, quanto magis conuenit nos . . . cum omni reuerentia eius adstare conspectibus eius mysteria celebrare?" (*Hom.* 2.10, *CCSL* 122:247, lines 30-41).

[11]"Mystice autem reuolutio lapidis sacramentorum est reuolutio diuinorum quae quondam littera legis claudebantur occulta. Lex enim in lapide scriptum est. Etenim et nobis singulis cum fidem dominicae passionis et resurrectionis agnouimus monumentum profecto illius quod clausum fuerat apertum est. . . . At uero Iudaeus ac paganus qui mortem quidem redemptoris nostri quam credunt inrident triumphum uero resurrectionis eius prorsus credere recusant quasi clausum lapide adhuc monumentum permanet" (*Hom.* 2.10, *CCSL* 122: 247-48, lines 59-70).

[12]"Eo amplius mente consternari quo nos uidemus longe adhuc peregrinari ab illo" (*Hom.* 2.10, *CCSL* 122:248, lines 79-80).

[13]*Hom.* 2.10, *CCSL* 122:248, lines 84-89.

[14]"Maxime tamen angelici nobis spiritus adesse credendi sunt cum diuinis specialiter mancipamur obsequiis, id est cum ecclesiam ingressi uel lectionibus sacris aurem accommodamus uel psalmodiae operam damus uel orationi incumbimus uel etiam missarum sollemnia celebramus" (*Hom.* 2.10, *CCSL* 122:249, lines 97-101).

[15]"Vbi nos quoque sua laudatione caeli ciues instituunt qualiter huius sacratissimae sollemnitatis gaudia celebrare quantas uerbo Dei laudes dicere debeamus quod in ea 'caro factum est et habitauit in nobis' ut nos ad suae gloriae uisionem subleuaret nobis participium gratiae et ueritatis qua ipse plenus est donaret" (*Hom.* 1.6, *CCSL* 122:44, lines 278-83).

[16]"Sit igitur nobis, fratres carissimi, communis ista sollemnitas sit terrestribus cum caelestibus nec tantum ista sollemnitas sed et omnis nostra conuersatio sit supernorum ciuium apta consortio. Meditemur interim in uia quod habere desideramus in patria concordemus etiam nunc in quantum ualemus uitae illi mundissimae beatorum spirituum qui tunc associari speramus internae puritatis mutuae dilectionis" (*Hom.* 1.6, *CCSL* 122:45, lines 318-25).

[17]*Hom.* 1.6, *CCSL* 122:41-42, lines 177-81.

[18]See Adolf Katzenellenbogen, *The Sculptural Program of Chartres Cathedral* (New York, 1959), pp. 8-15 and figures 10 and 13. Katzenellenbogen does not mention Bede's Homily 1.6 here, but he does note that two of Bede's other homilies (1.8 and 1.18) were contained in a twelfth-century lectionary of the Chapter of Chartres Cathedral (p. 108, nn. 17-18).

[19]"Magnae nostrae exemplum humilitatis" (*Hom.* 2.5, *CCSL* 122:215, line 48).

[20]"Lauatio pedum illa remissionem quidem peccatorum designaret non tamen eam quae semel in baptismate datur sed illam potius qua cotidiani fidelium reatus sine quibus in hac uita non uiuitur cotidiana eius gratia mundantur. Pedes namque quibus incedentes terram tangimus ideoque eos a contagione pulueris sicut reliquum corpus inmunes custodire nequimus ipsam terrenae inhabitationis necessitatem designant . . . qui ablutus est fonte baptismatis in remissionem omnium peccatorum non indiget rursus immo non potest eodem modo ablui sed cotidiana tantum mundanae conuersationis contagia necesse habet cotidiana sui redemptoris indulgentia tergantur" (*Hom.* 2.5, *CCSL* 122:217, lines 97-115).

[21]"Et pedes ungimus eius cum mysterium susceptae incarnationis debita laude praedicamus caput ungimus cum excellentiam diuinitatis digna uerbi opinione ueneramur. . . . Pedes ungimus domini cum pauperes eius uerbo consolationis. . . . Eosdem capillis nostris extergimus cum de rebus quae nobis superfluunt egentium necessitate communicamus. . . . Vbi aperte quid Maria semel fecerit typice autem quid omnis ecclesia quid anima quaeque perfecta semper faciat ostenditur" (*Hom.* 2.4, *CCSL* 122:210-11, lines 107-32). It should be noted that Bede's thought here shows the influence of both Gregory the Great and Augustine. See Gregory, *Hom. in evang.* 2, 33, 6 (*PL* 76:1242-43); Augustine, *Tract. in Ioh.* 50, 6 (*CCSL* 36:435, lines 12-19).

[22]See n. 4 above.

[23]G. W. H. Lampe, "The Exposition and Exegesis of Scripture: To Gregory the Great," in *The Cambridge History of the Bible,* ed. G. W. H. Lampe (Cambridge, 1969), 2:165-66.

[24]*Hom.* 2.10, *CCSL* 122:251-52, lines 182-217; cf. Adamnan, *De locis sanctis* (*CSEL* 39:227, lines 17ff.).

[25]*Hom.* 1.6, *CCSL* 122, pp. 38-39, lines 60-80.

[26]Mt 26:6-13; Mk 14:3-9.

[27]*Hom.* 2.4, *CCSL* 122:209-10, lines 88-94; cf. Ambrose, *Expos. evang. sec. Luk.* 6, 14 (*CCSL* 14:179, lines 142-53).

[28]See Christine Mohrmann, "Saint Augustin écrivain," *Recherches augustiniennes,* 1 (1958):60-61.

[29]"Quem illi in praesepio uidere uagientem nos in patris solio mereamur uidere regnantem" (*Hom.* 1.7, *CCSL* 122:47, lines 50-51).

[30]"Induit enim carnem ut nos uirtutem spiritus indueret descendit e caelo ad terras ut nos de terris eleuaret ad caelum soluit tributum Caesari ut nobis perpetuae libertatis gratiam donaret" (*Hom.* 1.6, *CCSL* 122:40, lines 130-33).

[31]Philip West, "Liturgical Style and Structure in Bede's Christmas Homilies," *American Benedictine Review,* 23 (1972):429, n. 7.

[32]West, "Liturgical Style and Structure," p. 431; cf. Jean Leclerq, *The Love of Learning and the Desire for God,* trans. Catharine Misrahi (New York, 1962), pp. 78-83.

[33]"Proinde necesse est, fratres mei" (*Hom.* 2.3, *CCSL* 122:205, lines 175-76).

[34]". . . inploret pietatem eius qui in nomine patris adueniens benedictionem mundo adtulit Osanna in altissimis proclamans saluari se superna in patria flagitet; sternat uestimenta sua in uia, id est membra sui corporis humiliet . . . ramos de arboribus caedat et sibi sternat in uia, id est sanctorum scripta sedulus ad memoriam reuocet" (*Hom.* 2.3, *CCSL* 122:206, lines 206-13).

Preaching and the Sermon in the Carolingian World

Thomas L. Amos

Historians of the early Middle Ages have written at great length about the Carolingian religious reforms. Despite the attention paid to the reforms, sermons of this period have been almost entirely neglected. Recently, it was suggested that we have no sources for Carolingian popular preaching because the surviving sermons are in Latin, while the reform legislation called for vernacular preaching. Yet royal and episcopal legislation on preaching provide a context for the use of the sermon and establish that sources for Carolingian popular preaching exist in relative abundance and can be used to investigate the religious life of the period. The sermons themselves provide evidence for how and when preachers used these texts to communicate with their lay audiences. Ultimately, it is content rather than language which allows us to identify sources for popular preaching. This study examines the conditions of popular preaching in Carolingian Europe.

Few editions of these works have been made. For now, most of the printed Carolingian sermons exist only in the volumes of J.-P. Migne's Patrologia Cursus Completus . . . series latina *devoted to the period 750-950. A bibliographical guide to this literature in editions and manuscripts can be found in chapter five of Thomas L. Amos, "The Origin and Nature of the Carolingian Sermon" (Ph.D. diss., Michigan State University, 1983). The reform legislation has been edited or is being edited by the* Monumenta Germaniae Historica, *in the series* Capitularia Regum Francorum, Concilia Aevi Karolini *and the recent* Capitula Episcoporum.

Historians studying sermons from any period face the difficulty of determining how those sermons were used by the people who composed them. This matter of what function the sermons served--whether they were preached or served as literary creations--is too often passed by without careful examination. After all, early medieval sermons took many forms and served many purposes. They ranged in nature from sermons intended to be preached to the people to more formal exegetical compositions intended for private study and meditation in a monastic setting. The question of how sermons were used, therefore, can indicate more about the nature of a church than whether or not it supported preaching, and the answer is not always readily apparent.

For the Carolingian Church, the matters of preaching and the sermon are central to much that we believe we understand about the nature of religious life during the period from roughly 750 to 950. Reform capitularies--royal and imperial edicts which took their name from the chapters or *capitula* into which they were divided--such as Charlemagne's *Admonitio generalis* and the canons of councils and synods tell us that religious reform was a vital interest of both rulers and clerics. These same legal documents also tell us that the sermon was to have served as the chosen means of communicating a new reform ethos to the people.

Yet medievalists who wish to use these sermons as sources are confronted, for the most part, with a body of Latin sermons, sermonaries, and homiliaries and with a populace that neither read nor spoke Latin. From these two facts it would be possible to argue, as indeed it has been argued, that no sermons preached to the people by the Carolingian clergy have survived.[1] For that reason, it is necessary first to examine the question of how sermons were used by the Carolingians. Since these Carolingian sermons were also used by Anglo-Saxon homilists as sources for their works, the answer to this question may also help to determine how both the Carolingians and the Anglo-Saxons used the sermons that they wrote.[2] The results of this examination will help to establish a context which will in turn permit identification of the sources for popular preaching that we do have.

Such an examination involves two distinct but related areas. We must begin with an understanding of what the Carolingian reformers expected of preachers and their sermons. Then, we should examine the mechanics of preaching in the eighth and ninth centuries, by which is meant the basic matters of when and how the sermons were delivered to the people for whom they were intended. While answers to these matters may seem simple or obvious, a re-examination of the sources will show how much of the surviving eighth- and ninth-century homiletic material should be regarded as having been used for popular preaching by establishing the context which the legislation created for sermon use in popular preaching, and by exploring how the surviving Carolingian sermons fit within that context. Such an understanding will make it possible to appreciate the place of preaching and the sermon in the Carolingian religious reforms.

Although religious reform in the Frankish world began with the councils organized by Boniface in the 740s with the support of the Carolingian mayors, it received a more fully articulated form in the reigns of Charlemagne and Louis the Pious. One component of Christian kingship, as the Carolingians understood it, involved the responsibility of the rulers for the religious life and, ultimately, the salvation of their people.[3] Not surprisingly, the Frankish rulers sought to invest their clergy with the actual work involved in carrying out this responsibility. As a result, the need for the clergy to instruct the Frankish people in the basic tenets of religion can be found as a theme running throughout the capitularies of this period beginning with the *Admonitio generalis* of 789.

The *Admonitio* marked the origin of a programmatic effort on the part of Charlemagne and his advisors to reform and improve the quality of the religious life of the Frankish people. The section of this capitulary devoted to an actual program of church reforms--chapters sixty to eighty-two--established the connection between regular preaching and improving the quality of religious life on the popular level. In chapters sixty-one and sixty-six, bishops and priests were ordered to preach regularly and especially to preach against the evils of hatred, envy, avarice, and greed.[4] These chapters made clear the interest taken by the reformers in the sermon's value as a means of communication and education. The final chapter of the *Admonitio*, however, spelled out more precisely what the sermon was supposed to accomplish.

The authors of the *Admonitio* cast chapter eighty-two in the form of a sermon with an exhortational opening and a sermon-like formulaic ending.[5] The chapter contained Charlemagne's program for preaching directed to both his bishops and priests. They were to preach belief in the triune God and to stress the orthodox nature of the Trinity.[6] Preachers were also to describe the incarnation of Christ and His death and resurrection and inform their people about the last judgment with its rewards and punishments.[7] The chapter also listed the capital sins from Galatians 5:19-21 and told the clergy to warn their people that any found guilty of such crimes could not gain the kingdom of heaven.[8] This list was followed by a list of the virtues necessary for salvation, including such things as love of God and neighbors, charity, and confession of sins.[9] The chapter concluded with the warning that the day of the false prophets, predicted in Scripture, might be at hand, and only sound preaching could prepare the Frankish people to resist them.[10] To the Carolingians, preaching came to mean teaching through oral instruction. Chapter eighty-two of the *Admonitio* set forth a sort of irreducible amount of religious knowledge which Charlemagne and his advisors expected the bishops and priests of the Frankish Church to pass on to the people through regular preaching.

The emphasis placed on the sermon as a vehicle of reformed religion can be found throughout the rest of Charlemagne's legislation. Of particular note in this regard are the capitularies issued to the *missi dominici*, royal and, after 800, imperial officials who inspected districts of the Carolingian state to see that the emperor's commands were carried out. Charlemagne ordered the *missi* to insure that bishops and priests preached regularly on Sundays and feast days.[11] The *missi* examined the clergy to assure themselves that sermons delivered covered the desired topics, such as the Creed and the Lord's Prayer, and the proper prayers to make in times of plague.[12] The *missi* also made sure that parish priests had the books necessary to perform their duties--sermonaries, copies of the canons, and Gregory the Great's *Pastoral Rule*.[13] While there has been some dispute over the nature of the capitularies, there can be little doubt that they served as expressions of the emperor's wishes and had at least that degree of force of law.[14]

The conciliar and synodal legislation of the period illustrated that the episcopate followed the lead of the reformers in letter if not always in spirit. The acts of the Council of Friuli of 796-97 presided over by Paulinus of Aquileia and the *Instuctio pastoralis* issued by Arno of Salzburg at the Council of Riesbach in 798 both showed a close relationship to the *Admonitio generalis*.[15] The synodal legislation also called for regular preaching. A chapter from the synod held by Theodulph of Orléans in 797 stated:

> We urge you to be prepared to teach the people. Those who know Scripture, let them preach Scripture: those who do not know it, at least let them say this, which should be well known, to the people: that they should turn away from evil and do good; that they should seek peace and follow it because the eyes of God are on the just and His ears open to their prayers. . . . Therefore no one can excuse himself that he does not have a tongue with which he can teach something. . . .[16]

Other synodal statutes advised priests to preach regularly on Sundays and feast days, to preach in the vernacular or at least "in a tongue which their hearers understand," to preach from Scripture, and to stress the Creed and the Lord's Prayer in their sermons, since these provided the key to salvation.[17] Priests should use prepared sermonaries--Gregory the Great's *Forty Homilies on the Gospels* was a favored collection--and they were advised to get someone learned in Scripture to explain to them difficult passages so that in turn their flocks could comprehend them.[18]

Of course the best known episcopal legislation on preaching came from the five great reform councils of 813. Canons of all five councils called for regular preaching.[19] The Council of Arles repeated the earlier permission given by Caesarius of Arles for priests to read prepared sermons and for deacons to be able to read sermons in case of the priest's illness.[20] This provision was also repeated by the *Concordia canonum* drawn up in Aachen after the councils had met.[21] Three of the councils called for preaching in the vernacular, as had some of the synodal statutes.[22] The most famous of these canons came from the

Council of Tours. It contained requirements for preaching very similar to those found in the *Admonitio generalis*:

> It should be seen to by all of us that each bishop has homilies containing the necessary admonitions which shall educate the people subject to him so that they can understand the Catholic faith: the perpetual reward of the good and the eternal damnation of the evil; the future resurrection and last judgment; and which deeds merit blessed life and which can exclude them from it. And let each bishop strive to translate these same homilies openly into the rustic Roman tongue or into Theodeutsch, so that all the people can understand what is said.[23]

Here again the assembled bishops stressed the role of the sermon as a means of educating the populace in correct religious beliefs and practices. The legislation from these councils illustrated the degree to which ideas from the *Admonitio generalis* had penetrated the various regions of the Frankish world by 813.

The capitular and episcopal legislation set forth a series of minimal requirements for the Carolingian clergy to meet. They were expected to preach regularly, that is on Sundays and feast-days of the liturgical year. Their sermons should be based upon Scripture and should provide basic religious education and moral exhortation for the people who heard them. Priests had a limited permission to preach, which consisted mainly of the right to read their flocks a sermon from a sermonary. The Carolingian reformers thought preaching too important a task to be restricted entirely to the episcopate, as has traditionally been believed.[24] The controlled involvement of priests was important for the success of the reforms because it would increase the amount of preaching. Finally, sermons were supposed to have been delivered in the language of the people listening to them.

However simple these requirements may seem, it is well known that in some regions of the Carolingian world the clergy could not meet them.[25] At the same time as legislation on preaching was promulgated, the Carolingians also attempted to raise the standards and educational level of their clergy.[26] The constant conflict between the ends which the reformers hoped to accomplish and their simultaneous struggle to create the means to achieve those ends typified much of the Carolingian period. Similar conflicts could be found in areas other than religion. However, if it would be naive to assume that the capitularies and canons were everywhere observed, it would also be foolish to overlook evidence that indicates widespread popular preaching activity.

One problem which stands in the way of understanding how the Carolingian clergy preached is the basic matter of deciding what they preached. Christine Mohrmann first noted the diversity of terms used by patristic authors to designate materials used for preaching, and the Carolingians certainly employed them all in giving titles to their sermons in manuscripts.[27] Recently, a distinction has been proposed between the exegetical homily, used largely for liturgical and monastic purposes, and the exhortational sermon used for popular preaching.[28] This distinction, however useful it might be to the historian, would not have been favored by Carolingian preachers. They were explicitly told to base their sermons on Scripture, and they seem to have used any materials that came their way as sources for new sermons or as prepared sermons to read.[29] Certainly, there were liturgical homiliaries and homiliaries intended for monastic usage--by which is meant private reading and meditation--such as the homiliaries of the school of Auxerre.[30] The decision as to what homiletic materials were used for popular preaching, however, must be made and defended on the grounds of the content of individual sermons.

A large number of Carolingian sermons used for popular preaching have survived. Most of these, however, remain in manuscript form. There has been only one recent edition--Paul Mercier's edition of the fourteen sermons from northern Italy--but several sermonaries have been analyzed in journal articles by Henri Barré, Raymond Etaix, J.-P. Bouhot, and others.[31] Such guides, and my own researches in work done elsewhere, have led me to identify over nine hundred sermons written or adapted by Carolingian authors as sources for popular preaching in the period 750-950.[32]

To cite only materials readily available in J.-P. Migne's *Patrologia cursus completus . . . series latina*, three sermon collections intended for popular preaching exist in the collections attributed to Eligius and Boniface and the homiliary which Rabanus Maurus wrote for Bishop Haistulf of Mainz.[33] These sermons combined scriptural exegesis with religious education and moral exhortation. Most of them began with an explication of the gospel lection or pericope--some are edited with the pericope at the head of the sermon--and then applied the text to a particular situation. Generally the exegesis used the scriptural references to point to an application for good works involving the traditional works of charity and mercy.[34] Sermons which explained moral issues in terms of positive external actions helped the Carolingian clergy explain religious ideas to the people in terms they could readily understand.

The Pseudo-Boniface sermons, in contrast, did not have pericopes attached to them in the Migne edition. All fifteen of them, however, speak directly to the items Charlemagne commanded his clergy to expound to the Frankish people in the *Admonitio generalis*. The first three sermons more or less summarize the major themes of chapter eighty-two of the *Admonitio*.[35] It is clear from the content and style of these three collections that they were written and used for popular preaching. The primary purpose of the Pseudo-Boniface sermons was the instruction of a people only recently become Christian on simple matters of faith and elements of correct moral action. Most of the other sermons and sermonaries composed by Carolingian authors spoke to these same themes. These works were ideal popular sermons for a Church much occupied with missions on the frontiers and reform at home.

The sermons and sermonaries just described were written or adapted by Carolingian authors. In addition to these collections, preachers could also use the many sermonaries copied by Carolingian scribes which contained the works of patristic authors such as Augustine, Maximus of Turin, Caesarius of Arles, and Gregory the Great. Some of these patristic sermonaries were compiled by Carolingian clerics, while other compilations, particularly of Augustine's sermons, date from the time of Caesarius of Arles.[36] These patristic sermonaries allowed bishops and priests to read sermons which would fulfill the same functions and address the same themes as the works written by the Carolingian clerics. A look into any modern edition of patristic sermons will reveal how much their manuscript traditions owed to the eighth and ninth centuries. The oldest surviving manuscripts of some patristic sermons, such as those of Pope Leo the Great and Zeno of Verona, are products of Carolingian scriptoria.[37]

Although it is fairly clear that the Carolingian popular sermon does indeed exist, part of the defense of its existence involves posing answers for the problems of when the people heard these sermons and how they were delivered. It has long been assumed that early medieval and Carolingian sermons were preached during the Mass on Sundays and feast days by the bishop in his cathedral or the priest in his parish church.[38] This traditional view is supported by the legislation and the sermons themselves. The capitularies connected sermons with the Mass as early as 785, and many other references can be found linking the two in royal legislation.[39] Episcopal statutes also depicted the sermon as part of the Mass.[40] The clearest statement of all in this regard came from an anonymous episcopal statute:

> We order that each of you in the church assigned to you, on two or three Sundays or feast days of the saints shall strive to teach the people subject to you the healthful doctrine from the Holy Scripture *after the Gospel has been read,* and that you order the people so that no one shall leave the church before the blessing, that is, "*Benedicamus domino*" or "*ite, missa est*," is spoken by the priest or deacon. (Emphasis mine.)[41]

The references in this statute to the reading of the Gospel and the blessing of the priest--the *Ite, missa est*--clearly place the sermon in the context of the Mass. The Carolingians, therefore, wrote their legislation with the understanding that sermons would be preached at Mass after the Gospel reading.

The sermons themselves reflected this fact. As previously noted, many sermons began with some reference to the pericope on which they were based.[42] Others referred back to the pericope internally, to support an argument or introduce a new section of development.[43] These sermons, all of which were intended for popular preaching, found their obvious context within the Mass. This would seem to be the case for the greater part of the Carolingian popular sermon literature.

The fact that few of the Carolingian *expositiones missae* place the sermon after the Gospel should not be too surprising. The period was, after all, one of great liturgical confusion. The Franks attempted to adapt various strands of a "Gallican" liturgy to the variety of "Roman" books they encountered, and none of the Roman *ordines* mentioned the sermon at all.[44] In the so-called "Romano-Frankish" missals they produced, the Carolingians followed the traditions they received. This does not mean, however, that the missals and *expositiones missae* always tell us what was happening on the local scene. Despite the best efforts of the Carolingians, no liturgical uniformity existed at this period.[45] A further problem lies in the fact that many of the surviving *expositiones* came from a monastic milieu, such as the *Liber officialis* of Amalarius. Works of this nature could hardly be expected to mention the sermon at all outside of its monastic context in the multiple lessons of the Night Office.[46]

Was there, then, a developing "[preaching] office in the vernacular" called the "prone," which could be detached from the Mass, as Milton McC. Gatch has suggested?[47] This does not seem likely. If the prone was a vernacular parish sermon joined to parochial prayers and announcements, it is unlikely to have existed much before the creation of a developed system of parishes in the eleventh and twelfth centuries.[48] Much of the secondary literature which uses the term "prone" to describe early medieval sermons employs as examples of prones sermons we know to have been used for popular preaching in the Mass.[49]

Although Gatch's suggestion concerning this vernacular preaching office is an interesting one, it has no documentary foundation. It also leaves one guessing at the meaning of a "preaching office." In the final analysis, the complete absence in contemporary documents of anything like a description of the new practice suggested by Gatch should make us hesitate before accepting a break in the continuity of preaching practices between the early eighth century and the tenth century.[50] On the best evidence available, Carolingian sermons were delivered in the context of the Mass.

Were they delivered in the vernacular? This question--how the sermons were preached--is more difficult to answer. Charlemagne's empire was essentially trilingual, since its people used the purified Latin of the clergy and the Romance and Germanic dialects of the nobles and common people.[51] Again, the traditional view held that most vernacular preaching came from sight translations of Latin sermons or schema for sermons.[52]

Certainly this view receives support in the survival of extended glosses such as the *Abrogans* gloss, spoken-language guides such as the *Pariser Gespräche*, and vernacular glosses in sermon manuscripts. In addition to these materials, the Carolingians also engaged in more formal translation work as indicated by the translated sermons in Old French and Old High German, and the translated Old High German catechetical materials which lent themselves for adaptation by preachers.[53] We also know that formal education in the Germanic vernaculars was available. Lupus of Ferrières sent his nephew and two other youths to such a school at Prüm, where they remained for some three years studying with the renowned Abbot Marcward. Similar schools existed at Fulda and Weissembourg.[54] Those priests who learned sufficient Latin--and just how great a minority they were is not clear--would have been able to perform such a feat of translation.

Recently, Roger Wright has put forward a new thesis concerning the Carolingian reforms of Latin which helps to explain the mechanical aspects of preaching in the Romance vernaculars. He contended that the changes between the purified Latin of the clergy and the evolving popular forms from which came the Romance languages took place largely in the area of pronunciation.[55] The striking differences in the appearance of the two in texts resulted from the fact that Carolingian scholars wrote out vernacular words phonetically.[56] Wright's interpretation would mean that preaching in one of the Romance vernaculars would have been a matter of returning to the old pronunciation. His views of the development of Latin in the Carolingian age go a long way toward sustaining the traditional view of how the Carolingian clergy communicated with their Romance-speaking congregations through the sermon. Clerics in

German-speaking areas of the Frankish world learned Latin as a completely foreign language and would thus be in a position to translate the words or sense of the Latin schemas into the vernacular.[57]

To sum up the arguments put forward here, the Carolingians produced a copious body of legislation which announced their intent to reform the religious life of the peoples of their empire. They sought to effect their reforms through the preaching of the reform ideas and practices to the populace. The message of reform was contained in the many sermons which the Carolingian clergy wrote and in the collections they adapted and compiled. These sermons were preached to the people at Mass after the Gospel reading, with the exception of missionary sermons, and provisions were made to ensure that they could be preached in the vernaculars. The Carolingian legislation concerning preaching and the content and style of most of the surviving sermons clearly support these contentions.

The Carolingian sermon was intended, as Walter Ullmann put it, to become the means of "effecting the rebirth of Carolingian society."[58] While the Carolingian religious legislation constituted an impressive legacy, it did not, and perhaps could not, achieve all the results hoped for by the reformers. The reformers adapted the sermon traditions they received in order to meet needs they perceived in educating the populace in those religious beliefs and practices which were felt necessary for them to achieve salvation. The ways in which the Carolingians used the sermons also derived from the importance of establishing communication between the educated elite of reformers and the populace.

As we have seen, the sermons they used were vehicles fully capable of communicating to the common people. The ultimate failure to implement fully the religious reforms cannot, therefore, be blamed on the sermon, the means selected to accomplish this goal. Rather, the failure seems to reflect a basic fact of Carolingian history in that, to paraphrase Robert Browning, the reformers' reach too often exceeded their grasp.

How, then, can we understand the effects which the Carolingian sermons did have on their own world and in societies such as Anglo-Saxon England where they were used as sources for sermons and homiliaries? It is first of all necessary to be able to determine what surviving homiletic materials were used for popular preaching. Such a determination is best made through a careful study of content and context. This study has described the broad context within which the popular sermons were preached and provided some suggestions as to the nature of their contents. As I have attempted to show, the Carolingian sermon can serve as a valuable source for the study of early medieval religious life. Like all historical sources, however, its proper use by historians must fall between the two extremes of simple belief that a source is what it says it is and hyper-criticism.

Notes

An earlier version of this study was given at the Twenty-first International Congress on Medieval Studies, Western Michigan University, May 1986. I would particularly like to thank Rev. Eugene Green, CO and Professor J. E. Cross for their thoughtful criticisms of that version.

[1] Milton McC. Gatch, *Preaching and Theology in Anglo-Saxon England: Aelfric and Wulfstan* (Toronto, 1976), pp. 30-39. Gatch examined Carolingian preaching as a natural background for his study of Aelfric and Wulfstan, Anglo-Saxon homilists who used Carolingian sermons as sources. He concluded, however, that the surviving Carolingian Latin sermons were all intended for liturgical or monastic functions, and that if we are to find any Carolingian materials for popular preaching, we must look for something which he calls a "prone" (on which see the discussion in the text).

[2] Modern work on the interrelationship between Carolingian and Anglo-Saxon sermons began with articles by Cyril Smetana (e.g., his "Aelfric and the Early Medieval Homiliary," *Traditio,* 15 [1959]:163-204) and has been continued by many others, most notably J. E. Cross in the recent *Cambridge Pembroke College MS 25,* Kings College Medieval Latin Studies, 1 (London, 1987). Recently, Mary Clayton, "Homiliaries and Preaching in Anglo-Saxon England," *Peritia,* 3 (1985) [1988]:207-42 treats some of the same matters first raised by Milton Gatch (see n. 1 above) as I will be examining here, but from a different perspective.

Preaching and the Sermon in the Carolingian World

[3]Walter Ullmann, *The Carolingian Renaissance and the Idea of Kingship*, The Birkbeck Lectures, 1968-69 (London, 1969), pp. 24-32, 43-44 and 53-54. For the early medieval Constantinian model of kingship upon which this idea was based, see Eugen Ewig, "Das Bild Constantins des Grossen in der ersten Jahrhunderten des abendländischen Mittelalters," *Historisches Jahrbuch*, 75 (1956):28-29.

[4]*Admonitio generalis*, cc. 61 and 66, ed. A. Boretius, *Monumenta Germaniae Historica, Capitularia regum francorum*, vol. 1 (Hanover, 1896), p. 59 (hereafter cited as *MGH* and *Cap. reg. franc.*; individual *capitula* references in the legislation are cited as c. and cc.). See also J. M. Wallace-Hadrill, *The Frankish Church* (Oxford, 1984), pp. 259-61; and Jean Longère, *La Prédication Médiévale* (Paris, 1983), pp. 46-48.

[5]It begins with a sermon-like incipit: "Sed etvestrum videndum est, dilectissimi et venerabiles pastores etrectores ecclesiarum Dei, ut presbyteros . . ." and ends with a sermon formula: "Pax praedicantibus, gratia oboedientibus, gloria domino nostro Iesu Christo" (*Admonitio generalis*, c. 82, *MGH Cap. reg. franc.*, 1:61-62). While these forms no doubt aided the material to be read aloud in large gatherings for its promulgation, it is difficult to believe that we do not see here a case of content influencing style.

[6]"Primo omnium praedicandum est omnibus generaliter, ut credant Patrem et Filium et Spiritum sanctum unum esse Deum omnipotentem, aeternum, invisibilem, qui creavit caelum et terram, mare et omnia quae in eis sunt, et unam esse deitatem, substantiam, et maiestatem in tribus personis Patris et Filii et Spiritus sancti" (*MGH Cap. reg. franc.*, 1:61).

[7]*MGH Cap. reg. franc.*, 1:61.

[8]*MGH Cap. reg. franc.*, 1:61-62.

[9]"Sed omni instantia ammonete eos de dilectione Dei et proximi, de fide et spe in Deo de humilitate et patientia, de benignitate et misericordia, de elimosinis et confessione peccatorum, et ut debitoribus suis secundum dominicam orationem sua debita demittant: scientes certissime, quod qui talia agunt regnum Dei possidebunt" (*MGH Cap. reg. franc.*, 1:62).

[10]*MGH Cap. reg. franc.*, 1:62. For other views on the nature of the *Admonitio generalis* in the Frankish Reforms, see Rosamund McKitterick, *The Frankish Church and the Carolingian Reforms, 789-895* (London, 1976), pp. 23-34; Étienne Delaruelle, "Charlemagne et l'église," *Revue d'Histoire de*

Thomas L. Amos

l'Église en France, 39 (1954): 181-84; and Ullmann, *The Carolingian Renaissance,* pp. 9-10 and 36-37.

[11]*Capitulare missorum generale* (802), c. 10; *Capitula a sacerdotibus proposita* (802), c. 4; *Capitula de examinandis ecclesiasticis* (802), c. 4; *Capitulare missorum Aquisgranense primum* (810), c. 6; *Cap. miss. Aquisgranense secundum* (810), c. 2; and *Pippini capitulare Italicum* (801-10), c. 1, in *MGH Cap. reg. franc.,* 1:93, 106, 110, 153, 154, and 209. See also Albert Hauck, *Kirchengeschichte Deutschlands,* 8th. ed., 5 vols. in 6 parts (Berlin, 1954), 2: 215-17; and F. L. Ganshof, "Charlemagne's Programme of Imperial Government," in *The Carolingians and the Frankish Monarchy,* trans. Janet Sondheimer (London, 1971), pp. 59-61 and 70.

[12]*Capitulare missorum item speciale* (802), c. 29; *Cap. miss. Aquis. primum,* c. 5; and *Capitula in diocesana quadam synodo tractata* (803-04), c. 1, in *MGH Cap. reg. franc.,* 1:103, 154, and 236.

[13]*Cap. de exam. eccles.,* c. 10; *Interrogationes examinationis* (post 803), c. 6; and *Quae a presbyteris discenda sunt* (805?), c. 12, in *MGH Cap. reg. franc.,* 1:110, 234, and 235.

[14]See the contrast between F. L. Ganshof, *Recherches sur les capitulaires* (Paris, 1958), pp. 20-25 and 31-32; and Janet L. Nelson, "On the Limits of the Carolingian Renaissance," in *Renaissance and Renewal in Christian History,* ed. Derek Baker, Studies in Church History, 14 (Oxford, 1977), pp. 56-58. I follow Ganshof's views.

[15]*Concilium Foroiuliense,* cc. 2 and 13; and *Concilium Rispacense, Arnonis Instructio Pastoralis,* in *MGH Concilia aevi karolini,* ed. A. Werminghoff, 3 vols. (Hanover, 1902-08), 2.1:190-95 and 198-201 (hereafter cited as *MGH Conc.*).

[16]"Hortamur vos paratos esse ad docendas plebes. Qui scriptura scit, praedicet Scripturas; qui vero nescit, saltim hoc, quod notissimum est, plebibus dicat: Ut declinat a malo et faciunt bonum, inquirant pacem et sequantur eam, quia oculi Domini super iustos, et aures eius ad preces eorum. . . . [Ps 33: 15-17]. Nullus ergo se excusare poterit, quod non habeat linguam, unde possit aliquem aedificare . . ." (Theodulph, *Capitula ad presbyteros parochiae suae,* c. 28, ed. Peter Brommer, *MGH Capitula Episcoporum, pars 1* [Hanover, 1984], p. 125).

[17]*Statut diocèsain de Vesoul,* c. 13, ed. C. de Clercq, *La législation religieuse franque* (Louvain, 1936), p. 371.

[18]Waltcauld of Liège, *Statut diocèsain,* c. 11, *La législation religieuse franque,* p. 365; Hincmar of Rheims, *Capitula presbyteris,* c. 8, *PL* 125:774D; and *Statut de Vesoul,* c. 13, ed. de Clercq, p. 371. Much of this legislation is digested in Guy Devailly, "La pastorale en Gaule au IXe siècle," *Revue d'histoire de l'Église en France,* 59 (1973):31-33. See also McKitterick, *The Frankish Church,* pp. 50-70. On this literature, see now Peter Brommer, *Capitula Episcoporum: Die bischöflichen Kapitularien des 9. und 10. Jahrhunderts,* Typologie des Sources du Moyen Age Occidental, 43 (Turnhout, 1985) for identifications and manuscripts.

[19]*Concilium Remense,* c. 13; *Concilium Cabillonense,* c. 1; and *Concilium Turonense,* c. 3, in *MGH Conc.,* 2.1:255, 274, and 287.

[20]*Concilium Arelatense,* c. 10, *MGH Conc.,* 2.1:250. This canon was based on the first canon of the council of Vaison (527) held by Caesarius of Arles, who seems to be the first western bishop to have given priests even a limited permission to preach. *Concilium Vasense,* c. 1, *Concilium Galliae A. 511-A. 695,* ed. C. de Clercq, CCSL, 148A (Turnhout, 1963), pp. 78-79.

[21]*Capitula e canonibus excerpta,* c. 13, *MGH Conc.,* 2.1:296.

[22]*Conc. Rem.,* c. 15; *Conc. Moguntinense,* c. 25; and *Concordia Episcoporum,* c. 10, in *MGH Conc.,* 2.1:255, 265, and 298. See also n. 23 below.

[23]"Visum est unanimitati nostrae, ut quilibet episcopus habeat omelias continentes necessarias ammonitiones, quibus subiecti erudiantur, id est de fide catholica, prout capere possunt, de perpetua retributione bonorum et aeterna damnatione malorum, de resurrectione quoque futura et ultimo iudicio et quibus operibus possunt promereri beata vita quibusve excludi. Et in eadem omelias quisque aperte transferre studeat in rusticam Romanam linguam aut in Thiotiscam, quo facilius cuncti possint intellegere quae dicuntur" (*Concilia Turonensis,* c. 27, in *MGH Conc.* 2.1:288). See also Werner Betz, "Karl der Grosse und die *Lingua Theodisca,*" in *Karl der Grosse: Lebenswerk und Nachleben,* vol. 2, *Das Geistige Leben,* ed. B. Bischoff (Düsseldorf, 1965), pp. 301-03 (hereafter cited as *Karl der Grosse*).

[24]For the traditional view, see Gatch, *Preaching and Theology,* pp. 31-33 and the works he cites.

[25]Pierre Riché, *Écoles et enseignement dans l'Occident chrétien de la fin du Ve siècle au milieu du XIe siècle* (Paris, 1979), pp. 102-18.

[26]The key text for clerical education is the *Epistola de litteris colendis, MGH Cap. reg. franc.*, 1:79-80. See also M. L. W. Laistner, *Thought and Letters in Western Europe AD 500 to 900*, 2nd. ed. (Ithaca, NY, 1957), pp. 193-96; and Ellen Perry Pride, "Ecclesiastical Legislation on Education, AD 300-1200," *Church History*, 12 (1943):242-45.

[27]Christine Mohrmann, "*Praedicare-Tractare-Sermo*: essai sur la terminologie de la prédication paleochrétienne," *La Maison-Dieu*, 39 (1954):97-107.

[28]Gatch, *Preaching and Theology*, pp. 28-29; and McKitterick, *The Frankish Church*, pp. 165-66.

[29]See, e.g., the 'Admonitio Synodalis,' c. 40: "Unusquisque vestrum quantum sapit plebi suae de evangelio vel apostolo die domenico vel festis diebus annuntiet" (ed. R. Amiet, "Une *Admonitio synodalis* de l'époque carolingienne. Étude critique et édition," *Mediaeval Studies*, 26 [1964]:51); see also n. 43 below.

[30]On these homiliaries see Henri Barré, *Les homéliaires carolingiens de l'école d'Auxerre: authenticité, inventaire, tableaux comparatifs, initia*, Studi e Testi, 225 (Vatican City, 1962), pp. 32-139.

[31]See, e.g., Henri Barré, "L'homéliaire carolingien de Mondsee," *Revue Bénédictine*, 71 (1961):71-107; Raymond Etaix, "Le sermonnaire carolingien de Beaune," *Revue des Études Augustiniennes*, 25 (1979):106-49; and Jean-Paul Bouhot, "Une sermonnaire carolingien," *Revue d'histoire des textes*, 4 (1974):181-223. The edition referred to is Paul Mercier, *XIV homélies du IXe siècle d'un auteur inconnue de l'Italie du Nord: introduction, texte critique, traduction et notes*, Sources chrétiennes, 161 (Paris, 1970).

[32]Thomas L. Amos, "The Origin and Nature of the Carolingian Sermon" (Ph.D. diss., Michigan State University, 1983), pp. 193-236. Much of this present study is based on work originally done for that dissertation.

[33]These works are found in *Patrologia cursus completus . . . series latina*, ed. J.-P. Migne, 221 vols. (Paris, 1844-1903), 87:593C-654C, *PL* 89:843C-872A, and *PL* 110:9A-134D respectively (hereafter cited as *PL* and volume number). On the sermonary of Rabanus Maurus, see now Raymond Etaix, "Le receuil des sermons composé par Raban Maur pour Haistulfe de Mayence," *Revue des Études Augustiniennes*, 32 (1986):124-37.

[34]See, e.g., Rabanus Maurus, *Homiliae* XIV and XXI, *PL* 110:29B and

42A; and *XIV homélies du IXe siècle,* II, 5 and VIII, 3, ed. Mercier, pp. 158 and 198.

[35]See in particular Pseudo-Boniface, *Sermo* I, *De fide recta, PL* 89: 844D-845B. The passage in question discusses the nature of the Trinity and covers in order the points of preaching set forth in c. 82 of the *Admonitio generalis.*

[36]See, e.g., Réginald Grégoire, "La collection homilétique du Ms. Wolfenbüttel 4096," *Studi Medievali,* 3rd. ser., 14 (1973):259-86; and Germain Morin, "L'homéliaire de Burchard de Wurzbourg," *Revue Bénédictine,* 13 (1896):97-111. On the use of Gregory the Great's Homilies, which were generally transmitted as discrete collections without additions of other works, see Patricia A. DeLeeuw, "Gregory the Great's 'Homilies on the Gospels' in the Early Middle Ages," *Studi Medievali,* 3rd. ser., 26 (1985):859-65.

[37]See, e.g., Leo the Great, *Sancti Leonis Magni Tractatus,* ed. Antoine Chavasse, CCSL, 138 (Turnholt, 1973), pp. xv-clii; and Zeno of Verona, *Zenonis Veronensis Tractatus,* ed. B. Löfstedt, CCSL, 22 (Turnholt, 1971), pp. 19*-40*.

[38]Rudolf Cruel, *Geschichte der deutschen Predigt im Mittelalter* (Hildesheim, 1966--reprint edition), pp. 3-5; and Anton Linsenmayer, *Geschichte der Predigt in Deutschland von Karl dem Grossen bis zum Ausgange des vierzehnten Jahrhunderts* (Frankfurt, 1969--reprint edition), p. 13.

[39]*Capitula de partibus Saxonibus,* c. 18; *Cap. de sacerdot. proposita,* c. 4; *Cap. de exam. eccles.,* c. 10; and *Quae a presbyteris discenda sunt,* c. 12, in *MGH Cap. reg. franc.,* 1:69, 106, 110, and 235.

[40]See, e.g., Theodulph, *Capitula ad eosdem*: "Commonendi sunt ut diebus Dominicis pro captu ingenii unusquisque sacerdos ad plebem praedicationis faciat . . . His et aliis quantum potest singulis diebus Dominicis plebem suam instruat" (*PL* 105:209D-210B).

[41]The Statute of Freising reads: "Praecimus vobis ut unusquisque vestrum super duas vel tres ebdomadas diebus dominicis seu festivitatibus sanctorum populum sibi subiectum doctrinas salutiferis ex sacra scriptura sumptis in ecclesia sibi commisa post evangelium perlectum instruere studeat et iubeat illis, ut nullus de ecclesia exeat, antequam a presbitero sive diacono laus, id est 'Benedicamus domino' aut 'ite, missa est' pronuntietur" (ed. Emil Seckel, cited in McKitterick, *The Frankish Church,* p. 71).

[42]See n. 34 above.

[43]Pseudo-Eligius, *Homiliae* II, IV, and VIII, *PL* 87:602C, 609A, and 615B; and the two sermons from North Italy cited in n. 34 above.

[44]Cyrille Vogel, "La réforme liturgique sous Charlemagne," in *Karl der Grosse,* pp. 217-24; and Louis Duchesne, *Christian Worship: Its Origins and Evolution; A Study of the Latin Liturgy up to the Time of Charlemagne,* 5th ed., trans. L. McClure (New York, 1949), pp. 102-04.

[45]Cyrille Vogel, *Medieval Liturgy: An Introduction to the Sources,* trans. and rev. William Storey and Niels Rasmussen, NPM Studies in Church Music and Liturgy (Washington, D.C., 1986), especially, on the nature of the documents, pp. 62-64.

[46]Duchesne, *Christian Worship,* pp. 170-72. See also Laistner, *Thought and Letters,* pp. 310-14. Gatch, *Preaching and Theology,* pp. 35-36, uses Amalarius's work, by "the most famous liturgical scholar of the age," and its silence regarding the homily to provide what he regards as rather conclusive evidence that there was no preaching at the Mass. In addition to the arguments made in the text, it should be pointed out that the *Liber officialis* had no official standing, was more of a commentary on the liturgy than an *expositio*, and was not well accepted by Amalarius's contemporaries.

[47]Gatch, *Preaching and Theology,* pp. 37-38.

[48]On the prone see Ulysses Berlière, "Le prône dans la Liturgie," *Revue Bénédictine,* 7 (1900):98-100, 242-46; and Henri Barré, s.v. "Prône," in *Dictionnaire d'archéologie chrétienne et de Liturgie,* vol. 14 (Paris, 1939), cols. 1898-1900 (hereafter cited as *DACL*).

[49]See, e.g., Paul Lejay, "Le rôle théologique de Césaire d'Arles," *Revue d'histoire et de littérature religieuse,* 10 (1905):158.

[50]The sermon is noted as part of the liturgy in the "Gallican" liturgical *expositio* written by Pseudo-Germanus of Paris sometime around 700 and in the tenth-century Ottonian *ordines*. See André Wilmart, s.v. "Germain de Paris," in *DACL,* 6:1049-1102; and Gatch, *Preaching and Theology,* p. 35 and n. 57.

[51]See c. 17 of the Council of Tours cited at n. 23 above; and Philippe Wolff, *Western Languages AD 100-1500,* trans. Frances Partridge (London, 1971), pp. 114-21.

[52]Albert Lecoy de la Marche, *La chaire française au Moyen Age* (Paris, 1868), pp. 221-37, esp. 225-26.

[53]Wolff, *Western Languages,* pp. 121-34; J. Knight Bostock, *A Handbook on Old High German Literature,* 2nd. ed., rev. K. C. King and D. R. McLintock (Oxford, 1976), pp. 92-125; Laistner, *Thought and Letters,* 382-85; and McKitterick, *The Frankish Church,* pp. 192-95. DeLeeuw, "Gregory the Great," pp. 867-68 examines the presence of lexical and etymological glosses in the surviving Carolingian manuscripts of Gregory's Homilies.

[54]On the school of Marcward at Prüm, the primary sources are Lupus of Ferrières, *Epistolae* 35, 58, 65, and 70, ed. Léon Levillain, *Loup de Ferrières Correspondence,* Les Classiques de l'Histoire de la France, 10 and 16, 2 vols. (Paris, 1927-35), 1:156-58, 224-28, 238-42 and 2:6. On schools which offered education in German generally, see also Wolfram Haubrichts, *Die Kultur der Abtei Prüm zur Karolingerzeit,* Rheinisches Archiv, 105 (Bonn, 1979), pp. 66-67. I would like to thank Professor John J. Contreni of Purdue University for calling my attention to Lupus's mention of vernacular education.

[55]Roger Wright, *Late Latin and Early Romance in Spain and Carolingian France,* ARCA Classical and Medieval Texts, Papers and Monographs, 8 (Liverpool, 1982), pp. 112-22.

[56]Wright, pp. 122-36 and 135-36.

[57]Amos, "The Carolingian Sermon," p. 282; and Wallace-Hadrill, *The Frankish Church,* pp. 377-87.

[58]Ullmann, *The Carolingian Renaissance,* p. 36.

Aelfric the Catechist

Eugene A. Green

Aelfric (c. 955-c. 1010), monk at Cerne Abbas in Dorset and abbot at Eynsham in Oxfordshire, is considered the greatest Anglo-Saxon prose writer of his time. Chief among his works are the Catholic Homilies *(in two series), the* Lives of the Saints, *the* Heptateuch, *and a* Grammar. *His writings were instrumental in disseminating learning during the late tenth-century revival of monasticism in England. Aelfric's sermons have been recently edited by Malcolm Godden (*Aelfric's Catholic Homilies: The Second Series, *London, 1979) and by John C. Pope (*Homilies of Aelfric: A Supplementary Collection, *2 vols., New York, 1967). A complete nineteenth-century edition was put forth for the Early English Text Society by Benjamin Thorpe (*The Homilies of the Anglo-Saxon Church. The First Part, containing the Sermones Catholici or Homilies of Aelfric, *2 vols. London, 1844; rpt. New York, 1971). Most of Aelfric's writing was completed and disseminated between 992 and 1005; in 992, at the earliest, he began composing the* Homilies, *and in 1005 he was elected Abbot of Eynsham. Even as abbot, however, he continued revising copy until his death.*

This present essay examines the catechetical curriculum of Aelfric's preaching, focusing on his pre-Lenten sermons and sermons for the Sundays in Lent. In his sermons for this season of reform, Aelfric expressed the hope that the spiritual lives of his audience would be "emended" by his sermons: ad animarum emendationem, *so he promised. Teaching the doctrine of the gospels was the chief concern of Aelfric's preaching and the chief explanation for its strong catechetical character. He returned to the major catechetical themes of the ancient catechumenate and shaped his patristic and early medieval sources to the understanding and needs of his countrymen: the crucial concerns here lie in his comprehensive* organization of materials, *his* sensitivity to the needs of his audience(s) and, above all, his *use of the vernacular. A glancing comparison of his*

> *Lenten sermons with other Old English sermons for the Sundays in Lent further demonstrates Aelfric's commitment to a systematic Lenten catechesis not found elsewhere. Aelfric's sermons stand as a sturdy milestone along the pilgrim path of Christian catechesis.*

Aelfric's homilies left a record of Christian education during the tenth and eleventh centuries that outdistances the efforts of anyone else for centuries on either side of his life.[1] In order that a congregation might listen to a homily twice monthly, he wrote a homily for approximately every second Sunday in a two-year cycle. To teach gospel truth or evangelical doctrine is the chief concern and motive force behind all of Aelfric's preaching and the chief explanation for its strong catechetical character. Aelfric's educational, catechetical goals and his orthodoxy are signalled strongly by his returning literally hundreds of times to the word *lare* (teaching); to preach on the scriptures is to teach divine doctrine. Within Aelfric's larger religious, educational plan, there exist subsets of sermons with a stronger than usual catechetical thrust. Such are the sermons for Rogationtide and the Lenten sermons. In this essay we will deal with the pre-Lenten sermons and the sermons for Lenten Sundays. We will consider how and why they can be studied as a unit, briefly survey the tradition on which they draw, elucidate their major catechetical themes, and compare them to other Old English sermons for the Sundays in Lent in order to learn further about Aelfric's commitment to systematic Lenten catechesis.

The Aelfric canon contains twenty-two homilies for the entire Lenten season. In the First Series of his *Catholic Homilies*, Aelfric composed five homilies for the Sundays in Lent (if we begin counting at Septuagesima and end with Palm Sunday). In the Second Series, Aelfric assigned eight homilies for the same liturgical period. In addition, there are two homilies in the *Lives of the Saints*: one for the beginning of Lent (Quinquagesima Sunday or Ash Wednesday) and one for Midlent Sunday. What remain are sermons for the five Fridays in Lent, one for the Third Sunday (not covered in either the First or Second Series), and one for the Wednesday after Midlent Sunday. Among these twenty-two Lenten sermons, something like sermon subsets emerge for the Fridays and Sundays in Lent; indeed, the Fridays of Lent have been variously studied as a group.[2]

During Aelfric's lifetime and shortly beyond, the Lenten homilies were variously grouped (in part, presumably, because of their catechetical usefulness). The manuscript tradition testifies to the special value Aelfric and his later editors saw in Lenten catechesis. No other season of the liturgical year enjoys the attention that Lent enjoys in these manuscripts.[3]

All of Aelfric's sermons, no matter how attentive to exegesis, are fundamentally catechetical.[4] In the first Latin Preface, Aelfric expresses the hope that the moral, spiritual lives of his audience will be "emended" by his sermons: *ad animarum emendationem*, with "emendation" taking on the sense of "freedom from error."[5] In the English Preface, Aelfric says he undertook his preparation of the homilies because of the unsettling errors he found in many books already turned out in English: books which did not adequately reflect "gospel truth" (*godspellican lare*), texts tinged with *gedwyld*, that is, heresy, or at least foolish speculation. In line with the great apostolic and prophetic tradition, Aelfric regards orthodox Christian training as a matter of the greatest urgency; instruction in "gospel righteousness" (*godspellican sothfaestnysse*) derives from the divine imperative to "go, teach all nations" (Mt 28:19).[6] Aelfric made available in the people's language Latin sermons of high quality and great authority. And while he translated, he shaped his patristic and early medieval sources to the understanding and needs of his countrymen. "Fortunate parish priests could rely on the cycles of sermons . . . ; the circulation and effort of his civil, gentle, and clear prose must have been considerable."[7]

The backdrop of our inspection of the catechetical curriculum in Aelfric's Lenten sermons is the needful state of tenth-century liturgy and religious education. Medieval catechesis, what there was of it, was designed for an adult and largely illiterate audience. Adults, in their turn, were charged with transmitting the faith to their children and godchildren. Most English Christians during the age of Aelfric owned little more than "the veneer of Christianity."[8] The structured and systematic catechesis of the ancient catechumenate was long since dead and had not been replaced as such.[9] Some form of comprehensive Christian education became all the more needed as liturgical rites grew more complicated and liturgical Latin less intelligible. Systematic preaching began to appear as an alternative form of religious education. Indeed, after the sixth century, catechetical preaching had begun to take on the characteristics of what today we might call continuing or on-going religious training.[10] Children were being baptized, and neither adult nor child was being trained according to the more rigorous standards of the ancient catechumenate.

While the formal catechumenate of the first six Christian centuries was in existence, it had an agenda, a kind of syllabus that was fairly well defined. Both the Creed and the Lord's Prayer were normally taught through a careful explication of each phrase. The Ten Commandments, the capital sins, and the works of mercy were also regarded as central teachings. Teaching the Creed effectively was especially critical. Lessons were designed to explain the fatherhood of God, the relationship of the three persons in God to one another, God's creation of the world, and his plan for the salvation of humankind; the virgin birth of Christ was expounded, as was the story of Christ's suffering, death, and resurrection; the second coming featured importantly, as did sin, death, heaven, and hell.

Such a presentation of doctrine was based on an overview of Judeo-Christian history as had been recommended by Augustine and outlined in the *De Catechizandis Rudibus*, a guide for priests entrusted with the *cura animarum*. Evidence of a catechetical *narratio* such as Augustine recommends can be found much simplified in various of Aelfric's works: the *Sermo de Initio Creaturae*, the *Hexameron*, and the beginnings of his *Letter to Sigeward* and his *Letter to Wulfgeat*.[11] The *Sermo de Initio Creaturae*, the opening sermon for the *Catholic Homilies*, outlines the divine economy and its history, beginning with the creation and rebellion of the angels and ending with the assignment of men to heaven and hell.[12] At the opening of his sermon, Aelfric concentrates on the Trinity (as he does in the *Letter to Wulgeat*, the *Letter to Sigeweard*, the *Hexameron*, and several of the Lenten homilies); just toward the end of the *Sermo de Initio*,

Aelfric summarizes another theme that will be repeated and dilated in almost every Lenten sermon: "that no man can be saved except he rightly believe in God, be baptized, and adorn his faith with good works."[13] Inspection of the pre-Lenten sermons and the sermons for the Lenten Sundays reveals many of the themes typical of the ancient catechumenate.

In the pre-Lenten sermons, we discern a pattern of favorite themes united with fidelity to a tradition of instruction. At Septuagesima, Aelfric bases his homily on the parable of workers in the vineyard and centers on the universal history of religious teaching from Adam until the second coming of Christ.[14] Here emerges a catechetical *narratio*--derived from Gregory through Haymo of Auxerre,[15] germane to Lent, and comparable to Aelfric's *Sermo de Initio Creaturae*. In this Septuagesima homily and in the homily for the Second Friday in Lent,[16] the image of vineyard is used to teach a catechetical lesson about Church unity.

In his Sexagesima sermon, based on the parable of the sower and his seed in Luke, Aelfric overviews the several chief vocations in the Church and recommends patience and chastity as good ground in which God's word can grow to its full potential.[17] The vocations are also dealt with in another Lenten sermon and in a Rogation sermon.[18] This theme of the vocations reflects the ancient catechesis's concern with the new believer's way of life and with the moral obligations appropriate to the various states.

At Quinquagesima or Shrove Sunday, Aelfric returns to the catechetical theme of Fall and Restoration.[19] Basing his commentary on the narrative of the man born blind, Aelfric describes humankind blinded by Adam's sin, with sight restored by Christ; Lent is viewed as an opportunity for vision refreshed through fasting and almsgiving or good works. Comparable is Aelfric's sermon for the First Friday in Lent.[20] Based on the miraculous healing at the Bethesda pool, this homily speaks of humankind--blind, halt, and deaf through Adam's sin--now restored to health through Christ's coming as man. It returns, also, to the catechetical emphasis on fasting and good works.

Equally catechetical in concern are the sermons for Lenten Sundays. The gospel for Lent's First Sunday recounts the temptations of Christ in the desert. Aelfric's First Series homily begins with Christ's response to the temptations themselves as a sign of Christ's dual nature. Not only does it provide Aelfric occasion to explain what the creed means by true god and true man, but it also allows him to look back to the beginning of the *narratio* and Adam's sin, now overcome through Christ's resistance to temptations of vainglory and covetousness. The Second Series homily shows further evidence of Aelfric's strong catechetical commitment to stressing good works. It recommends works of mercy in light of Christ's second coming and the final judgment; finding Christ among the needy is essential to salvation. "Mercy," he says, " is the medicine of sins."[21]

The Second Sunday of Lent draws upon the Canaanite woman's petition that Christ save her daughter to preach a message about faith, patience, and humility, especially faith.[22] She becomes an image of baptism, for just as her daughter was saved through her faith, so infants are now saved through the faith of their parents and godparents. Like the Canaanite woman, the Samaritan woman in the homily for Lent's Third Friday[23] brings Aelfric to the catechetical theme of faith; the deep mystery of election and the need to hold fast what the Church teaches.

The Third Sunday of Lent comprises a grand mixture of assorted catechetical themes: the Ten Commandments, the deadly sins, and the doctrine of the Trinity.[24] On this Lenten gospel story of a man possessed, dumb, and blind, Aelfric preaches the continuity of Christ's healing work throughout history; believers rendered mad, dumb, or blind by sin can likewise be cured by Christ. This catechetical theme of spiritual healing, a favorite with Aelfric, also appears at Quinquagesima and the First Friday in Lent.

The Fourth Sunday of Lent, Laetare Sunday, has four homilies assigned to it, if we count each composite sermon as two.[25] Given the importance of this Sunday in the ancient catechumenate, such lavish homiletic attention is not so surprising.[26] The four Laetare homilies differ from one another in structure, in handling of scripture, and in message; all four, nonetheless, are catechetical. The first, based on the multiplication of the loaves, preaches God's provident care for humanity's material and spiritual needs as well.[27] Like the five loaves of bread, the Pentateuch and all of scripture nourish the human soul. The second and third of these four homilies, much like Aelfric's homily for the Third Sunday in Lent, take up large catechetical themes. Depending heavily upon scriptural paraphrase, the first of these two focuses largely on the Ten Commandments, while the second preaches the Deadly Sins. Both prosecute catechesis in the course of recounting the history of salvation from Abraham to the end of Exodus and onward through the settlement of the Promised Land. As Aelfric comprehensively exclaims in conclusion, "who may ever in life recount the great powers of God which he has shown forth from the creation of Adam until the present day,"[28] an exclamation close to Augustine's definition: "Narratio plena est, cum quisque primo catechizatur ab eo quod scriptum est in principio . . . usque ad presentia tempora ecclesiae."[29] The fourth of these sermons for Midlent Sunday is likewise catechetical in the sense of *narratio*; its concentration on prayer and fasting is developed through a recapitulation of biblical narrative from Adam to Jonah.

Appropriately for Passion Sunday, Aelfric's sermon for the Fifth Sunday in Lent deals with the mortal conflicts between Jesus and the Jews.[30] A largely soteriological sermon, it catechizes its listeners to a deeper loathing of sin and a more profound appreciation of the price Christ paid to save humankind.

Finally, both Palm Sunday homilies recount the final week of Christ's life.[31] The First Series sermon limits its attention to Christ's triumphal entry into Jerusalem, explaining, as it goes, the typology of the donkey, the garments, the palms, and so forth. The longer Second Series sermon devotes its attention to the passion, death, and burial of Jesus. Because the gospel pericopes for these homilies are so strongly narrative and because the story told is so central to the larger catechetical *narratio*, Aelfric here is more simply expository than interpretive.

Taken as a group, these various sermons for the Lenten Sundays provide a comprehensive overview of the Church's central teachings in matters of faith and morals: "those things which have been accomplished among us (Lk 1:1)," as the Evangelist says. At the same time, they evidence Aelfric's fondness for such subjects as patience, good works, and spiritual healing: a fondness and perhaps even a principle of selection that he brought to reading his sources.

Something further can be learned about Aelfric's commitment to systematic Lenten catechesis from a comparison of his Lenten Sunday homilies with other Old English sermons for the Sundays in Lent: those of Wulfstan and the Blickling Homilist. The First Sunday provides a convenient point of reference; for that Sunday we have remaining to us sermons by Aelfric, Wulfstan, and the Blickling Homilist.[32] Aelfric's is the longest; Wulfstan's the shortest. Unlike Aelfric's address (First Series), a homily derived from the assigned pericope (Mt 4:1-11), Wulfstan's address, though incomplete, is more sermon than homily. Designed for use on the First Sunday (or on Ash Wednesday), it refers to the Lenten season but does not depend on seasonal scriptural texts for its initiation or development. It urges all Christians to live a life of prayer, fasting, and almsgiving; it then calls specifically upon public sinners to be reconciled with the Church. Parallels to the Blickling Homilist and Aelfric are here predominantly thematic.

Aelfric shares more with the Blickling Homilist than with Wulfstan. Both wrote homilies properly so called, that is, expositions of the assigned Gospel pericope--the account in Matthew of Christ's temptations in the wilderness. Both drew upon Gregory the Great's homily for the first Sunday in Lent,[33] and both revealed a hearty catechetical interest. Yet Aelfric wrote a more tightly structured exposition of the Gospel narrative, worked his borrowings from Gregory into a more logical pattern, and used the Gospel, along with Gregory and his own remarks, toward clearer catechetical goals. For instance, Aelfric attractively defines a catechetical context for his homily at the very beginning. Everything subsequent will develop around the theme of universal and personal salvation. "Jesus came to mankind," says Aelfric, "because he would overcome all our temptations by his temptations and overcome our eternal death with this temporary death."[34] There exists no such overarching statement in Blickling, and even the analogous passage in Gregory is less imposing.[35] The Blickling Homilist, instead, wanted to connect Christ's desert fast with his baptism and Christian baptism with Lent,[36] before moving into an explanation of the temptations and their spiritual significance; the homiletic form here is more loose than Aelfric's. Unlike Gregory, who examined each point in great detail and illustrated every idea with scriptural citations, the overall impression in the Blicking Homilist is more diffuse.

The structure of Aelfric's homily is clear and concentrated. Having explained in turn each of the three wilderness temptations, Aelfric then explicates the three ways in which temptation arises, the three ways in which Satan tempted Adam, and finally the three parallel ways in which Christ was tempted but proved victorious.[37] Aelfric's return at the end to his original notion of Christ's ultimate victory allows him to preach a lesson about avoiding greediness, vainglory, and covetousness: the three vices he has been talking about from the start and with which he now concludes. With sharper focus than either Gregory or the Blickling Homilist, Aelfric concentrates on the contrast between the Savior and Satan, then between Satan and the soul.[38] Aelfric's rhetorical commitment to opposition and contrast surely buttressed his catechetical goals. Much shorter than Gregory's homily, much better organized than the Blickling, Aelfric's homily teaches its lesson lucidly, economically, and forcefully.

In conclusion, Aelfric's homilies have left an unparalleled record of Christian education during the tenth and eleventh centuries. His hope that his sermons might serve to free the souls of his audience from error (*ad animarum emendationem*) is especially evident in his Lenten sermons. Lent, as well as Rogationtide, provided the early English preacher with special occasions for gathering together reflections and admonitions designed to assist the spiritual growth and development of his spiritual charges. Aelfric's pre-Lenten sermons and his sermons for the Sundays in Lent are readable as a set. They demonstrate a self-conscious commitment to sound doctrine and a comprehensive catechetical content. In addition, there is manuscript evidence of their use as a set. These Lenten sermons have a formal and ancient catechesis as their ancestor. Aelfric regularly returns to major catechetical themes such as: the three persons in one God, God's creation of the world, humanity's fall from grace, the promise of a redeemer, the two natures in Christ, the inevitability of death, the finality of judgment, and the ultimate importance of good works. Aelfric's commitment to Lenten catechesis is further clarified by a comparison of his homily for the First Sunday in Lent with those of Wulfstan and the Blickling Homilist, and with the common source for Aelfric and the Blickling homilist: Gregory the Great's homily for the First Sunday in Lent. Aelfric's exposition of the Gospel narrative is more tightly structured and is directed towards clearer catechetical goals. Notable is his use of a rhetorical contrast that sharpens his presentation. Aelfric's homilies demonstrate his concern for orthodox Christian training in an age when liturgy and religious education were in a needful state. His homilies and his own good works stand as a sturdy milestone along the pilgrim path of Christian catechesis.

Notes

[1] See Milton McC. Gatch, "The Achievement of Aelfric and His Colleagues in European Perspective," in *The Old English Homily and Its Backgrounds,* ed. Paul E. Szarmach and Bernard F. Huppé (Albany, NY, 1978), pp. 60-61.

[2] See, for example, Ann Eljenholm Nichols, whose chief concern is stylistic: "Methodical Abbreviation: A Study in Aelfric's Friday Homilies for Lent," in *The Old English Homily,* ed. Szarmach and Huppé, pp. 158-80. See also John C. Pope, ed., *Homilies of Aelfric: A Supplementary Collection,* 2 vols. (New York, 1967), 2:160, who notes that homilies for the Fridays in Lent "are very rare" and that the only two Latin sets he has encountered are in Haymo and in the Migne version of Paul the Deacon.

[3] For example, from among the first recension manuscripts, Cambridge, Corpus Christi College (CCCC) MS 162 contains sermons for all Sundays in Lent, beginning at Septuagesima. All Sundays have a sermon by Aelfric, while some, presumably to provide choice, have a second sermon by an author other than Aelfric. CCCC MS 303 collects one sermon each for all nine Sundays, with four by Aelfric. With some of the homilies by Aelfric, all nine Lenten Sundays are grouped together in three remaining manuscripts, one of which (CCCC MS 302) has, in addition, sermons for Ash Wednesday and three Lenten ferials. For more information on the manuscript tradition,

see Malcolm R. Godden, *Aelfric's Catholic Homilies: The Second Series* (London, 1979) pp. xx-lxxviii.

[4] See Milton McC. Gatch, "Basic Christian Education from the Decline of Catechesis to the Rise of Catechisms," in *A Faithful Church: Issues in the History of Catechesis*, ed. John H. Westerhoff III and O. C. Edward, Jr. (Wilton, CT, 1978), p. 94.

[5] ". . . nec tamen omnia Evangelia tangimus per circulum anni, sed illa tantummodo quibus speramus sufficere posse simplicibus ad animarum emendationem, quia seculares omnia nequeunt capere, quamvis ex ore doctorum audiant" (Benjamin Thorpe, *The Homilies of the Anglo-Saxon Church. The First Part, containing the Sermones Catholici or Homilies of Aelfric*, 2 vols. [London, 1844-46, rpt. New York, 1971], 1:1-2). See also Malcolm Godden, "Aelfric and the Vernacular Prose Tradition," in *The Old English Homily*, ed. Szarmach and Huppé, pp. 99-101; and *Eleven Old English Rogationtide Homilies*, ed. Joyce Bazire and James E. Cross (Toronto, 1982), pp. xvii-xxv.

[6] Thorpe, 1:2-8.

[7] Michael Alexander, *Old English Literature* (London, 1983), p. 188.

[8] Jill N. Claster, *The Medieval Experience: 300-1400* (New York, 1982), p. 165.

[9] On the formal catechumenate of the first six Christian centuries, see Josef Jungman, *Handing on the Faith: A Manual of Catechetics* (New York, 1953), pp. 1-19, and *The Early Liturgy: To the Time of Gregory the Great*, trans. Francis A. Brunner (South Bend, IN, 1980), pp. 74-86, 247-52.

[10] "Religious training" is here used in the sense defined by Jungman: "This term indicates that catechesis does indeed deal with instruction, but instruction which not only inculcates correct doctrine but also makes possible a genuine religious education. And this religious education implies more guidance as its natural correlative" (*Handing on the Faith*, p. xiii).

[11] The *narratio*, attributed to Boethius and his *De Fide Catholica*, is found importantly in Martin of Bracara's *De Correctione Rusticorum* and in Pirmin of Reichenau's *Scarapsus*. See Virginia Day, "The Influence of the Catechetical *narratio* on Old English and Some Other Medieval Literature," in *Anglo-Saxon England*, 3 (Oxford, 1973), pp. 51-61.

Aelfric the Catechist

[12]*Sermo de Initio Creaturae*, Thorpe, 1:8-28. Vercelli 19, assigned in some manuscripts to Rogationtide, discusses Trinity and creation in relation to the Three Persons. See Paul E. Szarmach, ed., *Vercelli Homilies IX-XXIII* (Toronto, 1981), pp. 69-76. Wulfstan relies significantly on *Sermo de Initio*. See *The Homilies of Wulfstan*, ed. Dorothy Bethurum (Oxford, 1957), pp. 293-98.

[13]". . . nán man ne mæg beon gehealden, buton he rihtlice on God gelyfe, and he beo gefullod, and his geleafan mid godum weorcum geglenge" (Thorpe, 1:26).

[14]Thorpe, 2:72-88; and Godden, pp. 41-51.

[15]Gregory's *XL Homiliarum in Evangelia*, No. 19 in *PL* 76:1154-59; and Haymo's Homily 21 in *PL* 118:154-63.

[16]See Pope, 2:247-58.

[17]Thorpe, 2:88-98; and Godden, pp. 52-59.

[18]Under the rubric of love and good works, Aelfric's sermon in the Second Series for Monday of Rogationtide deals more expansively with the variety of vocations within the church: "Let everyone now consider what befits his state" ["Smeage nu gehwá hwæt his hade gedafnige . . ."] (Thorpe, 2:318, and Godden, p. 183). Also the sermon for Midlent Sunday in *Lives of the Saints* outlines forms of behavior appropriate to various individuals in terms of their state in life. See Sermon 13 in Walter W. Skeat, ed., *Aelfric's Lives of the Saints*, 2 vols. (Oxford, 1966), 1:282-305.

[19]Thorpe, 1:152-64.

[20]Pope, 1:226-46.

[21]"Mildheortnyss is synna læcedóm" (Thorpe, 2:102; and Godden, p. 61). The first Lenten Sunday homilies are found in Thorpe, 1:166-80; Thorpe, 2:98-109; and Godden, pp. 60-66.

[22]Thorpe, 2:110-16; and Godden 2:67-71.

[23]Pope, 1:226-46.

[24]Pope, 1:259-85. All of Aelfric's sermon for Wednesday in Rogationtide

(First Series, Thorpe, 1:274-94) is dedicated to the Trinity, as is part of his sermon for Rogationtide Monday (First Series, Thorpe, 1:245-58) and part of his sermon for Friday in the fourth week of Lent (Pope, 1:303-32).

[25]Thorpe, 1:180-92; Thorpe 2:188-224; and Godden, pp. 119-26.

[26]On Laetare Sunday in the ancient catechumenate, see Jungmann, *The Early Liturgy,* pp. 257-59.

[27]Aelfric's sermon ("On the Lord's Prayer") for Tuesday in the First Series Rogationtide collection likewise deals with God's providential feeding of man: "He is your hand or your foot and cares for your needs. He is your eye and teaches you wisdom, bringing you along right paths. He who protects you like a father is, as it were, your head" ["Se bið ðin hand oððe ðin fót, seðe þe ðine neoda deð. Se bið þin eage, seðe þe wisdom tæcð, and on rihtne weg þe gebrincð. Se ðe þe múndað swa swa fæder, he bið swylce hé ðin heafod sy"] (Thorpe, 1:274).

In the Monday sermon for the First Series Rogationtide set, Aelfric again returns to the theme of providential feeding: "Now, therefore, everyone should arise from that ignorance, and go to his friend, that is, he should incline to Christ with all fervour, and pray for the three loaves, that is, belief in the Holy Trinity" ["Nu sceal forði gehwá arisan of ðære nytennysse, and gan to his frynd, þæt is, þæt he sceal gebugan to Criste mid ealre geornfulnysse, and biddan þæra ðreora hlafa, þæt is, geleafan þære Halgan Ðrynnysse"] (Thorpe, 1:248). He likewise compares the fish, egg, and bread of his gospel pericope with the theological virtues of faith, hope, and charity.

[28]"Hwá mæg æfre on life ealle gereccan godes mærlican mihta. ðe hé mannum cydde. fram Adames anginne. oð þisne andweardan dæg . . ." (Thorpe, 2:224; and Godden, p. 126).

[29]*De Catechizandi Rudibus,* 3.1, ed. I. B. Bauer, *Sancti Augustini Opera,* vol. 13, part 2, CCSL, 66 (Turnholt, 1969), p. 124.

[30]Thorpe, 2:224-40; and Godden, pp. 127-36.

[31]Thorpe, 1:206-18; Thorpe, 2:240-62; and Godden, pp. 138-49.

[32]Bethurum, ed., *The Homilies of Wulfstan,* 14 (17), pp. 233-35; and R. Morris, ed., *The Blickling Homilies of the Tenth Century* (London, 1868; rpt. London, 1989), no. 3, pp. 27-39.

[33] *PL* 76:1134-38.

[34] "Se Hælend com to mancynne forði þæt he wolde ealle ure costnunga oferswiðan mid his costnungum, and oferswiðan urne ðone ecan deað mid his hwilwendlicum deaðe" (Thorpe, 1:168).

[35] "Justum quippe erat ut sic tentationes nostras suis tentationibus vinceret, sicut mortem nostram venerat sua morte superare" (*PL* 76:1135CD).

[36] "But we must bear in mind that our Lord after his baptism fasted and was also tempted. It is needful then for us to fast, because we are often tempted by the devil after our baptism" ["Ac þæt us is to geþencenne, þæt ure Drihten æfter þæm fulwihte fæstte, & eac wæs costad. Us is þonne nédþearf þæt we fæston; forþon þe we beoð oft costode from deofle æfter urum fulwihte"] (Morris, *Blickling*, pp. 26-27).

[37] "The old devil tempted our father Adam in three ways: that is with greediness, with vain-glory, and with covetousness; and then he was overcome, because he consented to the devil in all those three temptations. . . . With the same three things with which the devil overcame the first-created man, Christ overcame and prostrated him" ["Se ealda deofol gecostnode urne fæder Adám on ðreo wisan: þæt is mid gyfernysse, and mid idelum wuldre, and mid gitsunge; and þa wearð he oferswiðed, forðon þe he geðafode ðam deofle on eallum þam ðrim costnungum. . . . Mid þam ylcum ðrim ðingum þe se deofol ðone frumsceapenan mann oferswiðde, mid þam ylcan Crist oferswiðde hine, and astrehte"] (Thorpe, 1:176-77).

[38] "But the devil was overcome by Christ by the same means with which he had of yore overcome Adam; so that he departed from our hearts made captive by the entrance at which he had entered and made us captives" ["Ac se deofol wæs þa oferswiðed ðurh Crist on þam ylcum gemetum þe he ær Adam oferswiðde; þæt he gewite fram urum heortum mid þam innfære gehæft, mid þam þe he inn-afaren wæs and us gehæfte"] (Thorpe, 1:176-79).

Archbishop Stephen Langton and his Preaching on Thomas Becket in 1220

Phyllis B. Roberts

> *Stephen Langton (ca. 1155-1228), master of theology in the schools at Paris, author of numerous biblical commentaries, and archbishop of Canterbury from 1206-28, was also a preacher whose renown was echoed in the contemporary phrase, "Stephanus de lingua-tonante." His reputation as a preacher to audiences, clerical and popular alike, is well attested by the chronicles of the period and by the large number of sermons attributed to him. The first major study of Langton's sermons was* Stephanus de lingua-tonante: Studies in the Sermons of Stephen Langton *(Toronto, 1968) by P. B. Roberts, who has also edited several of the sermons in* Selected Sermons of Stephen Langton, Toronto Medieval Latin Texts *(Toronto, 1980). While many of Langton's sermons belong to his Paris period and are linked to the growth of popular preaching in the late twelfth century, several noteworthy sermons survive from the time of his archiepiscopate.*
>
> *The two sermons examined here represent Archbishop Stephen Langton's preaching on Becket in 1220. As historical sources, the sermons shed light on Langton's interpretation of Becket as martyr, saint, and defender of the liberties of the Church to audiences at Canterbury and Rome.*

The year 1220 marked the jubilee celebration of the martyrdom of St. Thomas of Canterbury. In commemoration of this event, Stephen Langton, then archbishop of Canterbury, preached about Becket on at least two occasions: to mark the translation of the relics at Canterbury in July 1220 and in Rome late in December on the fiftieth anniversary of Becket's martyrdom.

This essay will examine the texts of Langton's two sermons

on Becket with a view to understanding the ways in which Langton, himself an embattled archbishop, interpreted Becket's earlier defense of ecclesiastical liberty. Langton's preaching on Becket in 1220, as we shall see, varied according to his audience, the occasion, and the setting. The two sermons illustrate that the significance of sermons as historical sources lies, first, in the importance of the preacher; second, in the subject matter of the sermons themselves; and finally, in the occasions and settings in which they were preached.

The value of sermons as historical sources has attracted the attention of many distinguished scholars who have argued the importance of research into sermons and have, furthermore, demonstrated how sermons can contribute to our knowledge of medieval social and intellectual life. The French scholar Langlois, for example, called the sermon a particularly important source for the history of manners and popular fables. Likening the sermon of the thirteenth century to the popular press, Langlois wrote that for a knowledge of the "spiritual state" and the customs of the age, there are no contemporary texts as alive as those sermons addressed to laity and clergy.[1] Owst, the author of studies on medieval preaching in England, has also emphasized the important contribution of sermons to our knowledge of social life and thought.[2] Other writers, such as Lecoy de la Marche, stress the value of the sermon as a source for the study of medieval Latin and "modern" French as well;[3] and Grabmann has noted its importance for the history of theological thought.[4]

There is also the potential in the study of medieval sermons for information about relations between Church and State. Preachers of the twelfth and early thirteenth centuries attacked enemies of the Church in biblical language and metaphor, but they kept within an ecclesiological framework.[5]

A noted commentator on the Bible, Stephen Langton was also one of the great preachers of the high Middle Ages and author of these sermons. His reputation in the art of preaching is attested by the chroniclers of his day and by the large number of sermons attributed to him in the manuscripts. As archbishop of Canterbury, Langton was a principal in the events surrounding the drafting of the Great Charter. The years of his archiepiscopate from 1207 to his death in 1228 were also marked by persistent efforts to effect in the English church the reforms articulated at Lateran IV in 1215. Langton's role as an active preaching archbishop was not the least of his achievements. His preaching career had its beginnings in the years he had spent in Paris as a student and master of theology. Born in Lincolnshire ca. 1155, the young Langton came to Paris about fifteen years later and remained there studying, teaching, writing, and preaching for over thirty years, until his consecration as archbishop in 1207.

The sermons preached by Archbishop Langton which are the subject of this study culminated a career which drew on the Becket image for its inspiration. His student days in Paris had been spent with a group that was strongly pro-Becket. In his years of exile, from 1207 to 1213, Langton found a temporary refuge with the Cistercians at Pontigny who had welcomed Becket many years earlier. By the time of his return to England in 1213, Langton may well have been convinced that he was himself a successor to Becket in spirit as well as title. Langton's long struggle with King John and his stubborn efforts to achieve the freedom of the English church from royal interference were well in the tradition of Thomas Becket, who had earlier declared his independence and that of the Church from John's father, Henry II.[6]

The first of these sermons on Becket belongs to a ceremony of dedication marking the translation of the relics. The theme is a saint's martyrdom and a sinner's penitence. The style shows remarkable affinities with biblical commentary and the senses of scriptural use. The tone is cautious, perhaps conciliatory. Becket here is the martyr whose relics were to be translated and whose shrine was to be dedicated. Details of his persecution, exile, and death are notably muted or absent. The setting was Canterbury, and the audience included a mixed assembly of notables, lay and ecclesiastic.

The second sermon was preached in Rome by papal invitation on the anniversary of the martyrdom, December 29, 1220. The sermon, very likely addressed to a monastic congregation, is marked in the manuscript for public reading and stylistically adheres to the methods of the *ars praedicandi*. Here Langton recalls not only Becket's martyrdom but also his travail and suffering as defender of the liberties of the Church.

By 1220, when Langton spoke, fifty years had passed since Thomas's martyrdom. Over the years, however, Thomas had not gone unnoticed. Quite the contrary. On March 12, 1173, less than three years after Thomas's murder, Pope Alexander III inscribed Thomas in the catalogue of saints. The pope, in a letter to the prior and monks of Canterbury, also urged them to arrange a ceremony for the elevation of the remains of the martyr. Pilgrimages to Canterbury began soon after the martyrdom and quickly attracted some illustrious visitors including the count of Flanders, Philip of Alsace; King Richard the Lion Heart of England; King Louis VII of France; the archbishops of Cologne and Lyon; and Lothar of Segni, the future Innocent III who visited Canterbury while still a young student in Paris.[7]

Despite the vogue of the pilgrimage, certain obstacles prevented the carrying out of the translation that had been projected as early as 1173. At the time of Thomas's canonization, the church of Canterbury was without leadership, the see being vacant from 1170-74. Distractions of war in the continental Angevin provinces and a fire in the cathedral in September, 1174 (although not damaging Thomas's tomb) also contributed to the delay. After the death of Archbishop Richard of Dover, the time seemed ripe for the translation, but it was not to be. There were difficulties between Baldwin and the Canterbury chapter over the building of a collegiate church dedicated to St. Thomas and to St. Stephen Protomartyr at Hackington near Canterbury. The monks balked at the proposal and claimed that the archbishop had not obtained papal authorization to remove the body of the martyr. Appeals and counter-appeals to Rome lasted for fifteen years. Further delays were created by Henry II's troubles with his sons, the events of Richard's reign, and especially John's reign as he encountered the opposition of the barons and the controversial archbishop, Stephen Langton.[8]

By the later years of Langton's archiepiscopate, circumstances had finally changed and created a more auspicious time for the carrying out of the translation. In 1218, Honorius III, whose confidence Langton enjoyed, succeeded to the papal throne. There was relative peace in England during the minority of Henry III. The church of Canterbury had been restored to order and prosperity so that preparations could, at last, be made to mark the solemn translation of the relics. The date was set for 1220 on Tuesday, July 7. Langton, who obtained a promise of special indulgences, spared nothing to make this a grand occasion.[9]

From the night of Saturday, July 4 to Sunday, July 5, having observed the fast and prayed, the aged Archbishop Langton, assisted by his suffragan, Richard of Salisbury, and some monks of Christ Church, opened the tomb and removed the bones of the saint. Some of the bones were set aside as relics to honor certain churches, and a relic was chosen for the pope himself.[10]

On Tuesday, July 7, the relics of St. Thomas the martyr were solemnly elevated at Canterbury Cathedral. Stephen Langton, archbishop of Canterbury and primate of all England, presided at this grand occasion, attended by the young king, Henry III, and the justiciar, Hubert de Burgh. The remains of the martyred saint were raised and placed in a gold reliquary chest adorned with precious stones and mounted on a marble altar in the new Trinity Chapel,[11] whose vaults were decorated with paintings of saints and of the hallowed kings of England--Canute, Ethelred, Edward the Confessor, and with them Henry III.[12] The archbishop of Reims celebrated the pontifical mass. Suffragan bishops from the archdiocese were gathered together. The chroniclers mention the presence of three archbishops: Canterbury, Reims, and an archbishop from Hungary. York was apparently absent. It was a magnificent occasion. The reception was held in the hall of the archbishop's palace, and the menu included the finest meats and wine.[13]

The occasion of the translation in 1220 was widely noticed by the chroniclers.[14] Associated with the translation is a well-known sermon ostensibly preached by Langton on this occasion. The sermon, which was probably preached in French, is extant in a Latin text in a unique fourteenth-century Vatican manuscript (lat. 1220, fols. 257^r-262^v). It was first published in a collection of materials on Becket, called the *Quadrilogus*, by Christian Wolf (or Lupus) at Brussels in 1682. The "Lupus" edition was reprinted by J. A. Giles in 1845 and the "Giles text" reprinted by Migne in 1854.[15] There is a new edition of the text in *Selected Sermons of Stephen Langton* published in 1980 in the Toronto Medieval Latin Texts Series.[16] The sermon text, in its present form, probably represents an amalgam of Langton's preaching on Becket in July 1220 (at the translation itself) and July 1221 when Langton, on his return from Rome, preached at a synod that was held at Canterbury to commemorate the anniversary of the translation. As Raymonde Foreville has ably demonstrated, there are close resemblances between portions of the sermon and the Office of the Translation which was composed before July 7, 1221 by Langton or by someone in his immediate circle.[17]

The year 1220 marked the fiftieth or jubilee year of Thomas's martyrdom. This sermon is an elaboration on the theme of jubilee which in ancient Hebrew law marked a year-long celebration held every fifty years in which all bondsmen were to be freed, mortgaged lands were to be restored to the original owners, and land was left fallow (Lev 25:8-17). In the medieval church, the jubilee came to be identified as a year of plenary indulgence in which remission of punishment for sin might be obtained by those who complied with certain conditions and performed certain acts.

Langton had been one of a group of Paris masters who had a special interest in the teaching of sacred scripture and in the sacramental theology of penitence. These interests came together in this sermon on the translation, which has been described as an extended anagogical or spiritual gloss of the various portions of the Old Testament that Langton apparently believed especially appropriate to the occasion.[18] In addition to his prominence as a preacher, Langton was an important biblical scholar and is credited by some with responsibility for the present arrangement of the books of the Bible.[19]

At the outset of the sermon, Langton immediately sets the tone of commemoration, emphasizing the virtues of Becket. He identifies the martyred Becket with Judah Maccabee who was an example of a fighter who dedicated himself to resisting temporal tyranny and to the renewal and rededication of the temple of the Lord. "Thus," says Langton, "we should emulate Matthias and his sons who struggled against Antiochus. We should prudently and bravely resist those enemies who disturb our Sabbaths and our spiritual joy."[20]

In a lengthy section, Langton then outlines the qualities of joy, good works, and aid (*subsidium*) that come from the celebration of the saints' feastdays: "First is joy, that we should rejoice in the Lord; second is the example of good works given us by the saints; and third is the aid given us by the saints."[21] "Today," says Langton, "we recall what a great stone was Thomas the martyr, as his relics are raised from the tomb."[22]

Exempla and similitudes describing the attributes of saints and just men abound: the minds of the faithful are likened to the *tabulata*, the stories of the ancient temple: narrow and lowly are they as they contemplate worldly things; broader and higher, as they contemplate heavenly things.[23] The hearts of good men are likened to incense burners that are closed on the lower part but are open above.[24] The mind is compared to a bird which soars on high, but the serpent, in contrast, is lowly because it provokes lust.[25]

Langton links various qualities of the saints with St. Thomas of Canterbury: those who abound in spiritual joy and rejoice in the service of the Lord,[26] those who in their humility reach a higher level of perfection,[27] and those who are filled with the memory of the Lord's passion.[28] In all this, however, Langton emphasizes Becket's role as a martyr whose translation, solemnly celebrated, will assure forgiveness for sins and perpetual salvation. "Martyrs," says Langton, "are represented by stones and we translate this most precious stone as we translate the relics of the martyred saint."[29] He also notes that it is meritorious that this translation be celebrated on a Tuesday since it was on a Tuesday (i.e., Tuesday, December 29) that Becket died, fifty years earlier.[30]

Langton does not, however, dwell here on the bitterness of past disputes which led to Thomas's martyrdom. The aim of the sermon was to exalt sainthood and this St. Thomas, in particular. There is no retelling here of the Becket story nor is there any account of the conflict between the martyred archbishop and King Henry II, who gets scant attention as the villain of the piece.[31] That passion was muted for this occasion when all--king, nobles, clergy, and commoners--could now come together to honor the memory of their martyred saint.

Still, Langton could not totally ignore the central lesson of the martyrdom on such an occasion, especially if the young king Henry III sat before him.[32] Politely and obliquely, in the spirit of the festive occasion, he reminds the audience that kings may come and go while the Church endures, enriched by the blood of its martyrs. To teach the lesson, he turns to Job 14:18: "And surely the mountain falling cometh to nought, and the rock is removed out of his place." In a reference to Henry II, who, coincidentally, was buried on July 7, Langton says:

> Just as the mountains stand on high and tower over the plain, so are the mountains kings and princes who dominate over their lands. But the mighty mountain fell when King Henry died, and the earth took in the body of the dead king when King Henry was buried."[33]

The "rock that is removed from its place" is fulfilled in this solemn translation of the relics of the martyred saint.

The blessed Thomas is then likened to a burning and radiant lamp:

> The Lord kindled this lamp when He raised him to the head of His Church; He purified this lamp when He allowed His martyr to suffer exile and affliction by insults, abuses, and countless injuries. . . . The Lord extinguished this lamp when His servant was martyred, but though He extinguished it corporally, the more does it burn spiritually as a symbol of sanctity for us all to follow.[34]

As one can see, Becket was portrayed in his role as saint and martyr to the assembly at Canterbury. To the audience of monks in Rome later that year, however, Langton emphasized Becket's role as defender of the liberties of the Church against its enemies. Walter of Coventry tells us that Langton set out for Rome in the autumn of 1220 on matters of Church business.[35] Apparently, the archbishop brought to the pope a request from the prior and chapter at Canterbury that the indulgences granted earlier on the occasion of the translation be extended. To this the pope replied on December 18, 1220 that the extraordinary indulgences granted earlier be enlarged and confirmed in perpetuity. Langton probably reported this information back to the monks at Canterbury in the summer of 1221, at the synod commemorating the translation.[36] The chronicler further tells us that Langton took with him some relics of the blessed martyr Thomas and that, at the request of Pope Honorius III, he preached a sermon. Presumably, this was on the occasion of the fiftieth anniversary of the martyrdom which fell on Tuesday, December 29, 1220.

So far as is known, only a single copy of this sermon is extant and is found in an anonymous book of sermons contained in the thirteenth-century manuscript Arras 222, fols. 13^r-15^r. I believe, as I have shown elsewhere, that we can, with reasonable certainty, identify the sermon as Langton's sermon on Becket preached in Rome in the winter of 1220. The sermon is one of a large number of authentic Langton sermons in the Arras manuscript.[37] External evidence furnished by the chronicler Walter of Coventry indicates the setting and circumstances for its delivery. Moreover, the text itself provides internal evidence that this was indeed the sermon preached on this occasion. Langton takes as his theme Song of Solomon 2:3-4: "I sat down under his shadow with great delight, and his fruit was sweet to my taste. He brought me to the banqueting house and his banner over me was love." Langton cites the appropriateness of these words: first, to the martyr who was being commemorated on that day; second, to the time of the Lord's nativity, i.e., to the Christmas season; and third, to an audience of religious.[38] Thus the Christmas season provided the circumstance; a monastic congregation, very likely, the audience; and the anniversary of the martyrdom, the theme for this previously unknown text of Langton's preaching on Becket.

Unlike the sermon on the translation that we examined earlier, this text more closely adheres to the methods of the *ars praedicandi*: the setting forth of the theme and its systematic development by similitudes and *exempla*; the insertion of protheme and subordinate themes (with their explication); and the citation of sources which are here almost exclusively scriptural.[39]

The dominant motif in the sermon is, of course, Becket's martyrdom by which he imitated the Lord's passion. The imagery of the main theme repeats the motif again and again. The "shadow beneath which he sat with great delight" symbolizes Becket's emulation of the Lord in the affliction of His body. The "fruit sweet to the taste" was the Lord's passion when, for the Lord's sake, Becket endured exile, proscription, insults, and opprobrium.[40]

Becket's travail and martyrdom obtain fresh emphasis in the secondary theme whose text is Ecclesiasticus 50:1-8: "Behold the high priest was as the flower of roses in the days of the spring and as the lilies that are on the edge of the water."[41] Here the lily symbolizes Becket's suffering, and the six leaves of the lily remind Langton of Becket's six years in exile. The red seed at the top of the lily denotes his martyrdom.[42]

Langton then introduces the "banqueting-house" motif of the main theme as he discusses Becket's martyrdom:

> Just as the banqueting-house is a place of temporal feasting, so is the glory of Becket's martyrdom a spiritual banqueting-house, wherein Becket, by returning from exile and then suffering martyrdom released his soul to the glory of eternal beatitude.[43]

In a second explication (i.e., relating the theme to the Christmas season and the faithful soul), the banqueting-house is the Church, the wine jars are its martyrs, and the wine, the blood of their sufferings:

> So does the Lord introduce the faithful soul in the Holy Church and proposes that he drink the wine of love marking St. Stephen's day [December 26]; the wine of purity for the feastday of St. John the Evangelist [December 27]; the wine of innocence for the feastday of the Holy Innocents [December 28]; and the spiced wine marking the martyrdom of the blessed Thomas [December 29] who was a zealot in the cause of ecclesiastical liberty.[44]

Finally, in a third explication (i.e., the suitability of the theme to this audience of religious), the banqueting-house is the cloister in which the wine ought to be the wine of compunction, abstinence, and religion.[45]

This sermon also includes specific references to Becket's persecution, to England, and to the English church. The "rose" of the Ecclesiasticus passage Langton compares with the martyr, and the thorn on which it grows is England, since there is no end to the sting of persecution that afflicts the Church. "Yet," he notes,

> the thorn produces men such as St. Alphege or St. Edmund the Martyr. The rose which most lately adorns this thorn is the glorious martyr Thomas. This thorn should not be spurned since, God willing, it may produce other roses.[46]

The example of the blessed Thomas is thus offered in this sermon as one who defended the Church, his flock, and fearlessly faced the tyrant in the preservation of ecclesiastical liberty.

A parenthetical comment is in order on the saints whom Langton mentions here. St. Alphege, who died in 1011, was abbot of Bath and later bishop of Winchester and was apparently involved in the conversion of the Danelaw. Slain at Canterbury by the Vikings, whose attacks on England were led by the Danish king, Swin, Alphege was regarded as a martyr of righteousness. In fact, St. Thomas of Canterbury is reported to have invoked the aid of this saint when he was slain.[47] St. Edmund the Martyr was a ninth-century king of East Anglia who had led his people against the heathen Danes. Tradition has it that he refused to compromise the Christian religion and the people's welfare when he was offered a peace treaty and was put to death. He was thereafter regarded as a holy king who apparently performed many miracles. Many churches were subsequently dedicated to him.[48]

The tradition in the Church of preaching about Becket on the anniversary of the translation thus began in 1220 with Langton's sermon. Preaching on Becket's feastday, however, appears to have had earlier precedents. Beryl Smalley describes two sermons that were preached by Gervase of Chichester on St.

Thomas the martyr: the first on December 29, 1172 anticipating the canonization, the second in 1173 on the first solemnity of St. Thomas Becket's feastday.[49] Indeed, as Dr. Lawrence C. Braceland demonstrated in his recent edition, as early as December 26-28, 1171, Master Gilbert, Abbot of Hoyland, preached three sermons, apparently on St. Stephen, but the second and third were really on Thomas Becket who is called our protomartyr.[50]

The cult of Becket spread rapidly across western Europe in the years following the saint's martyrdom in 1170. So well known was the story of his life and murder that in the generations and centuries that followed, his cult flourished in all parts of Latin Christendom. Latin sermons preached about Thomas Becket in the thirteenth and fourteenth centuries were a part of a rich medieval Latin preaching tradition that contributed to the diffusion of the cult of Becket.[51] Becket was a complex figure who could be portrayed in many ways. He was the worldly chancellor who became priest and archbishop. A former friend and associate of King Henry II, he became the king's most stubborn opponent. He died a martyr for the sake of the liberties of the Church. How did the Church, embattled as it usually was by its Henrys great and small, use this vivid and compelling image? The great Canterbury pilgrimages to the shrine of Becket are evidence that the myth took hold with vigor. Indeed King Henry VIII, many centuries later, found the Becket shrine so powerful a symbol that he had it utterly destroyed. That shrine dated back to the year 1220 when Archbishop Stephen Langton, in the last years of his life, preached about Thomas Becket. He saw in the martyred archbishop an example which inspired extensive commentary in these two sermons which as historical sources tell us much about Langton the preacher and his subject, Becket: saint, martyr, and defender of Church liberties. Archbishop Stephen Langton and his preaching on Thomas Becket in 1220 have much to tell us about the attraction of both the Becket image and of its example for the society of medieval Europe.

Notes

A version of this essay was originally presented at the Seventeenth International Congress on Medieval Studies, Western Michigan University, May 1982. This research was supported (in part) by a grant from the City University of New York PSC-CUNY Research Award Program.

[1] Ch.-V, Langlois, "Sermons parisiens de la première moitié du XIIIe siècle contenus dans le ms 691 de la Bibliothèque d'Arras," *Journal des Savants*, nouv. sér. (1916):549. See also his "L'Eloquence sacrée au moyen âge," *Revue des deux mondes*, 115 (1893):170-201.

[2] See Gerald R. Owst, *Preaching in Medieval England* (Cambridge, 1926) and *Literature and Pulpit in Medieval England*, 2nd ed. (Oxford, 1961).

[3] Albert Lecoy de la Marche, *La chaire française au moyen âge, spécialement au XIIIe siècle* (Paris, 1886), p. 269.

[4] M. Grabmann, *Die Geschichte der katholischen Theologie* (Freiburg-im-Br., 1933), p. 48. Examples of more recent works that show the usefulness of sermons as historical sources include John W. Baldwin, *Masters, Princes and Merchants: The Social Views of Peter the Chanter and his Circle*, 2 vols. (Princeton, 1970); Nicole Bériou, *La Prédication de Ranulphe de la Houblonnière: Sermons aux clercs et aux simples gens à Paris au XIIIe siècle*, 2 vols. (Paris, 1987); David L. D'Avray, *The Preaching of the Friars: Sermons Diffused from Paris before 1300* (Oxford, 1985); and Jean Longère, *Oeuvres oratoires de maîtres parisiens au XIIe siècle: Étude historique et doctrinale*, 2 vols. (Paris, 1975). See also Louis J. Bataillon, "Approaches to the Study of Medieval Sermons," *Leeds Studies in English*, n.s. 11 (1980):19-35.

[5] See examples in Beryl Smalley, *The Becket Conflict and the Schools: A Study of Intellectuals in Politics in the Twelfth Century* (Oxford, 1973), esp. chap. 8 on interpretations of Becket's martyrdom.

[6] See Phyllis B. Roberts, *Stephanus de lingua-tonante: Studies in the Sermons of Stephen Langton* (Toronto, 1968), chap. 1 on the life of Stephen Langton (hereafter cited as *Studies*).

[7] Raymonde Foreville, *Le jubilé de Saint Thomas Becket du XIIIe au XVe siècle (1220-1470)* (Paris, 1958), pp. 3-4.

[8] *Le jubilé de Saint Thomas Becket*, pp. 4-7.

[9] *Le jubilé de Saint Thomas Becket*, pp. 7-8.

Archbishop Stephen Langton

[10]*Le jubilé de Saint Thomas Becket*, p. 8.

[11]*Le jubilé de Saint Thomas Becket*, p. 9.

[12]See Madeline H. Caviness, "A Lost Cycle of Canterbury Paintings of 1220," *Antiquaries' Journal*, 54 (1974):66-74.

[13]*Le jubilé de Saint Thomas Becket*, p. 9.

[14]See, e.g., Matthew Paris, *Chronica Majora*, ed. H. R. Luard, 7 vols. (London, 1872-83), 3:59; and Walter of Coventry, *Memoriale*, ed. W. Stubbs, 2 vols. (London, 1872-73), 2:245-46.

[15]J. A. Giles, "Vita S. Thomae," *Herberti de Boseham . . . opera quae extant omnia*, ed. J. A. Giles, *Patres ecclesiae Anglicanae*, 2 vols. (Oxford, 1845-46), 2:269-97 reprinted in *PL* 190:407-24.

[16]See *Selected Sermons of Stephen Langton*, ed. P. B. Roberts, Toronto Medieval Latin Texts (Toronto, 1980), Sermon 4, pp. 65-94. Hereafter, references to the Latin texts in this edition use the following form: TMLT, Sermon no.[period]section no., page no. in the sermon.section, page reference.

[17]See *Le jubilé de Saint Thomas Becket*, pp. 11, 38 and the Appendix, pp. 89-95 for comparisons between this sermon and the Office of the Translation.

[18]*Le jubilé de Saint Thomas Becket*, p. 29-31.

[19]See Roberts, *Studies*, ch. 5.

[20]"Imitemur ergo, karissimi, Mathathiam et filios eius, qui cum fidelibus Antiocho resistentibus prouide statuerunt ut contra gentes que tempore Sabbatorum in eos insurgerent unanimiter dimicarent. Nos namque prudenter et fortiter hostibus resistamus qui Sabbata nostra perturbant et iniquis surreptionibus machinantur ut spirituale gaudium in perniciem transeat animarum quod ad earum remedium est statutum" (TMLT, 4.2, pp. 67-68).

[21]"Prima causa est gaudium, ut in Domino gaudeamus . . . Secunda causa est exemplum, ut nos, qui sanctorum merita recensemus, in sensu bonorum operum eorum uestigijs insistamus . . . Tercia cause est subsidium, ut qui de sanctorum meritis gratulantur de eorum patrocinio glorientur" (TMLT, 4.4, p. 69).

[22]"Cum igitur hodie recolamus qualiter lapis grandis in sanctuario sit erectus, id est Thomas martir gloriosus de tumulo eleuatus, ad hunc lapidem cordis dirigamus intellectum, et defigere studeamus in eo nostre mentis affectum, ut deuotionis nostre testis esse possit et uelit" (TMLT, 4.9, pp. 72-73).

[23]"Tabulata, quibus templi parietes decorantur, sunt fideles ecclesie qui eam uestiunt et ornant . . . Huic sensui bene congruit quod tabulata fuerunt in superioribus latiora, quia fidelium mentes ad temporalia se constringunt et ad celestia se expandunt" (TMLT, 4.23, pp. 80-81).

[24]"Sunt enim corda bonorum thuribulo ualde similia, quod cum sit clausum inferius, superius est apertum" (TMLT, 4.24, p. 81).

[25]"Nam et auis domestica, alijs auibus capiendis assueta, se premit cum predam conspicit quam ardenter appetit, et ad quam dirigendam sese sentit. Quis ergo miretur si mens hominis in humilitate se comprimat quando predam beatitudinis eterne considerat, ad quam inhianter aspirat? . . . Regulus aues uolantes inficit, coluber autem latibula querit et colit. Bene ergo uinum colubro comparatur et regulo: colubro, quia libidinem prouocat. . ." (TMLT, 4.28, pp. 83-84).

[26]"Post ista premissa, sequitur competenter: 'Comedite amici, etc.' Decenter enim exultant qui talibus obsequijs Deum placant. Quoniam autem inebriatio, sicut diximus, spiritualis leticie notat habundantiam, recte qui Dominum in sanctorum memoria uenerantur inebriandi dicuntur, ut aperte notetur quod sancti leticia debeant habundare" (TMLT, 4.14, pp. 75-76).

[27]"Hac consideratione uir iustus, quanto magis in perfectionem se erigit, tanto per humilitatem amplius se substernit, ne superba de se sentiat, et per presumptionem precipitatus corruat, aut per inanem gloriam euanescat" (TMLT, 4.20, p. 79).

[28]"Illorum autem mentes memoria martiris imbuit quorum conuersatio fortitudinis eius formam in se ostendit. Imitantur enim martyrem, quibus licet non sit datum pati pro Christo, pro eius tamen amore labentia cuncta despiciunt, carnem affligunt, et ad promerenda celestia se potenter accingunt" (TMLT, 4.30, p. 85).

[29]"Lapidum nomine martires figurari sequentia declarabunt. Lapides ergo transferunt qui translationi martirum obsequia sue deuotionis impendunt, qui scilicet eorum reliquias de locis humilibus eleuant, ut sullimius et sollempnius cum debita ueneratione reponant. Nos igitur lapidem preciosum trans-

tulimus, cum translationi martiris obsequium qualem potuimus exhibere curauimus" (TMLT, 4.31, p. 85).

[30]"Prouisum namque fuerat ab hijs qui martyrem transtulerunt ut feria tercia transferretur, quia tercia feria passus fuit, ut talis dies eius glorie deseruiret qualis eius passioni ministerium suum impendit" (TMLT, 4.35, pp. 88-89).

[31]See the reference to Henry II in note 33, below. There are more specific references to Becket's persecution, to England, and to the English church in the second sermon discussed later in this paper.

[32]*Le jubilé de Saint Thomas Becket*, p. 9.

[33]"Martir enim fuit ea die de terra translatus qua rex Henricus, cuius tempore passus est, fuit in terra sepultus, ut impleretur hoc modo quod legitur in scriptura: 'Mons cadens defluit, et saxum de loco suo transfertur.' Montes sunt qui terram planam altitudine sua transcendunt et in sullimitate cacumen suum attollunt. Montes itaque sunt reges et principes, qui terrarum dominium optinent, et sullimiores sunt ceteris eminentia potestatis. Mons ergo magnus cecidit cum rex Henricus occubuit. Mons autem iste defluxit, cum regem mortuum sinus terre suscepit" (TMLT, 4.37, pp. 89-90).

[34]"Quod beatus martyr cuius sollempnia celebramus lucerna fuerit ardens et lucens. . . . Dominus hanc lucernam accendit, cum electum suum in apicem eximie prelationis erexit. Hanc etiam lucernam emunxit, cum martyrem suum exilio diuturno, contumelijs, dampnis et iniurijs innumeris affligi permisit. . . . Dominus hanc lucernam extinxit, cum seruum suum martyrio consummauit. Set dum corporaliter eam extinxit, spiritualiter eam magis accendit, quia sanctitatis eius titulum post mortem ipsius crebris miraculorum testimonijs illustrauit" (TMLT, 4.38, pp. 90-91). This image from John 5.35 is used frequently. Bernard of Clairvaux, for example, used it for John the Baptist. See J. Leclercq and H. Rochais, *Sancti Bernardi Opera,* 7 vols. (Rome, 1968), 2: 176: "In nativitate Sancti Ioannis Baptistae, De lucerna ardente et lucente." My thanks to Beverly Kienzle for this reference.

[35]*Memoriale,* 2:246.

[36]*Le jubilé de Saint Thomas Becket,* pp. 37-43.

[37]For a complete description and analysis of the contents of this MS, see Roberts, *Studies,* pp. 152-54 and 262. The text is edited in *Selected Sermons*

of Stephen Langton, here, 3, pp. 53-64.

[38]"'Sub umbra illius quem desideraueram sedi, fructus eius dulcis gutturi meo. Introduxit me rex in cellam uinariam, ordinauit in me caritatem.' Horum uerborum seriem tripliciter exponemus, ut primo congruat martiri cuius sollempnitas hodie agitur; secundo dominice natiuitatis tempori; tercio etiam uestre religioni" (TMLT, 3.1, p. 55).

[39]For a survey on sermon construction see Roberts, *Studies,* chap. 4. There are sixteen references to Scripture in the sermon and one to a classical source, Horace, *Satires* 2.2.73-74. See TMLT, 3.15, line 31, p. 62.

[40]"Sequitur: 'fructus eius dulcis gutturi meo.' Fructus desiderati est passio ipsius. Tunc enim dulcis fuit ei passio Ihesu Christi: quod rei euentu ostendit, quando pro eo exilium sui suorumque proscriptionem, contumelias et opprobria mente hylari sustinuit" (TMLT, 3.2, p. 56).

[41]"Vnde bene huic martyri competit quod dicit Ecclesiasticus de commendatione magni sacerdotis: 'Ecce sacerdos magnus quasi flos rosarum in diebus uernis et quasi lilia in transitu aquarum'" (TMLT, 3.4, pp. 56-57).

[42]"Flos lilij sex folijs distinguitur, et gloriosi martyris exilium per .vi. annos dilatatum est. Semen rubicundum in summitate lilij est martirium, quod summitas floris per .vi. folia distincti pretendit, quia in fine annorum quibus exulabat secutum est martyrium" (TMLT, 3.7, p. 58).

[43]"Sequitur: 'introduxit me rex in cellam uinariam.' Cella uinaria est gloria martirum. A torculari defertur uinum in cellarium. Vinacium porcis relinquitur conculcandum. Vinum est anima; vinacium est corpus. Tunc ergo introductus est in cellam uinariam, quando ab exilio rediens a torculari passionis ferebatur anima ad gloriam eterne beatitudinis" (TMLT, 3.3, p. 56).

[44]"Cella uinaria est ecclesia; dolia martyres; vinum passiones eorum. Similiter Dominus noster introducit animam fidelem in sanctam ecclesiam, proponit ei uinum caritatis in passione beati Stephani qui legitur affectuose pro inimicis orasse, vinum mundicie in festiuitate sancti Iohannis Euuangeliste, vinum innocentie in festo sanctorum innocentum, vinum gariophilatum in passione beati Thome, qui dici potest zelus libertatis ecclesiastice" (TMLT, 3.12, pp. 60-61).

[45]"Cella uinaria est claustrum in quo debet esse uinum conpunctionis, abstinentie, religionis" (TMLT, 3.16, p. 63).

[46]"Rosa designat martyrium. Rosa crescit super spinam. Spina est caro; rosa super spinetum est martyrium in corpore afflicto. Vel spinetum potest dici Anglia, quia aculeo persecutionis non cessat ecclesiam infestare. Certe uilissimum esset hoc spinetum nisi rosas aliquas procrearet. Ab hoc spineto namque prodijt sanctus Elfegus, sanctus Eadmundus et multi alij. Rosa que ultimo decorauit hoc spinetum fuit gloriosus martyr Thomas; et ideo non est spernendum hoc spinetum, quia si Domino placuerit adhuc poterit et alias rosas procreare" (TMLT, 3.4, pp. 56-57).

[47]Sabine Baring-Gould, *Lives of the Saints*, 16 vols. (Edinburgh, 1914), 4:229-32.

[48]Baring-Gould, 14:462-66. For a "Life of St Edmund" see *Three Lives of English Saints*, ed. M. Winterbottom, Toronto Medieval Latin Texts (Toronto, 1972).

[49]Smalley, *The Becket Conflict*, pp. 222-23 and 248.

[50]Lawrence C. Braceland, S.J., ed. and trans., *Gilbert of Hoyland 4: Treatises, Epistles, and Sermons*, Cistercian Fathers Series, no. 34 (Kalamazoo, MI, 1981), pp. 132-81.

[51]I have prepared a detailed inventory (soon to be published) of over 180 Latin sermons about St. Thomas of Canterbury belonging to the period from the 1170s to ca. 1400. These texts were intended for the use of preachers on Becket's feastday, December 29, and the Feast of the Translation of the Relics, July 7.

Maternal Imagery in the Sermons of Hélinand of Froidmont

Beverly Mayne Kienzle

Hélinand (1160-1237), monk at the Cistercian monastery of Froidmont, authored the French poem Les Vers de la Mort *and numerous Latin works, chief among them the* Chronicon *and a collection of liturgical sermons. The sermons were first edited by Bertrand Tissier in the* Bibliotheca Patrum Cisterciensium *and then reproduced by J.-P. Migne in volume 212 of the* Patrologia Latina. *Additional sermons are found in two Paris mss, Bib. Nat. ms lat. 14591 and Bib. Maz. 1041. The complete sermons are now being edited by Beverly Mayne Kienzle for the series* Corpus Christianorum, Continuatio Medievalis. *Most of the sermons were probably composed at Froidmont for a monastic audience, but several were delivered in Toulouse for the 1229 synod and the founding of the new university. The style of Hélinand's sermons varies from harsh denunciation of abuses of wealth and power to gentle praises of Christ and Mary. The form is transitional, ranging from the simple emotive passages characteristic of the monastic homily to the structural complications of the school sermons. Notable are the numerous* exempla *which found their way into the writings of many later authors.*

In the sermons examined here, Hélinand, like other Cistercian writers, has recourse to maternal imagery. With it, he describes the relationship between the word and preacher or listener who must strive to show God's word some measure of the divine love he or she receives. He also employs it to evoke the deep sentiment of his own conversion, the moment when he was overwhelmed with the power of God's love. Tracing Hélinand's use of this imagery broadens our understanding of the Cistercian tradition of employing feminine imagery and enhances our appreciation of his place in that tradition.

Maternal Imagery

While Hélinand of Froidmont urged that the word be preached with force and acerbity,[1] he also counseled preachers and listeners to relate to the word with gentleness and sweetness. The relationship between preacher and word includes a maternal dimension, involving affection and caring. The preacher is to model his own spiritual motherhood of the word (*divini Verbi mater spiritualis est, PL* 212:534B) on the example of the Blessed Mother who cared for the living Word. The listener, too, must relate to the word with maternal attention. Simeon's enthusiastic and affectionate reception of the infant Christ demonstrates how the word should be received. The listener's responsibility is also described with maternal imagery, an obligation to prepare the heart as a mother hen does her nest (*verbo Domini Facere nidum, ubi ponat pullos suos, et foveat, PL* 212:531D).

The usage of maternal imagery has precedence in twelfth-century Cistercian references to a mothering quality in authority figures.[2] The affectionate relationship to the word also has a personal source in Hélinand's own conversion. In order to convey the depth of God's love for him, Hélinand included among his chosen images that of Christ as mother hen and himself as chick ([me] *duxit ut gallina pullos suos congregans sub alas et fovens, PL* 212:592B).

My study of preacher and listener's relationships to the word begins with texts concerning the preacher: the maternal affection and preparation of self patterned on the Blessed Mother. The role of the heart, home and destination for the word, provides the transition between preacher and listener, the bearer and the receiver of the word. I next focus on the listener's responsibility to the word, modeled on Simeon's receiving the infant Christ but described with feminine imagery. Finally, Hélinand's own conversion with his description of a maternal Christ leads to the personal source for this affection for the word, the preacher's devotion to the person and example of the living word.

That any sermon writer and especially a Cistercian would choose Mary's love as a model for deep affection would not surprise us. Hélinand, however, marked his texts devoted to Mary with a very personal stamp. His enthusiasm moved him to pursue certain images with little grace. For example, he compares Mary at length to an elephant (*PL* 212:661-68). At even greater length, he belabors a tedious comparison between Mary and the parts and attributes of a rose (*PL* 212:636-46). Yet devotion overflows with beauty from a shorter passage where Hélinand refers to himself and fellow Cistercians as Mary's vassals (*PL* 212:495D).

The language of courtly tradition is evident as Hélinand calls Mary the great sovereign lady (*magnae . . . dominae*) to whom the Cistercians pay homage (*faciunt homagium*). She alone is the order's advocate, and all its churches are named for her. Dutiful Cistercians (*qui . . . cum bona conscientia defunguntur*) receive the earth in a sort of feudal agreement (*in foedum*) with reciprocal benefits. In return for the service promised this queen in their profession of vows, the Cistercians receive protection. Her seal is confirmed in the prayers for the dead[3] and is described with martial language, for the sweet name of this queen (*dulce nomen Mariae*) is mighty. Reciting prayers in her name casts off all slanderers' depravity, blocks every mouth from speaking iniquity, breaks off every controversy, and vanquishes every possession.

Vassal of Mary, our Cistercian preacher looks to her for advice on delivering the written word. Hélinand describes the future preacher as spiritual mother of the divine word: *praedicator . . . divini Verbi mater spiritualis* (*PL* 212:534B).[4] This analogy is developed in sermon six, the first for the feast of the Purification (*PL* 212:530-35).[5] Mary's self-purification and bringing her infant to the temple figures the preacher's self-preparation and offering of the word. Preparation begins in the heart, then cleanses the life and purges the conscience.

Three aspects of Mary's offering deserve the preacher's special consideration: the time, the manner, and the place; or when, how, and where (*tempus, quando; modus, quomodo; locus, ubi*, *PL* 212:534AB). For Mary, the time of offering involved a waiting period. The living word was not offered immediately after birth, but rather when Mary's cleansing was complete. The manner required careful attention, for the word was brought forth neither in fearful majesty nor in contemptible nudity. He was dressed by tender hands (*indutum membris teneris*) and wrapped in very pure cloths (*pannis mundissimis involutum*). The place where the infant word was offered, the midst of the temple, not outside it, indicates that the preacher ought to preach publicly in a church. However, he must first cleanse his conscience and fully purify his way of life.

Hélinand elaborates further on how to deliver a sermon: the type of language and the tone of voice. The preacher should not offer the word in philosophical majesty, nor rough simplicity; rather, he must show it a mother's care and gentleness, clothing it with affectionate utterances (*affectuosissimis adornatum sententiis*) and wrapping it in sweet sayings (*dulcissimis sermonibus involutum*). Accordingly, the preacher's voice ought not to make a loud noise in the people's ears, but reach the depths of their hearts as Jesus entered into the midst of the temple (*PL* 212:534C).

The heart, site of preparation in the preacher, is also then, in the listener, the target for the sermon. In another sermon, Hélinand borrows the metaphor of the preacher as archer, shooting arrows into the hearts of his listeners (*PL* 212:546).[6] Here he discusses where the preacher ought not to aim his sermon, and he distinguishes four types of preaching and preachers.

A bothersome multitude of preachers address purses, tongues, and ears; few take on the more difficult task of preaching to hearts. The purse preachers ask for nothing but money; the tongue preachers seek nothing but fame; the ear preachers do not know how to ask for anything;[7] and the heart preachers do not want to lose anything. Their type of preaching is to be pursued with great effort, and its pursuit is hard work. Purity of heart is required for entering and not merely piercing the listener's heart. The instrument for entrance is a eucharistic tongue (*lingua eucharis*), prepared on the altar of a pure heart, and found only in a good person (*PL* 212:534D).

Hélinand again draws on maternal imagery to underscore the preacher's intimate responsibility to speak with and out of holiness. Here the image becomes somewhat complicated when Hélinand combines the roles of conceiver and begetter in the person of the preacher.[8] He says that a woman who conceives a child in sin gives birth in sin. Correspondingly, one who conceives the divine word in impurity is necessarily an unworthy sower and a useless distributor of holy seed. Conception, when tinted with sin, results in a sinful giving birth for the woman; for the preacher, sinful conception of the word leads to corrupted begetting of the word. Conception requires fertility for the woman and also for the preacher in the form of fruitful doctrine (*fecunditas doctrinae*). Development of the fertility parallel between woman and preacher stops when Hélinand, perhaps like the tongue preacher he criticizes, takes the occasion to demonstrate his own talent by exploiting *fecunditas* and *facundia*. He states that fruitful doctrine is unfruitful unless fluency of speech makes it fruitful ([*fecunditas doctrinae*] *semper infecunda est, nisi eam fecundit linguae facundia*, *PL* 212:535A). The preacher's fertility is then self-contained, made fruitful only by his own eloquence.

Receiving the fruits of the preacher's efforts also involves the heart and includes a preparation that is maternal, described with the nest image. The listener should come to meet the word and show it affection just as Simeon came to meet the child Jesus in the midst of the temple and embraced and kissed him. Coming to meet the word means coming to the preacher's word with an alert mind, a ready spirit, and a prepared heart (*PL* 212: 531C). The heart must open its door as soon as the preacher begins to speak, for the heart is the home for the divine word. It is: *domicilium, domus, mansio, hospitium*, and *nidus*. Home and affection are drawn together in the nest image, and the listener is counseled to imitate the hen. Hélinand borrows, he says, from Augustine when he states that the hearer ought to make a nest for the word of God, a place to put the chicks and keep them warm (*verbo Domini facere nidum, ubi ponat pullos suos, et foveat*).[9] Simeon's receiving Jesus in the midst of the temple means accepting the word into the heart, an *hospitium* where the word, offered by the preacher, is like a small boy knocking at the door and seeking a place to stay (*PL* 212:531D-532B). Final signs of affection are seen in Simeon's taking the infant in his arms, embracing him, and kissing him. Taking the child is interpreted as carrying out the salvific word with good works, embracing as doing what is commanded and more, and kissing the feet of the Lord as looking down upon all that is ours and attributing everything to God (*PL* 212:532CD).

In showing affection to the word, preacher and listener try to reciprocate and emulate the divine love God lavishes on them. For Hélinand, the overpowering intensity of that divine favor was felt at the moment of his conversion, when the Lord he calls kind Jesus (*bone Jesu*) touched his heart. The heart turning to God experienced divine power but also divine affection. To express the caring protection of the Lord who called him, Hélinand again uses the maternal imagery of the nest.

In sermon fourteen for the Ascension, various birds are mentioned--hen, eagle, vulture, crow and dove--and two--the mother hen and the mother eagle--are selected to represent Christ's guiding his little ones to a virtuous life and calling upon them to aspire to a life beyond. One takes charge of the nest, the other of leaving it.[10] The hen, drawn in over her chicks, teaches us to live in moderation, integrity, and devotion on earth. We live under wings that represent an example for living and a message for teaching, both in humility (*PL* 212:592C). In the manner of the hen, Christ is occupied with our earthly life, leading us around, teaching us, and guarding us like the pupil of his eye (Dt 32:10) (*PL* 212:593). The hen changes the earth into the gate to salvation (*PL* 212:593C). We dream of moving from under the hen's wings onto the shoulders of the eagle (*de sub alis gallinae super humeros aquilae*, *PL* 212:593B). In Hélinand's text, Christ is the eagle of Dt 32:11, calling her young to flight and hovering over them (*PL* 212:593D, 594B).[11]

From the sermon's aviary,[12] the hen and the eagle provide images for Christ's intervening actions in Hélinand's life. Indeed, Hélinand begins the sermon speaking to Jesus with a lyric beauty imitating the imagery of the psalms:

> Kind Jesus, you who protect me under the shadow of your wings, you who cast a shadow over me with your shoulders, you who draw me in with the perfume of your ointments, you come to meet me and with hand [outstretched] take me up into your arms; you first taught me to walk humbly after you on earth; today you teach me how to soar sublimely after you into heaven (*PL* 212:591D).

In the same way that Christ cared for the little children, he showed concern for Hélinand (*PL* 212:592A); like the mother hen, he led the sinful poet under his wings. First the devil found and surrounded Hélinand, and then Christ found and succoured him. The devil's serpent led him astray, and the Lord's messenger, finding him in darkness, could not bring him home. Then a pure man, a sort of Moses, found Hélinand toiling in vain in the mud and serving the devil with debauched excess and hardened, stubborn wickedness (*effeminata luxuria, dura et obstinata malitia diabolo servientem*). This Moses led Hélinand out of his desert but did not guide him to peace. Only God as man in Christ could do that. He brought the poet onto the mountain of holiness. Like the hen gathering and warming the chicks under her wings, Christ led Hélinand.

When Hélinand describes the hen's behavior, he implies that Christ is a diligent seeker of souls. Like the woman in Luke's gospel who searches diligently for her silver coin (Lk 15:8-10), the hen scratches, turns the home upside-down, and turns over the whole nest-covering to look for a sick chick. Hélinand illustrates this determined searching with the example of the abbot who should imitate the hen and the eagle. The abbot is like Christ and the hen when he checks the beds of monks not present for a particular task. A prelate is also like an eagle; he ought to rise above his monks as the eagle flies above her young (*PL* 212:594BC).[13]

In summary, Hélinand describes with maternal imagery the relationship between preacher and listener and the word. His devotion to the Blessed Mother warms his counsel that the preacher emulate her preparation for sending forth the living Word. In imitation of her self-purification, the preacher is spiritual mother of the divine word (*praedicator . . . divini Verbi mater spiritualis*, *PL* 212:534B). As conceiver and begetter of the word, he combines male and female roles. His fertility depends only on his own eloquence. The listener's obligation to the word, although modeled on Simeon's reception of Jesus in the temple, also involves a maternal dimension. A hearer of the word must prepare a nest in the heart, placing the word there and keeping it warm (*verbo Domini facere nidum . . .* , *PL* 212:

531D). Both preacher and listener strive to show God's word some measure of the divine love they receive.

Hélinand's usage of maternal imagery follows a tradition in twelfth-century Cistercian writers, and at the same time, seems distinctive and personal. Whereas in many sermons his style shows the structuring influence of the new school sermons,[14] here his language reflects the emotive quality of the monastic homily where the words of scripture give natural expression to thought.[15] Hélinand's Cistercian predecessors developed that sort of preaching with a special emphasis on the tenderness of a loving God. Hélinand's feminine imagery, based in nature, also exemplifies what M.-D. Chenu has called the "symbolist mentality" of the twelfth century. Writers in the tradition of Cîteaux and Saint Victor made use of metaphoric analogy to find messages of divine love flowing from the most lowly creatures in nature.[16] This familiar natural imagery is extended to encompass Hélinand's own concern with preaching. The tenderness he describes is directed primarily toward the word by both preacher and listener, or toward humankind by God. Unlike the earlier Cistercian abbots, here he does not mitigate the prelate's authority with images of maternal tenderness. His abbot as hen searches for negligent chicks and as eagle, rises above others. Furthermore, Hélinand extends the imagery to include the preacher and a non-authority figure, the listener.

Hélinand again has recourse to maternal imagery to describe the moment when he himself was so overwhelmed with the power of God's love that he entered the monastery.[17] Christ as mother hen led and warmed him under protective wings. As mother eagle, Christ teaches him how to soar into heaven. Having journeyed from sinful poet to signal preacher, Hélinand now aspires that his preacher's offering may be pleasing and well-received, like Mary's offering of the word. To deliver the word, a preacher must bring a cleansed life, abundant knowledge, and accomplished eloquence to the task of persuading others to undertake the journey toward salvation. His speech, instrument of holy persuasion, should be pure and simple, honest and useful, holy and salvific, gracious and sweet, just as the Psalmist sings: "grace is poured from your lips" (Ps 45:2). Hélinand's speech, seldom pure and simple, undoubtedly reached its highest graciousness when he recalls the affectionate concern of divine love and emulates its manifestation in the Blessed Mother's care for the living Word.

Notes

[1] Beverly M. Kienzle, "The Sermon as Goad and Nail: Preaching in Hélinand of Froidmont," in E. Rozanne Elder, ed., *Goad and Nail*, Studies in Medieval Cistercian History 10, CS 84 (Kalamazoo, 1985).

[2] See Caroline Walker Bynum, *Jesus as Mother: Studies in the Spirituality of the High Middle Ages* (Berkeley, 1982), pp. 110-69. Bynum states that Hélinand uses little feminine imagery and that he is "the only Cistercian [she has] found who lacks the intense interiority and sense of incorporation with God that characterizes his fellow Cistercians [and] lacks also any interest in the cloister (either as solitude or as community)." For Bynum, Hélinand "was far more interested in the organization of the church and the life of the clergy" and employed building imagery popular with some regular canons (p. 165). While Hélinand doubtless used less feminine imagery than his Cistercian predecessors, I consider it not insignificant that he employs maternal imagery to describe his own conversion, to soften the definition of his own role, that of preacher, and to describe a non-authority figure, the listener.

[3] "Et ipsa nobis securitatem facit de foedo nostro in charta sua, id est in brevibus quae fiunt pro defunctis: ubi dulce nomen Mariae, et ejusdem inviolabilis sigilli confirmatio hoc modo recitatur: Eo die obiit frater ille monachus vel conversus sanctae Mariae de Fremont" (*PL* 212:495D).

[4] Gregory the Great drew a clear parallel between preaching and motherhood in Homily 3, *40 Homiliarum in Evangelia*, Liber I: "Sed sciendum nobis est quia qui Christi frater et soror est credendo, mater efficitur praedicando. Quasi enim parit Dominum, quem cordi audientis infuderit. Et mater ejus efficitur, si per ejus vocem amor Domini in proximi mente generatur" (*PL* 76:1086D). Henri de Lubac cites three commentaries on the Song of Songs, those of Gregory, Aponius, and Honorius, where preachers are compared to two breasts of scripture. Hélinand is the only source given for the phrase "mater spiritualis" (*Exégèse médiévale* [Paris, 1959], 1.2:409-10). As mentioned in Bynum (p. 118), Bernard also employs breasts and nursing as symbols of preaching: feeding the needy with the milk of doctrine (Sermon 41.5-6, *S. Bernardi Opera*, ed. J. Leclercq, C. H. Talbot, and H. M. Rochais,

Maternal Imagery

5 vols. [Rome, 1957], 2:31-32), trans. Kilian Walsh in *On the Song of Songs II*, CF 7 (Kalamazoo, MI, 1983), p. 208.

[5]Other sermons for the Purification include sermon seven (*PL* 212: 535-44) and an unedited sermon in Bib. Nat. ms lat. 14591, fol. 32, summarized briefly by A. Lecoy de la Marche, *La chaire française* (Paris, 1868), pp. 167-68.

[6]An arrow image is used by Hugh of Saint-Cher--"First the bow is bent in study, then the arrow is released in preaching"--and inspires the title of the *Liber Pharetrae*, a collection of authorities probably compiled by a Paris Franciscan working before 1264. See Richard H. and Mary A. Rouse, *Preachers, Florilegia, and Sermons: Studies on the Manipulus florum of Thomas of Ireland* (Toronto, 1979), p. 41.

[7]Alain of Lille states that preaching designed to delight the ear rather than to edify the soul is to be condemned (*PL* 210:112C; trans. Gillian A. Evans in *The Art of Preaching*, CF 23 [Kalamazoo, MI, 1981], p. 18).

[8]Bynum, p. 148, distinguishes stereotyped male and female roles in Cistercian usage of imagery and includes engendering (either begetting or conceiving) as both a male and female role. This example in Hélinand is an interesting combination of the two aspects of engendering.

[9]The hen image has its scriptural source in Mt 23:37. Anselm is possibly the source for twelfth-century Cistercians and may have taken the image from Augustine's exegesis of Ps 101:7. See *A Book of Showings to the Anchoress Julian of Norwich*, ed. Edmund Colledge and James Walsh, 2 vols. (Toronto, 1978) 1:153-54; and Bynum, pp. 113-15.

[10]Adam of Perseigne, in a letter possibly written in 1192, exhorts the bishop of Le Mans to take better care of those entrusted to him. In stressing the prelate's paternal and maternal responsibilities, Adam uses the hen and the eagle: "Alioquin quo pacto se patrem parvulorum aut matrem nominatur qui pullis suis affectu tenero more galline non incubat, aut sicut aquila provocans ad volandum pullos suos super eos volitet, et in alis tam verborum quam operum commendatos sibi parvulos sursum portet?" (*Correspondence*, ed. J. Bouvet, *Archives historiques du Maine*, 13 [1952], letter 4, p. 30; see also Bynum, p. 125).

[11]This eagle is somewhat confusedly juxtaposed with the vulture (also "aquila") in Pr 30:17 whose offspring, with the crows, attack those who mis-

treat their father and mother. Hélinand deals briefly with the significance of the crows' and eaglets' violent behavior and then returns to the image of Christ extending his wings of forgiveness over all (*PL* 212:594C).

[12] These aviary images relate to the probable use of aviary and bestiary books for instruction in Cistercian monasteries; see Willene B. Clark, "The Illustrated Medieval Aviary and the Lay-Brotherhood," *Gesta*, 21 (1982): 63-74.

[13] Comparison of the abbot and the hen is also found in Adam of Perseigne; see note 10 above.

[14] On Hélinand's style, see my "Erudition at God's Service: Hélinand's Toulouse Sermons II," in *Erudition at God's Service*, ed. John R. Sommerfeldt, Studies in Medieval Cistercian History 11, CS 98 (Kalamazoo, MI, 1987), pp. 277-90.

[15] Richard N. and Mary A. Rouse cite Hélinand as a preacher whose works show the impact of the school sermon on the cloister homily; see *Preachers, Florilegia, and Sermons*, pp. 71-72.

[16] See M.-D. Chenu, *Nature, Man, and Society in the Twelfth Century* (Chicago, 1968), pp. 113-19.

[17] On the language and meaning of monastic conversion, see Marie-Bernard Saïd's introduction to Bernard of Clairvaux, *Sermons on Conversion*, CF 25 (Kalamazoo, MI, 1981), pp. 13-15.

Humbert of Romans's Material for Preachers

Simon Tugwell, OP

> *Humbert of Romans (ca. 1200-77), fifth Master of the Dominican Order (1254-63) and one of the outstanding churchmen of his age, wrote a large work designed to help preachers understand and practice their vocation, known under the title* De Eruditione Praedicatorum. *The structure of this work, not all of which survives, and much of which has never been printed, has been generally misunderstood. This is not surprising, since the work is very awkwardly constructed; subsection nine of section seven of the work consists of sermon material for nearly four hundred different kinds of occasions.*
>
> *This article considers the structure of* De Eruditione Praedicatorum *and the difficulties that would be involved in using Humbert's material in creating an actual sermon. The difficulties are illustrated by a comparison between a surviving sermon, which is almost certainly to be ascribed to Humbert, and the corresponding section in the sermon material. Since neither text has previously been published, a provisional edition is given of both.*

Humbert of Romans's massive work *De Eruditione Praedicatorum* has never been printed in its entirety, nor is there any known surviving manuscript which contains the whole of it. Not surprisingly, its structure and the scope of its contents have been generally misunderstood.[1]

Internal references show that *De Eruditione Praedicatorum* was completed after Humbert's collection of *exempla*, *De Dono Timoris*, after the *Instructiones* on the officials of the Order, and after the *De praedicatione crucis*; thus, it can be dated to the period after Humbert's retirement from being Master of the Dominican Order in 1263.[2] Its purpose was similar to that of the *Instructiones* on the officials: Humbert intended to inform preachers what is involved in being a Dominican preacher. His book is therefore quite different from the *artes praedicandi* which were beginning to proliferate.

As part of his attempt to provide all the help he could to preachers, Humbert suggested material for sermons for a huge variety of different occasions, and this accumulation of sermon material took on a life of its own, so that most of the surviving manuscripts omit the rest and contain only the sermon material, in varying degrees of completeness. This part of the work has accordingly come to be treated as "book two,"[3] but this is not in fact what Humbert intended.

There is, unfortunately, a textual puzzle about the index to the whole work. In MS Avignon, Musée Calvet 327 (hereafter cited as A), the sections of the work are listed as follows (fol. 1^r):

> Sex sunt circa hoc notanda:
> Primum est de condicionibus huius officii.
> Secundum est de necessarii predicatori ad hoc officium exercendum.
> Tertium est de modo accendendi ad hoc officium.
> Quartum est de execucione huius officii.
> Quintum est de effectu huius officii.
> Sextum est de effectu huius officii.
> Septimum est de annexis isti officio.

It will be noticed that although six items are promised, seven are in fact listed. The number six is firmly established in the tradition. Only three other manuscripts of this part of the work survive, and they all have the same reference to *sex . . . notanda*. Two related manuscripts, Segovia, Cathedral, Estanceria B 331 (=S), and Salamanca, Bibl. Univ. 773 (=T), have the same list of contents as A, but omitting *de annexis isti officio*. Madrid, Bibl. Nac. 19423 (=M), has *de annexis* but omits *de effectu*, which could be simply an oversight, though *de annexis* is duly listed as number six.

It is conceivable that the seventh section, *de annexis,* was not part of Humbert's original plan for the work, but it contains material which is obviously important for preachers, so we should perhaps infer that *sex sunt notanda* is a mistake for *septem sunt notanda*.

Simon Tugwell, OP

In any case, all four manuscripts contain a lengthy section seven, whose contents are listed at the beginning of the section as follows:

> Circa annexa predicationi sciendum est quod ista sunt decem, scilicet discursus per mundum, conuersacio inter homines, collocuciones familiares, hospitacio apud extraneos, occupaciones circa aliqua negocia hominum, requisicio consiliorum, auditus confessionum, prothemata, materie sermonum seu collacionem, iniuncciones oracionum.

per mundum conuersacio: per modum conuersacionis ST

The whole collection of sermon material is therefore subsection nine of section seven of the work as a whole!

The final piece, headed *iniuncciones oracionum*, seems not to have survived at all. The sermon material survives in a fair number of manuscripts, but nowhere completely.

An introductory paragraph leading into the sermon material is found in most manuscripts. The commonest form of it is this:

> Circa materias sermonum siue collacionum notandum est quod interdum multis difficilius est inuenire materias utiles et laudabiles de quibus fiat sermo quam inuenta materia de ipsa sermonem contexere. Ideo expedit quod predicator semper habeat in promptu materias ad predicandum uel conferendum de deo siue ad omne genus hominum siue in omni diuersitate negociorum siue secundum uarietatem temporum siue secundum uarietatem omnium festorum.

de deo: diuidendo ST

This is how the text features in M and, also, with insignificant variants, in Bologna, Bibl. Univ. 2323, Donaueschingen 342, Michelstadt 685, Munich Clm 186, Nürnberg Cent. II 17, Rheims 612, and Vatican Pal. lat. 368.

In three manuscripts, however, A, S, and T, an extra two sections of sermon material are promised:

> siue secundum proprietates missarum temporis siue secundum proprietates sanctorum in festis eorum.

And the general index in M also contains these two sections (fol. 86ᵛ):

> Speciales materie secundum uarietates missarum pertinencium ad tempus sub titulis lxxi.
>
> Speciales materie secundum proprietates sanctorum sub titulis lxvii.

Michelstadt 685 actually contains the material for individual saints, under sixty-seven headings, as announced in M.

The final index in M is very much more complete than the actual text contained in the manuscript (all the sermon material is in fact omitted from the text), and the specification of how many headings are included in each section of the sermon material indicates that the index was based on a complete text of the work, as there is no reason to suppose that Humbert composed an index of what he proposed to do before he finished writing it. The fact that the *iniuncciones oracionum* do not feature in M's final index can perhaps be taken as an indication that Humbert forgot to write this concluding section, or that if he did, it soon dropped out of circulation.

The disagreement, then, between the introductory paragraph found in most of the manuscripts and the final index in M may be regarded, cautiously, as a hint that Humbert added two extra sections of sermon material which were not originally part of his plan. And this hint is perhaps confirmed to some extent by the disagreement between A and ST over the text. A has the last item as:

> siue proprietates sanctorum in festis eorum.

ST have:

> siue secundum uarietates et proprietates eorum in festis (eorum S).

Eorum obviously needs to be emended to *sanctorum*, but otherwise it could be suggested that the readings of A and ST are due to divergent ways of incorporating a notice of sections found in the text but previously missing in the introductory paragraph.

The contradiction in the Michelstadt manuscript between the introductory paragraph and the actual contents of the text is easily explained, as we know that the scribe, Johannes Merstetter of Ehingen,[4] referred to more than one manuscript. At the end of his section four (on *diuersa negocia*), he notes (fol. 167ᵛ):

> Finis libri quarti sed in aliis exemplaribus est finis secundi, ita quod illa quarta in eisdem est pars 2a.

The agreement between what is announced in the index in M and what is actually contained in the Michelstadt manuscript makes it more or less certain that the sermon material on individual saints is an authentic part of Humbert's work. The section *secundum proprietates missarum temporis* is apparently missing, although it is quite possible that it is lurking somewhere anonymously in some manuscript waiting to be identified.

It is possible, then, that Humbert added some extra material which was not originally envisaged, but the work as it finally emerged almost certainly contained six sections of sermon material, all six sections constituting subsection nine of section seven of the book as a whole. It would be hard to imagine a more implausible structure.

The sermon material has a quite precise purpose in Humbert's mind. He is not providing ready-made sermons or model sermons; rather, he is suggesting ideas for the content of sermons. In most sections, he proposes one or two scriptural texts which could be used as a *thema*, but he makes little or no attempt to indicate how the arrangement of ideas he presents could be fitted to the normal *divisio* of the *thema*. In section six, on individual saints, he does not even propose any texts that could be used for a *thema*; instead, he always includes an *exemplum* designed to show that devotion to the saint in question is profitable. Since Humbert insists that sermons should be "woven" out of the words of scripture, his suggested *materia* gives a strictly limited assistance to the preacher, who has to devise some way of taking the *materia* to bits and re-assembling it around a scriptural text.

in iubilo,[f] scilicet angelorum, quia angeli multum gauisi sunt uidentes quod cum multitudine ueniret ad reparandum sedes suas. Et *similiter*[6] in prima preparatione ad hanc restaurationem multum gauisi sunt, scilicet incarnatione, unde cantauerunt, Gloria in excelsis deo.[g]

Tertio gauisi sunt de hostis antiqui deiectione. Quando aliquis intuetur duellum et uidet illum qui magis diligitur uictorem esse, multum gaudet. Militia est uita hominis super terram.[h] Iob VIIa. Intuentur angeli pugnam ipsam et multum diligunt nos et ideo multum gaudent cum uincimus diabolum. De prelio inter Michaelem et diabolum in Ap. XII, Ipsi uicerunt eum, id est diabolum. Propter hoc dicit uox in celis, Letamini celi etc.[i]

Quarto gaudent de domini sui honoratione plus quam de proprio. Quid est illud in quo summe honoratur deus de hac uita? Istud(?) sunt laudes diuine, scilicet quando promimus et psallimus laudes dei. Tunc principes celi et mundi et prouinciarum angeli ueniunt et adiungunt se nobis. Unde Ps., Preuenerunt principes coniuncti psallentibus.[j] Bernardus. Quam felix esses si oculis spiritualibus uidere posses qua cura, quo tripudio assunt orantibus, intersunt psallentibus.[k] Iob. Ubi eras cum me laudarent astra matutina, que habent certas horas quibus apparent et surgunt--hii sunt sancti qui deum laudant certis horis--et iubilarent filii dei, id est angeli, qui expressius imitantur deum.[l]

Quinto gaudent de nostra conuersione. Et exemplum habetur de quodam uiro sancto cui facta est reuelatio cuiusdam hominis in peccato existentis, et uidebat quod animam illius miseri duo demones alligatam duxerunt et angeli sancti a longe steterunt quasi compatientes et pio affectu gementes. Intrauit ille ecclesiam, audiuit uerbum dei et proposuit bene facere. Postea uir sanctus uidit animam lucidam, que prius deformissima erat, uidit demones lugentes et a longe stantes, angelos uero gaudentes et quasi manibus plaudentes. Et ideo gaudium fit in celo etc.

Instruxit nos apostolus gaudere cum gaudentibus.[m] Si ipsi etiam angeli gaudent et nos gaudere debemus in hoc festo. Unde et officium huius festi in aliquibus ecclesiis est, Gaudeamus omnes in domino etc.,[n] de cuius conuersione etc. Unde hec est una ratio quare sancta ecclesia fecit festum de conuersione beati Pauli. Sed nonne alii peccatores conuersi qui postea confecti sunt et de morte sanctorum facimus festum, non de conuersione ipsorum? Ideo uidete non fuit hoc sine causa.

Karissimi conuersio Pauli induxit maius gaudium in ecclesia quam alicuius alterius, quia ante conuersionem eius in magna tristitia erat primitiua ecclesia, sed conuersio beati Pauli magnum induxit gaudium in ecclesiam, quia conuersio Pauli fuit desperatior et uiri boni qui diligunt salutem animarum plus gaudent si contingat aliquem conuerti de quo nulla spes erat quam si aliquis alius conuerteretur. Quis [n]umquam speraret quod ille conuerteretur qui habuit animam ita crudelem quod persequebatur discipulos Christi? Quis etiam crederet quod tam cito conuerteretur? Unde tanto maius fuit gaudium quanto minus sperabatur. Unde Augustinus in lib. Confess., Gaudemus magis de salute desperate anime quam si spes fuisset de ea. Nec mirum, quia tu pater gaudes magis super uno peccatore penitentiam agente quam XC[IX] etc.[o] Gaudemus igitur de conuersione eius ut conformemus uoluntatem nostram uoluntati diuine.

Secunda causa est quia exemplo excellentior, magne enim auctoritatis erat. Unde si homo magne auctoritatis modo conuerteretur, omnes gauderent propter exemplum bonum quod monstraret. Paulus bonus clericus fuit ante conuersionem suam. Unde aliquando dictum fuit ei, Insanis Paule, multe littere te ad insaniam perducunt.[p] Magne etiam auctoritatis fuit quoad religionem que erat in iudaismo, in qua (fol. 226[r]) irreprehensibiliter uixit. Unde quando talis conuertebatur qui tante erat auctoritatis, tanto maius gaudium erat quanto maius dedit exemplum. Unde Augustinus, Multis noti multis [te] auctoritati[s] sunt ad salutem multosque preeunt sequentes.[q] Hec est secunda ratio.

Tertia ratio est quia quanto eius aduersio erat periculosior, tanto conuersio eius erat gratiosior. Unde Augustinus, Triumphat [impera]tor uictor et quanto in bello maius fuit periculum, tanto maius est gaudium in triumpho.[r] Pugnauit Christus pro ecclesia contra illum et prostrauit illum, et tanto maius gaudium quanto peius erat ecclesie periculum.

Quarta ratio est quia fructuosior fuit eius conuersio. Quis umquam fuit ita fructuosus ecclesie sicut Paulus? Nullus. Non enim fuit arbor infructuosa, immo fructuosa. Unus erat de illis quibus dicit dominus, Posui uos ut eatis etc.[s] Et dicit Gregorius in quadam omelia, Petrus post se Iudeam conuersam adducet, Thomas Indiam, Andreas Achaiam, Iohannes Asiam, sed Paulus post se totum mundum adducet.[t]

Quinta ratio est quod eius conuersio maius gaudium induxit, quia eius conuersio usque hodie est ad profectum ecclesie et nichil ita attrahit cor humanum conuersum ad spem uenie sicut conuersio Pauli. Effudit enim deus misericordiam suam super eum et peccatorem existentem in actu peccati conuertit et conuersionem eius insigniuit miraculo celesti. Unde circumfulsit eum lux de celo. Et omnes bestie currunt ad odorem pantere.⁷ Hoc etiam quod dicitur Cant. I, Curremus in odore unguentorum tuorum.ᵘ Et Bernardus, Omnino propter mansuetudinem quam audimus predicari de te curramus post te bone Ihesu, scientes quia non despicis peccatorem penitentem, non horres mulierem lacrimantem, non mulierem Chananeam, non sedentem in theloneo, nec deprehensam in adulterio, non negantem discipulum, non persecutorem discipulorum, id est Paulum, nec proprios crucifixores.ᵛ In odore illorum unguentorum curremus.

Item conuersus fuit non semiplene sed ua[l]de perfecte. Aliqui sunt qui de facili redeunt[ur], et si non corpore tamen mente retro redeunt. Egredere inquit dominus Abrahe de terra tua.ʷ Cum esset extra corpore uoluit quod exiret mente secundum illud Ps., Obliuiscere populum tuum et domum patris tui.ˣ Et apostolus, Posterorum oblitus etc.ʸ

Item quod perfecte conuersus fuit patet in perfecta uoluntatis mutatione. Prius erat uoluntas sua contraria Christo, modo omnino conformis. Unde dixit, Domine quid me uis facere?ᶻ Et dicit Bernardus, O uerbum breue sed efficax etc. Plures inuenimur imitatores illius ceci euangelici cui dixit dominus, Quid uis ut faciam tibi, quam qui dicunt cum Paulo, Domine quid me uis facere?ᵃᵃ

Tertium est quia statim cepit impugnare partem aduersam pro Christo. Unde fecit sicut miles aliquis conuersus ad regem aliquem statim incipit impugnare inimicos eius. Et ideo legitur hodie euangelium perfectionis, Ecce nos reliquimus omnia etc.ᵇᵇ Rogemus.

[a] Lk 15:7.
[b] Jn 20:20.
[c] Job 33:26.
[d] Matt 18:10.
[e] 1 Cor 13:12.
[f] Ps 46:6.
[g] Lk 2:13-14.
[h] Job 7:1.
[i] Apoc 12:7-12.
[j] Ps 67:26.
[k] Bernard, *Ep.* 78:6.
[l] Job 38:7.
[m] Rom 12:15.
[n] E.g., *Corpus Consuetudinum Monasticarum*, 9:146 (Fleury).
[o] Cf. Augustine, *Conf.*, 8, 3:6.
[p] Acts 26:24.
[q] Augustine, *Conf.*, 8, 4:9.
[r] Augustine, *Conf.*, 8, 3:7.
[s] Jn 15:16.
[t] *Hom. Ev.*, 1, 17:17 (*PL* 76:1148B).
[u] Cant 1:3.
[v] Bernard, *In Cant.*, 22:8.
[w] Gen 12:1.
[x] Ps 44:11.
[y] Phil 3:13.
[z] Acts 9:6.
[aa] Bernard, *Serm. de Sanctis, In Conv. S. Pauli*, 1:6.
[bb] Matt 19:27.

Simon Tugwell, OP

Michelstadt 685 fol. 176[r]
De conuersione sancti Pauli.

Notandum quod beatus Paulus ante conuersionem fuit magne auctoritatis aput iudeos cum haberet potestatem alligandi omnes christianos ubicumque inuenirentur,[a] et magne litterature cum propter illam dictum fuit ei quod insaniret,[b] et maximus ecclesie dei inimicus cum eam supra modum sit persecutus,[c] ut ipsemet dixit. Sicut igitur esset maximum gaudium fratribus in aliqua religione noua quando aliquis magne auctoritatis et magne litterature et eorum persecutor intrat ad eos, ita et in primitiua ecclesia maximum gaudium fuit de conuersione Pauli. Propter quod post conuersionem eius immediate ecclesia sancti spiritus consolatione replebatur.[d]

Item aliqui conuertuntur de quorum conuersione non sequitur nisi propria salus eorum. Aliqui uero sunt qui in aliqua parte mundi post conuersionem suam salutem aliquorum operantur. De conuersione uero Pauli secuta est conuersio totius mundi. Unde Gregorius de fructu quem presentabunt *apostoli*[g] domino in die iudicii dicit, Ibi Petrus post se Iudeam, Thomas Indiam, Iohannes Asyam, Andreas Achaiam, Paulus uero ut ita dicam totum fere mundum post se conuersum adducit.[e]

Item post ascensionem domini dominus aliquando homines misit ut apostolus, quandoque uero angelos ut patet in Cornelio.[f] Ad conuertendum autem Paulum nullum alium misit, sed ipsa in persona propria uenit apparens ei in uia qua ueniebat,[g] quod fuit maxime dignationis in Christo et honoris in Paulo.

Item dominus sciens quod Paulus erat durus ad conuersionem, ideo non est usus solis uerbis, sed et miraculis ad eius conuersionem, quia circumfulsit eum lux de celo, audita est uox et diuina potentia eum prostratum excecauit.[h]

Item Paulus fuit maximus peccator, sicut ipse dixit dicens, Quorum ego primus sum et maximus,[i] et tamen numquam quieuisset a malo uel in aliquo bono se preparasset nisi dominus eum conuertisset, ymo in ipso actu peccati cum esset in uia ad faciendum malum conuertit eum dominus, quod cedit ad maximam spem peccatoribus. Quis enim peccator hec audiens audeat desperare?

Item conuersio eius fuit ualde perfecta. Non enim solum sua et suum sanguinem reliquit, sed suam omnino uoluntatem subiciens eam omnino uoluntati diuine, cum dixit, Domine quid me uis facere?[j] Omnem etiam malitiam statim mutauit in bonitatem, factus de lupo agnus ut dicit Augustinus.[k] Ipsum quoque Christum contra quem pugnabat pro iudeis statim incepit defendere contra iudeos, confundens eos et affirmans quoniam hic est Christus. Et hec tria pertinent ad conuersionem perfectam et ueram.

Sic ergo patet quod sex sunt prerogatiue huius conuersionis. Nullius enim conuersio tantum gaudium induxit in primitiua ecclesia, nec tantum fructum in mundo, nec ita honorata fuit a persona diuina post recessum eius de mundo, nec sic decorata miraculis, nec in qua illuxerit tanta diuina gratia ad dandum spem peccatoribus, nec in qua fuerat tanta perfectio ut esset bonum exemplum ad ymitandum. Et ideo iustum est ut potius fiat festum de istius conuersione quam Magdalene uel Mathei uel alterius cuiuscumque.

Exemplum. Legitur in legenda Pauli quam descripsit *Linus*[9] quod post mortem suam quam cito Paulus cum innumerabili turba candidatorum apparuit Plantille que capitegium suum ei tradiderat euntí ad passionem ut de eo ligaret oculos suos et reddens illud ei dicens, Illud tu michi Plantilla in terris obsequium tradidisti et ego tibi quam citius ad regna celestia pergenti deuotissime obsequar et in proximo pro te reuertar et regis mundi tibi gloriam demonstrabo.[l] Ex quo patet quam sit utile seruire beato Paulo et esse deuotum ei.

[a] Acts 9:14.
[b] Acts 26:24.
[c] Gal 1:13.
[d] Acts 9:31.
[e] *Hom. Ev.*, 1, 17:17 (*PL* 76: 1148B).
[f] Acts 10:3.
[g] Acts 9:3-5.
[h] Acts 9:3-8.
[i] 1 Tim 1:15.
[j] Acts 9:6.
[k] Cf. *PL* 39:5008 (in the Dominican Lectionary: AGOP XIV L 1 fol. 194ʳ).
[l] *Passio S. Pauli,* 17 (ed. Lipsius, 1:41-2).

Notes

[1] Two sections of the sermon material were published in Hagenau in 1508, and the text of this edition has been reprinted in whole or in part quite frequently; the whole work up to the end of the second section of sermon material was first printed in Barcelona in 1607. Currently the most accessible edition of the work, up to but excluding the sermon material, is contained in J. J. Berthier, *Humberti de Romanis Opera de Vita Regulari* (Rome, 1888; rpt. Turin, 1956), 2:373-484. A translation of the work, with a selection of the sermon material, based on an edition in progress is included in Simon Tugwell, *Early Dominicans,* Classics of Western Spirituality (New York, 1982), pp. 183-370. I am preparing a critical edition of the whole work for Oxford University Press.

Simon Tugwell, OP

[2]Cf. F. Heintke, *Humbert von Romans* (Berlin, 1933), pp. 114-16; and E. T. Brett, *Humbert of Romans* (Toronto, 1984), pp. 153-54.

[3]This is already a feature of one manuscript (Salamanca 773).

[4]The scribe identifies himself on fol. 210^r. I am informed by Dr. Sigrid Krämer that two other manuscripts of his are known, but almost nothing has so far been discovered about the scribe himself, who presents himself as a secular priest in Speyer.

[5]After this sentence the manuscript contains the beginning of another sentence, which is then cancelled: "uidebant ciuitatem Iherusalem et istud significat in hoc quod iudei multum gaudebant quando. . . ."

[6]The manuscript has "sunt."

[7]The manuscript has "pancete." Cf. Thomas Cantimpratensis, *De Natura Rerum*, ed. H. Boese (Berlin, 1973), p. 159: "Cetere bestie cum vocem eius (sc. panthere) audierint, congregantur et sequuntur odoris suavitatem, qui egreditur de ore ipsius."

[8]The manuscript has "angeli."

[9]The manuscript has "Lucas."

The Rethorica nova *of Ramon Llull:*
An Ars praedicandi *as Devotional Literature*

Mark D. Johnston

Ramon Llull (1232-1316) is one of the most remarkable figures of the Scholastic era: a Catalan nobleman turned evangelist in a mid-life reform, he labored for over fifty years to convert Jews and Moslems in Spain and abroad, to obtain support from princes and popes for his missionary enterprises, and to compose a single theological and philosophical system capable of "proving" Christian doctrine to unbelievers, the so-called "Great Universal Art of Finding Truth." Self-educated, he composed in Latin, Arabic, and Catalan nearly three hundred works based on his Great Art, using a highly idiosyncratic terminology and cryptic symbolic arguments whose methods have long puzzled scholars. Among these many works, one that offers a perhaps unique insight into the verbal processes basic to Llull's whole enterprise is his still unpublished Rethorica nova *(cited here from Paris Bib. Nat. MS lat. 6443c, 14th cent., fols. 95va-109va).*

One of several treatises that attempt to rectify received Scholastic learning by reinterpreting it through the Great Art, the Rethorica nova *is nominally an* ars praedicandi *composed first in Catalan (1301) and then translated into Latin (1303). It uses sequences of allegorical interpretations* (distinctiones) *to combine commonplace precepts regarding popular preaching with traditional moral instruction concerning speech. The result is a sort of comprehensive art of Christian discourse, a model for the exercise of verbal* caritas *that would make all speech one great sermon or moral exhortation, and thereby promote the universal renewal of the* vita apostolica *that Llull sought so fervently. The* Rethorica nova *suggests how all Llull's writings function not as learned exposition, but rather as spiritual edification. It especially suggests how both the*

The Rethorica nova *of Ramon Llull*

moral ideals and discursive techniques of popular preaching may have broadly and profoundly guided the communication of lay devotion and learning in the late thirteenth century.

It is a truism of medieval studies, proclaimed by scholars from Owst to Murphy,[1] that preaching must have been one of the most pervasive influences upon the development of popular culture in the Middle Ages. The contribution of Franciscan sermon style to the growth of vernacular literature is a commonly cited example of such influence.[2] Other less obvious examples undoubtedly exist, awaiting scholarly recognition of their exact relation to particular aspects of sermon technique and preaching method. The writings of the Catalan lay philosopher and theologian Ramon Llull (1232-1316) constitute one especially unusual, yet previously unacknowledged, example. His work has long been regarded as one of the most idiosyncratic and marginal products of Scholastic culture.[3] Nonetheless, recent advances in our understanding of medieval popular religion and literature, notably the studies of Michel Zink[4] and J. B. Allen,[5] allow us to recognize that at least two fundamental features of Llull's seemingly unique work do in fact reflect techniques and methods basic to the practice of popular preaching in his day. The first of these, suggested by Zink, is the written redaction of popular sermons as devotional literature for those *laici religiosi* who formed an "intermediate public" between the illiterate audiences of popular preaching and the learned forums of the university sermon.[6] The second, argued by Allen, is the widespread use in later medieval literature of *distinctiones*, the lists of the various (typically tropological) senses of words. Although originally composed as preaching aids, the collections of *distinctiones* were so successful that they competed with other types of compendia and encyclopedias as popular sources of received wisdom.[7] Allen argues that the most important consequence of these collections' popularity was the habits of discursive organization that they encouraged. They legitimized the practice, especially common in narratives employing *exempla*, of treating the mere collocation of data under a single distinctive heading as immediate evidence of the innate mutual reference and relevance of that data.[8]

The writings of Ramon Llull display exhaustively the features noted by Zink and Allen; in many cases, recognizing them is the only way to make sense of Llull's arguments. No work of his demonstrates this more clearly than his treatise on preaching, the *Rethorica nova*. Taken at face value, his recommendations concerning the composition of sermons are grossly impractical. Examined in the light of Zink's and Allen's conclusions, however, Llull's *Rethorica nova* becomes comprehensible as a work devoted not to the academic education of learned clerics in the rhetorical precepts of the *ars praedicandi*, but rather to the moral edification of devout laymen in the use of language as an exercise of spiritual truth and Christian charity.

To the modern reader unfamiliar with Llull's life and work, the *Rethorica nova* must appear as peculiar as his entire career: a nobleman-turned-evangelist in a mid-life religious awakening, he devoted his life to proselytizing Jews, Moslems, and even Orthodox Christians from Spain to Armenia.[9] The chief weapon in this campaign was his singular philosophical and theological system, the so-called Great Universal Art of Finding Truth, which he continuously revised throughout his career. Although he received no formal university training, he eventually wrote nearly three hundred works covering virtually all fields of Scholastic learning, composing them in his native Catalan, Latin, and Arabic. The method of Llull's Great Universal Art has long puzzled scholars. Its most notorious feature is its use of letters of the alphabet to symbolize the basic principles that Llull defined as the common foundations of all knowledge and being. By combining these letters in square or circular diagrams, Llull claimed to generate true formulations of all possible philosophical and theological propositions. The success of his methods depends chiefly on the values of the basic categories that Llull chose as the foundation of his entire Art: these are the Divine Dignities or fundamental attributes of God, which all creatures share as likenesses of the Creator. The most basic of these attributes are the nine Absolute Principles--*Bonitas, Magnitudo, Duratio, Potestas, Sapientia, Voluntas, Virtus, Veritas, Gloria*. Their possible interrelations are the nine Relative Principles--*Differentia, Concordantia, Contrarietas, Principium, Medium, Finis, Maioritas, Aequalitas, Minoritas*. Llull adds as well a group of nine inventional questions--*Utrum, Quia, De Quo, Quare, Quantum, Quale, Quando, Ubi, Quomodo et Cum quo*.

Some modern scholars have sought a formal logical basis for Llull's system in the *ars combinatoria* of its letter symbolism.[10] Others have concluded, however, that those symbolic diagrams serve a purely mechanical or mnemonic function, and that the truth value of any proposition that they generate depends instead on their discursive interpretation.[11] This interpretation does not employ the Aristotelian syllogistics of Llull's Scholastic peers, but instead applies exhaustively analogical, allegorical, proportional, and figural arguments all devoted to showing how any philosophical or scientific truth reveals the one truth of Christian doctrine. In my own recent work I have attempted to show how Llull offered this spiritual reinterpretation or "moralization," to use the Scholastic term, of the rudiments of medieval logic.[12] Here I want to suggest how Llull pursued the same tropological enterprise in his treatment of rhetorical theory, as presented in the *Rethorica nova*.

The *Rethorica nova* is by far the longest of Llull's theoretical accounts of the *ars praedicandi* and constitutes a sort of omnibus of preaching precept and sermon aids, including several short collections of *exempla* and proverbs with directions for their use. Llull moralizes all this material, with the result that his text most resembles the allegorical sections on biblical figures of the preacher from Humbert of Romans's *De eruditione praedicatorum*,[13] whose rudimentary level of stylistic and dispositional precepts it also imitates.

The colophon states that Llull composed this work in Catalan during September of 1301 while staying at the monastery of Saint John Chrysostom in Cyprus; in 1303 it was translated into Latin at Genoa, perhaps by one of Llull's companion amanuenses.[14] The Catalan version no longer survives, except for the list of fifty proverbs,[15] which appears in another vernacular work, his *Proverbis d'ensenyament*.[16] The spelling "rethorica" in the title reflects common Scholastic orthography. The Greek etymology of the word apparently did not have much influence in preserving the more correct spelling: even though Isidore illustrated the derivation of "rhetorica" with the Greek "rhetor,"[17] this word appears as "rethor" in, for example, manuscripts of Gundissalinus's popular *De divisione philosophiae*.[18] The adjective "nova" indicates this work's contribution to Llull's project for refounding all the arts and sciences on the "new" principles of his own Great Art--during this same period he also wrote a *Logica nova*, *Geometria nova*, *Metaphysica nova*, and so forth.[19] As Samuel Jaffe has pointed out, the claim to offer a "new" Rhetoric is virtually a *topos* of prescriptive rhetorical theory.[20] The best-known example from the fourteenth century is probably the *Rhetorica novissima* of the Bolognese *dictator* Boncompagno, who was noted for his "scurrilous and eccentric" personality.[21] Llull's title alludes not to his claims for special professional aptitude, but rather to his new conception of artful speech as an essential skill for the Christian *homo novus*.

Llull divides his text into a Prologue and four sections (*distinctiones*) entitled "Order," "Beauty," "Knowledge," and "Love." The following pages use the Prologue alone as a framework for analyzing the doctrines advanced in the complete treatise, chiefly because Llull's introductory section establishes the fundamental concepts necessary to understanding the rest of the work's somewhat disorganized and repetitive precepts. It is not coincidental, for reasons that will become clear, that Llull's Prologue offers no formal definition of the foundations of preaching as a branch of rhetoric or of its relationship to the other language arts. The definitions of rhetoric or the *ars praedicandi* found scattered in Llull's other, typically encyclopedic works are rarely more than tersely formulaic, as when he states in his *Ars generalis ultima* of 1308 that rhetoric is "the art invented for the rhetorician to color and ornament his speech" or that preaching is "the form with which the preacher informs the people to pursue good morals and avoid bad ones, and especially if that mode of discourse is through the Principles and Rules of this Art."[22] Virtually all of Llull's learning in any field is equally superficial and probably reflects his own exclusive education from popularizing *florilegia* and manuals. Despite his frequent recourse to popular compendia of Scholastic learning, Llull does not imitate their usual definition of an art according to its Aristotelian four causes, the common practice in thirteenth-century *introductiones ad artes*.[23] Llull's favorite theological authorities are usually pre-Scholastic, and his opening remarks in the *Rethorica nova* may imitate some of the introductory formats popular in the twelfth century, such as the *didascalica* recommended by Boethius,[24] or the seven circumstances of Hermagoras listed by the Pseudo-Augustinian *De rhetorica*.[25] Whatever his model of exposition might have been, his comments nonetheless reveal his conviction, intimated as well in the terse definitions of rhetoric or preaching from his encyclopedic works, that the affective force of language depends on verbal ornament:

> Since speech is the means and instrument through which speakers and listeners accord in one end, it follows that insofar as words are more fully ordered and more ornate, so much more fully are they made attractive with beauty, and insofar as words are more beautiful, so much more pleasing are they rendered to the listeners. And truly insofar as they are more pleasing, so much more necessary it is that through them the speakers and listeners are joined agreeably in one end. And since the art of rhetoric is ordained to this, the subject of the said art will be ordered, ornate, and beautiful speech.[26]

The three functional terms in this Prologue are "end," "order," and "beauty." In regard to the first, the one end that Llull's speaker should seek is, of course, Christian love, and his entire conception of the affective force of speech remits to Augustine's advocacy of a Christian rhetoric of verbal *caritas*.[27] Llull's stress on the common accord of speaker and audience, rather than the speaker's persuasion of his audience to his own ends, reflects the participational conception of speech that underlies his extraordinary proposal of speech as a sixth sense called *affatus*.[28] Within the metaphysical system of his own Great Art, all the components of communication--including speakers, audiences, and messages--realize a communicative act thanks to their common participation in Llull's universal Absolute and Relative Principles. Llull's phrase "rendered more pleasing to the listeners" is the first of many echoes in the *Rethorica nova* of the precept "render the audience well-disposed, attentive, and receptive" that the *artes dictaminis* adapted from Cicero[29] in order to describe the function of the exordium in a speech; beginning with the *Dictaminum radii* of Alberic of Monte Cassino,[30] this phrase becomes a shibboleth of dictaminist doctrine. In other passages of the *Rethorica nova*, several references to plans for epistolary composition clearly show Llull's familiarity with at least the rudimentary teachings of the *ars dictaminis*. The collocation of so much disparate and even extraneous precept is a notable consequence of his exclusive reliance on *distinctiones* as the means of developing his arguments.

In regard to the second and third key operative terms introduced in Llull's opening lines, his focus on the order and beauty of speech appears at least to parallel similar concerns in medieval literary theory. The virtual identification of rhetoric with ornament seems to reflect the conventional distinction of rhetoric as ornate speech from grammar as correct speech and logic as true speech,[31] as well as the treatment in certain *artes praedicandi* of all rhetorical recourses and devices as forms of ornament.[32] Llull's mention of ordered as well as ornate speech may be an allusion to the conventional Ciceronian rhetorical canon of arrangement (*dispositio*), which he nominally treats under the heading of Order in this treatise. Llull devotes most of his attention, however, to word-order, an emphasis that perhaps reflects the association of word-order with ornament. This association appears in John of Garland, who states that "the fitting and elegant arrangement [*ordinatio*] of the parts of speech renders sentences fitting and elegant."[33]

Despite their apparent literary connections, Llull's categories of order and beauty owe far more to the traditional Scholastic definition of beauty as "due proportion" or "order."[34] For Llull, the order of speech is its beauty and its beauty is its order. Moreover, that order is necessarily extra-linguistic: it is the order of things. Since words are tokens of things for Llull, they must consequently express that order. In a passage from his *Libre de contemplació en Déu* [Book of Contemplation of God] of 1276 where he explains methods for "saying words rhetorically ordered" when meditating, he declares that "insofar as one speaks of the things that are most beautiful and greater and more virtuous, thus are the words more beautiful and more pleasing to hear and to be understood."[35] This order of things is of course theocentric; therefore the order of words must be so as well. The ontic, cognitive, affective, and linguistic statuses of things are perfectly aligned in one system organized according to the values of Christian ethics. This system simply extends principles already set forth by the twelfth-century pre-Scholastic authorities whom Llull evidently had read copiously. For example, Walter of Saint Victor declares that "Truly similar symbols [of God] are not however called similar symbols as though they had no dissimilarity, but rather because of their greater excellence."[36] The beauty that Llull seeks in words is precisely this "excellence," dignity, or nobility that a creature bears according to its relative approximation to the Creator. Llull moralizes rhetorical precepts by organizing them in *distinctiones* that allow their recognition as *symbola similia*. The result is an exposition of the rhetorical doctrine of the *ars praedicandi* oriented chiefly toward the spiritual edification of its audience. Such results are evidently perfectly consonant with the goals and objectives of Llull's own evangelistic program, according to his remarks on the genesis of the *Rethorica nova*:

> Desiring therefore, which we had long sought, to offer knowledge of well-ordered and ornamented speech and to compose sermons according to the General Art--but not being able because of certain other affairs that we could not avoid, especially because these sermons require much writing since they are very diverse in subject matter--we composed compendiously this book, in which is disclosed an easy and most useful way of composing and arranging beautiful and natural sermons for many and various subjects with due order and procedure maintained.[37]

The *Rethorica nova* thus purports to be an *ars praedicandi* organized according to the principles of Llull's Art, although these principles really play only a minor role in the elaboration of his rhetorical program as a whole; in the *Rethorica nova* they serve chiefly as ready-made *distinctiones* for classifying various aspects of artful speaking. There is no reason to doubt Llull's claim that he had long planned such a work, and the absence of any allusion to his doctrine of *affatus* indeed suggests that he might have composed most or all of it before 1295, when he introduced his peculiar theory of speech as the sixth sense. Llull's reference to the "compendious" character of his treatise invokes conventional distinctions between the *forma tractandi* and *forma tractatus* of a work.[38] His remarks about writing sermons are difficult to understand, since the *Rethorica nova* does not include any actual specimens of the preacher's art. Perhaps Llull originally intended to include a collection of sermons such as that accompanying his later *Liber de praedicatione*.[39] The sermons from that work display little affinity, however, with the preaching methods expounded in his *Rethorica nova*, whose practical utility is slight, given the work's overwhelming moralizing function of developing its reader's awareness of the ethical imperatives governing all uses of speech.

Llull concludes his Prologue by naming the four sections of the *Rethorica nova*. Llull commonly includes such an explanation of his text's divisions in all his later writings, a practice that reflects his attention to the creation of *distinctiones*, a term that he often uses, as here in the *Rethorica nova*, to name textual divisions, in the manner of his Scholastic peers. He briefly suggests a rationale for recognizing these particular divisions, which correspond in no way to the conventional canons of Ciceronian rhetoric:

> In order moreover that the teaching of this book offer itself more clearly to the readers, we have divided the book in parts so that the order of the doctrine will be patent and anyone who seeks anything in it will be able easily to find it. Thus the parts of this book are four, namely [1] order, [2] beauty, [3] knowledge, and [4] love. And therefore order is set as a part of this knowledge because in it is offered instruction for speakers. Here they are taught to maintain due order and avoid disorder in any sermons and speech, so that from this might be procured the mutual peace and amity of speakers for listeners, which beautiful and orderly speech initiates, since according to Seneca "let speaking well be the beginning of friendship." Similarly indeed we set as a part beauty--which we also said to be the subject of this art--because we wish to declare it as a

subject of this rhetoric. Thus through it we might be able to offer instruction in which through it and with it each one might be able to ornament his speech and beautify it with fitting ornament. Moreover, we set knowledge as a part of this rhetoric of ours in order to offer instruction through which is made understood to its readers how through it and with it the beauty and ornament of speech should be sought, and how ornate and beautiful words ought to be found. Thus may be distinguished the beautiful and orderly from the foul and disorderly, so that the beautiful are accepted for use and the foul avoided. We also assign a fourth part of this art and call it love, because here teaching should be drawn from it, whether in speech or not. Because words proferred from love shine with so much loveliness of beauty that in the end they cannot be beautiful without love.[40]

Since Llull rarely cites any authorities in his works but his own writings, his explicit reference here to Seneca is very unusual, if not improbable, even though it appears in all three of the best manuscripts of the *Rethorica nova*. Jordi Rubió has suggested that this phrase is very likely a marginal gloss that was copied into the text early on in the manuscript tradition.[41] However, Seneca's acknowledged position as the *magister moralitatis* for the medievals made references to him ubiquitous in medieval moral literature such as the collections of *distinctiones*.[42] This particular aphorism appears to remit ultimately to Isocrates's oration *Ad Demonicum*;[43] Albertano da Brescia includes it in his *Ars loquendi et tacendi*,[44] and Brunetto Latini after him in his *Tresor*.[45] Since Llull obviously relies on existing *distinctiones* in composing his own, it is just as likely that he imported this quotation himself from one of his sources.

Llull's reference to Seneca in connection with order in fact gives little idea of the precepts actually advanced in that part of his treatise. His account of order comprises a fairly brief exposition of three *distinctiones* that he recognizes for it. These correspond broadly to word association, word order, and sentence order. Llull's comments on the appropriate combination of words superficially recall the practice of *determinatio* described by authors of *artes poetriae*,[46] but express more directly the ethico-metaphysical perspective or "moralization" defined by his idiosyncratic doctrine of two universal "intentions." As set forth in his early *Libre de intenció* [Book of Intention][47] and integrated into all his subsequent work, this doctrine asserts that every created being possesses a primary intention or end of directly serving, honoring, and knowing its Creator, and a secondary intention or end that contributes indirectly to the first. This doctrine evidently synthesizes various arguments from the rich Patristic and Scholastic literature concerning the ultimate good or moral finality.[48] The most obvious precedents are Augustine's famous distinction between use and enjoyment[49] and Anselm's principles of *rectitudo* and *ordinatio*.[50] Llull's demonstration of these universal "intentions" effectively generates his entire program of moralizing argument, since they define a dynamic status for any real or rational being as the realization of those intentions. As applied to word-order in the first part of the *Rethorica nova*, Llull's doctrine produces such difficult precepts as his claim that words must be arranged in a sentence in order of their "dignity." For example, the sentence "the queen and servant-girl have great beauty" is more "rhetorically spoken" than the sentence "the servant-girl and queen are lovely with great beauty" because the word-order of the former rightly recognizes the precedence of a queen over a servant.[51] This qualitative determination of word order has a parallel in the rules for composing the greeting of a letter that the *artes dictaminis* prescribed.[52] Nonetheless, a more immediate precedent is the allegorical interpretation of word-order in Scriptural exegesis. Alford gives various examples, such as Hugh of St.-Cher's explanation why the phrase *regnum sacerdotale* from Exodus 19.6 appears as *sacerdotium regale* in 1 Peter 2.9.[53]

The first part of the *Rethorica nova* on order ends with a lengthy discussion of the parts of speeches or letters devoted to requesting, exhorting, defending, denouncing, admonishing, or accusing. These are the oratorical goals typically described in the Northern Italian *artes concionatoria, arengandi*, and *dictaminis*.[54] Llull's explanation of these genres is very rudimentary, and consists largely in recounting *exempla* appropriate to each part of such a letter or speech. When explaining how to earn the goodwill of a superior from whom one seeks a favor, he suggests using the widely repeated story of Alexander the Great offering a city to a faithful soldier.[55] When Llull turns to expounding the composition of an accusation, the *exemplum* that he recommends is an account of how a soldier composed his accusation when speaking before his lord. This infinite regress of exemplification extends both in and out of Llull's own text: his explanation itself becomes an *exemplum*, fusing or collapsing the functions of "showing" and "telling" or "illustrating" and "expounding" in his treatise. Llull's need to explain *distinctiones* embracing very disparate elements compels him to exemplify them repeatedly in order to demonstrate their analogical relation to each other. The representative illustrations that he offers effectively become *exempla* of their own exemplarity. When he concludes the entire section on order by observing that "there are many other modes that could be narrated," his use of the verb "to narrate" aptly recognizes that fusion of exemplary method and exemplary material in his own discourse.[56] His account of order illustrates perfectly how his analogical methods create a single system of ethical, metaphysical, and discursive *rectitudo*.

The distinction regarding beauty treats the ornament of discourse under seven headings, which evidently comprise seven *distinctiones* of the term "beauty"--*vocabula, principia, comparationes, exempla, congruum ornatum, coniunctiones et disiunctiones*, and *proverbia*. The chapter on beautiful *exempla* gives twenty-five edifying stories, some quite garbled, divided into the commonplace categories of natural and moral used by contemporary preceptists.[57] The chapter on beautiful proverbs lists fifty sayings, most of which deal with speech, like those found in similar lists from medieval ethical and courtesy literature.[58] The other chapters illustrate Llull's axiom that the beauty of words derives from the status of their referents, with examples such as "angel," which Llull calls a beautiful word (*dictio vel vocabula*) because it possesses the beautiful end of serving and knowing God.[59] The chapters on beautiful comparisons and disjunctions and conjunctions enumerate further instances of the fitting word combinations already treated in the first part on order. The repetition of similar or identical precepts in different chapters of the *Rethorica nova* perhaps suggests hasty composition, but also reflects the re-association of ideas and terms bred by the elaboration of *distinctiones*. The chapter on beautiful principles identifies these as *veritas, audacia, affectio, humilitas,* and *continuatio*.[60] These categories recall, on the one hand, traditional Ciceronian rhetorical precepts regarding delivery and display of the speaker's own good character as a means of "securing goodwill and rendering the audience attentive."[61] Llull employs many variations on this formula throughout his treatise. On the other hand, it obviously recalls as well the medieval sermon theorists' habitual emphasis on the preacher's good moral character.[62] Character acquires a virtual symbolic or communicative function in Llull's program from its analogical correlation with language in the commonplace precept *docere verbo et exemplo,* which was especially developed among the twelfth-century pre-Scholastic authorities[63] whom Llull evidently knew well.

The overall distribution of material and the exposition of individual terms in Llull's account of verbal beauty displays the moralizing pursuit of *distinctiones* at every level. This exercise consists in correlating the senses of three groups of terms. The first group includes metaphysical categories--such as form, matter, and end or the Absolute Principles--from Llull's own Great Art; the second group includes linguistic or literary categories common in medieval accounts of rhetoric or grammar; the third group includes ethical categories taken from popularizing works of medieval moral theology, especially virtue and vice treatises.[64] Llull interprets each group as an expression of the sense of the others, thereby correlating them and achieving the peculiarly moralized account of language, grounded in a theocentric metaphysics, that his rhetorical program seeks.

The section devoted to knowledge likewise distributes its material under various headings, in this case the nine Absolute Principles, nine Relative Principles, and nine Questions of Llull's own Art. This explicit use of his own terminology, which does not figure so prominently in earlier sections of the *Rethorica nova,* suggests that these portions were composed later. The application of the nine Lullian Questions displays es-

The Rethorica nova *of Ramon Llull*

pecially well Llull's moralization of learned terminology, in this case through a series of "grammatical metaphors" like those often found in contemporary exegetical literature, as noted already. Llull, however, does not simply assign tropological interpretations to common grammatical terms such as "noun" or "case," but instead finds grammatical answers to each of his nine Questions. For example, he offers the commonplace logical definition *vox significativa* in response to the question, "*Quid est verbum?*"[65] Although some of Llull's nine Questions give answers about the nature of language that plausibly reflect conventional Scholastic doctrines, this plausibility disappears completely in the exposition of his Absolute and Relative Principles as linguistic categories. The insistent tropological focus and predilect analogical form of his moralizing method completely determine his account of verbal *Virtus*, where he argues that

> If God placed virtues in plants and stones, much more [would He place them] in words that are virtuous through the moral and theological virtues existing in the speaker. And thus when the speaker has virtuous words, whose virtue is their subject or material, it colors their form, thanks to which coloring the form is beautiful. And those hearing the beautiful form receive the words with pleasure, and incline their ears and heart to listening with good will.[66]

Llull confects this little piece of moralized linguistic theory from two commonplace *distinctiones*. The first is simply the multiple senses of *virtus* frequently developed in contemporary exegetical manuals.[67] The second is the metaphor of "spiritual ears" found in St. Augustine[68] and especially developed after him by monastic authors.[69] It is especially revealing to see how the collocation of these *distinctiones* has probative value for Llull: the association of their terms explains the power of words by comparison to that of plants or stones, and the impression on the spiritual faculties by comparison to that of the physical senses. Both comparisons support Llull's conception, already noted, of the strongly affective force of language.

This chapter on *Virtus*, though brief, is also notable for its emphasis on the value of the speaker's own character as a contribution to successful persuasion. Llull's concern for this issue is evident from his development of it under several other headings in the chapter on knowledge. For example, verbal "wisdom" consists in ten "conditions" of thinking before speaking, avoiding undue brevity or superfluity, opportune time, fitting place, regard for the audience's level, useful speech, just words, honest discourse, virtuous and true speech, and a viable objective.[70] Verbal "will" consists in the love between speaker and audience and requires the six "conditions" of useful, fruitful, and just speech: appropriate length of speech, a fitting time with beautiful and useful words, an appropriate place, truth, and "concordant qualities of speakers and listeners."[71] "Glorious" speech depends on eight "principles": promising rewards, praise, narrating good works, truth, goodness, greatness, utility, and friendliness.[72] These enumerations display the Scholastic practice of *distinctiones* in an almost pure form: they collect under one heading various senses for a single term, where the collection itself serves to reinforce the recognition of a common factor in all the senses enumerated. These collections are not merely fortuitous, but depend "intertextually" on established associations of--usually very elementary--terms from the common vocabulary in a given field of learning. Because Llull typically never cites other authors, his dependence on existing lists of this kind is especially obvious and noteworthy when he incorporates known glosses or maxims. For example, when he explains the "goodness" of "glorious" speech, he cites Aristotle's famous dictum "the good is what all things seek."[73] His conflation in these lists of rhetorical and moral lore regarding speech resembles most the *De eruditione praedicatorum* of Humbert of Romans, whose use of *distinctiones* is equally evident in many parts of his manual on the training of Dominican preachers. Llull's treatise, though nominally an *ars praedicandi*, generalizes that same lore to cover all uses of speech, regarded under the single end of Christian charity that he treats in the last portion of his text.

The concluding section on love defines the paramount importance of charity in Llull's rhetorical program as a whole, reaffirming Augustine's precept that the end of all Christian instruction is love.[74] In this section Llull displays perfectly his pursuit of exemplary argument, setting forth ten proverbs on loving speech, illustrating each with an appropriate *exemplum*, and adding a brief indication of the situation in which a speaker might profitably employ the proverb and its exemplary exposition. The classification of sermons by their audience was of course one of the oldest axioms of the *ars praedicandi*, and thirteenth-century *exempla* collections still often organize their material through reference to appropriate categories of sinners and their vices.[75] Llull offers nine stories for such purposes as commending the altruistic, consoling the dejected, or upbraiding the avaricious, and one for reproving "those who in their preachings attend more to the arrangement of words and loftiness of ideas than to the good of the audience."[76] In his presentation of these *exempla,* Llull takes material originally collected for preachers to use in exhorting their audiences, and offers it as arguments suitable for anyone to use in exhorting anyone else on any occasion. In Llull's hands, the preacher's special imperative *docere verbo et exemplo* becomes the Christian's general obligation *diligere verbo et exemplo,* in which his analogizing moralization treats words and deeds simply as two *distinctiones* of one common spiritual exercise.

This summary review of the Prologue and four parts of Ramon Llull's *Rethorica nova* should demonstrate, even in the few examples cited, how his methods of argument and procedures of interpretation consist largely in the development of *distinctiones*. This practice ideally suits Llull's project for referring all creatures to their Creator, since its probative force lies, as J. B. Allen suggests, in its simultaneous assumption and demonstration of unity in diversity, of a multivocity that necessarily reduces to the univocity of one, inevitably moral, truth.[77] The common medieval view of the world and language as a single system of signs possessing a capacity for mutual "assimilation"--in the literal sense of "being likened one to another"-- allows any verbal or real thing to be a sign of any other verbal or real thing, as long as some higher meaning embraces them both. The precepts and doctrines of Scholastic learning formed for Llull part of this universal order, whose organization and truth were guaranteed by God, who is the ultimate meaning or transcendental signified in the medieval Christian universe. Llull's system seeks no "new" knowledge, but rather discovers truths that already exist.[78] Thus he rightly calls his philosophy "an art of finding truth." The theocentric organization of this system of assimilated signs, guaranteed in Llull's Great Art by the Principles that all beings share from God, assures its moral truth. As Allen so acutely observes, the structure of metaphor in medieval discourse always implies the structure of morality.[79]

Now in moralizing rhetorical precepts according to that structure, Llull manifests what Allen calls "the pervasive medieval willingness to submit empirical to devotional or interpretative necessities."[80] Although Llull undoubtedly regarded this enterprise as an effective means of combating the misuse of knowledge by his contemporaries in the schools, it is difficult to imagine how a revision of rhetorical practice that proposed using words in order of their morally determined "dignity" would find a very enthusiastic reception among his university-trained peers. Thus it is hardly surprising that, while Llull did obtain permission to expound his philosophy in various universities and *studia*, there is no evidence that he gained any followers there. We do know, however, of various devout laymen, Franciscan friars, and cloistered religious (notably the Carthusian house of Vauvert at Paris) who welcomed and supported Llull's schemes.[81] The work of Zink and of other historians of medieval popular religion allows at least educated speculation about the reasons for Llull's success among these groups. Most obviously, they all share a common engagement in the promotion of lay spirituality generally and in the encouragement of popular preaching specifically. Zink notes that the "intermediate public" of *laici religiosi* often obtained their copies of pious literature from the collections of convents or monasteries that evidently lent them out to their patrons and devotees.[82] J. N. Hillgarth has suggested that Llull himself gained his still-mysterious education at the libraries of the Dominican and Franciscan houses in his native city of Palma de Mallorca.[83]

Whatever the sources of its doctrine, Llull's *Rethorica nova*, like all his writings, displays many of the signal traits that Zink identifies in *La prédication en langue romane* with the religious literature fostered by popular preaching. A basic characteristic is the presentation of doctrines at a level less sophisticated than that of university sermons, but more developed than that of mass popular sermons.[84] A frequent practice is the organization of material as meditational *distinctiones*,[85] just as in the 365 chapters of Llull's own *Libre de contemplació en Déu*. There is a common tendency to imitate Scholastic styles or formats, though not content.[86] Most texts of this type make extensive use of allegory, analogy, and word-play,[87] including many well-known patristic allegories already introduced into vernacular preaching by the Victorines in the twelfth century.[88] Abuse of these devices typically leads to the reduction of the four recognized exegetical senses to the literal and spiritual alone,[89] and confusion in levels of allegory, resulting in "mixed metaphors" in allegorical figures.[90] The authors of popular devotional literature display the characteristic medieval facility for undifferentiated (this term is less judgmental than "uncritical") acceptance of any written material as equally authoritative doctrine.[91] More ambitious writers in this field offer elaborate contemplative schemes,[92] such as Llull's Great Art itself. Finally, there is the widespread development of material for strictly private use as "armchair preaching."[93]

With the *Rethorica nova* or any other of Llull's works viewed in this context, it becomes difficult to oppose F. R. Durieux's characterization of Llull as a "lay catechist," an educated non-cleric responding to the rising demand for popular spiritual instruction among the middle classes of the Midi in the later thirteenth century.[94] The term "popular religion" admits a range of meanings wide enough, as Jacques Paul has noted,[95] to include Llull's semi-educated activities. Still, it would be easy to dismiss Llull's methods as so perversely idiosyncratic that they bear little wider relevance to our understanding of the *ars praedicandi* in Scholastic culture. Close examination of his *Rethorica nova* nonetheless suggests that his methods, no matter how unusual, do adapt practices common in contemporary popular spirituality, especially the "moralizing" interpretation fostered in lay religious literature by popular preaching. In this regard, Llull's work allows several broad insights into the popular reception of Scholastic learning in general and of preaching theory in particular. The first is a very precise definition of the level of theoretical rhetorical knowledge possible among laymen not trained in the subtle techniques of the university sermon *ad cleros*, but educated instead through the example of the great popular preachers, such as Ramon de Penyafort, who personally counseled Llull about his plans. The second is the clear demonstration of how profoundly this example could shape the intellectual and spiritual character of devout laymen such as Ramon Llull: inspired by a Franciscan sermon to renounce the world and become himself an evangelist, he naturally adopted the style, method, and doctrines of the literature generated by popular preaching as the basis for his own personal philosophy and theology. Third and last, with respect to sermon theory itself, Llull's account of the *ars praedicandi* shows how the reflexive application of one of its fundamental practices--the tropological elaboration of *distinctiones*--could transform exposition of the theory alone into yet a further means of pursuing the moral persuasion sought in actual preaching. The reader of Ramon Llull's *Rethorica nova*, literate but not licensed to preach, learns from this account of the *ars praedicandi* a general lesson about all use of speech as spiritual truth, moral virtue, and contemplative science. Llull offers a medieval answer to the ancient question of the relationship between rhetoric and ethics: he identifies preaching as the exemplary Christian speech act and distinguishes all other uses of language as analogous exercises in moral virtue.

Notes

[1] G. R. Owst, *Literature and Pulpit in Medieval England: A Neglected Chapter in the History of English Letters and of the English People* (Cambridge, 1933; 2nd rev. ed., 1961); James J. Murphy, *Rhetoric in the Middle Ages: A History of Rhetorical Theory from St. Augustine to the Renaissance* (Berkeley and Los Angeles, 1974).

[2] As in John V. Fleming, *An Introduction to the Franciscan Literature of the Middle Ages* (Chicago, 1977) and David L. Jeffrey, *The Early English*

Lyric and Franciscan Spirituality (Lincoln, 1975).

[3] A typical assessment is Gordon Leff's in *Medieval Thought: St Augustine to Ockham* (Harmondsworth, 1958), p. 238.

[4] Michel Zink, *La prédication en langue romane avant 1300* (Paris, 1976).

[5] Judson Boyce Allen, *The Ethical Poetic of the Later Middle Ages: A Decorum of Convenient Distinction* (Toronto, 1982).

[6] Zink, *La prédication romane*, pp. 151-71.

[7] Richard and Mary Rouse, "Biblical Distinctions in the Thirteenth Century," *Archives d'Histoire Doctrinale et Littéraire du Moyen Age*, 41 (1974): 27-37.

[8] Allen, *Ethical Poetic*, pp. 101-04.

[9] The best recent summary of Llull's career is Jocelyn N. Hillgarth, *Ramon Lull and Lullism in Fourteenth-Century France* (Oxford, 1971), pp. 1-134.

[10] Notably Erhard-Wolfram Platzeck, *Raimund Lull: Sein Leben--Seine Werke: Die Grundlagen seines Denkens (Prinzipienlehre)*, 2 vols. (Rome and Düsseldorf, 1962-64).

[11] Most persuasively by Robert D. F. Pring-Mill, "The Analogical Structure of the Lullian Art," in *Islamic Philosophy and the Classical Tradition: Essays presented to Richard Walzer* (Columbia, 1973), pp. 315-26, and *El microcosmos lullià* (Oxford, 1961).

[12] Mark D. Johnston, *The Spiritual Logic of Ramon Llull* (Oxford, 1987).

[13] Humbert of Romans, *De eruditione praedicatorum*, ed. Joseph Berthier in *Opera de vita regulari*, vol. 1 (Rome, 1888), pp. 373-484; at pp. 407-11 and 450-51.

[14] All references to the still unpublished *Rethorica nova* are from the fourteenth-century copy in Paris Bibliothèque Nationale MS latinus 6443c, fols. 95va-109va, which I have collated with the less reliable and later copies in Kues, Codex Cusanus 83, fols. 77^v-89^r and Munich, Bayerische Staatsbibliothek, Cod. lat. 10529 (Pal. 526), fols. 1^r-29^v and 10544 (Pal. 544), fols. 164^r-196^v. The passage cited appears on fol. 109va.

Mark D. Johnston

[15]*Rethorica nova*, fols. 102vb-103va.

[16]Ed. Salvador Galmés in *Obres de Ramon Lull*, vol. 14 (Palma de Mallorca, 1928), pp. 375-89; at pp. 386-89.

[17]*Etymologiarum sive originum libri XX*, 2.1.1, ed. W. M. Lindsay (Oxford, 1911).

[18]Dominicus Gundissalinus, *De divisione philosophiae*, ed. L. Baur, *Beiträge zur Geschichte der Philosophie des Mittelalters*, Band 4.2-3 (Münster, 1903), pp. 63-69.

[19]The available editions of these works are *Liber de geometria nova*, ed. J. M. Mills Vallicrosa (Barcelona, 1953); *Logica nova*, in *Logica nova jam Valentiae impressa anno 1512: Et nunc Palmae cum libris Logica Parva . . .* (Palma de Mallorca, 1744; rpt. Frankfurt a. Main, 1971); *Metaphysica nova et compendiosa*, ed. Helmut Riedlinger, *Raimundi Lulli Opera latina*, vol. 6, Corpus Christianorum, Continuatio medievalis, no. 33 (Turnholt, 1978), pp. 10-51.

[20]"Rhetorica vetus--rhetorica nova: Remarks on the History of a Topos" (Paper presented at Colloquium "Tradition and Innovation in the History of Rhetoric," International Society for the History of Rhetoric, American Branch, Chicago, 12 November 1986).

[21]Murphy, *Rhetoric in the Middle Ages*, p. 254.

[22]In *Raymundi Lulli Opera ea quae ad adinventam ab ipso Artem Universalem scientiarum artiumque omnium brevi compendio, firmaque memoria apprehendendarum, locupletissimaque vel oratione ex tempore pertractandarum, pertinent* (Strasbourg, 1617), pp. 218-663; at pp. 536-37 and 554-56.

[23]Described by R. W. Hunt, "The Introduction to the 'Artes' in the Twelfth Century," in *Studia mediaevalia in honorem admodum Reverendi Patris Raymundi Josephi Martin* (Bruges, 1948), pp. 85-112.

[24]Boethius, *In Isagogen Porphyrii Commenta*, ed. Samuel Brandt, Corpus Scriptorum Ecclesiasticorum Latinorum, vol. 48 (Vienna, 1906), pp. 4-5.

[25]Pseudo-Augustine, *De rhetorica*, ed. Karl Halm in *Rhetores latini minores* (Leipzig, 1863), pp. 135-51; at pp. 141-42.

The Rethorica nova of Ramon Llull

[26]"Cum verbum sit medium et instrumentum per quod loquentes et audientes in unum finem conveniunt, consequitur ut quanto verbo fuerint amplius ordinata magisque ornata, tanto ampliori pulchritudine venustentur, quantoque verba fuerint pulcriora, tanto etiam audientibus placibiliora reddantur. Quanto vero sunt placibiliora, tanto necesse est ut per ipsa loquentes et audientes in finem concorditer uniantur. Et cum ad hoc ars rethorice ordinetur, erit dicte artis subiectum verbum ordinatum, ornatum et pulcrum" (*Rethorica nova*, fol. 95vb; all spelling and usage appear as found in the MS).

[27]On Augustine's views, see Murphy, *Rhetoric in the Middle Ages*, pp. 290-91.

[28]Llull apparently devised this classification of speech as a sixth sense by moralizing conventional Scholastic linguistic doctrine in order to assert more prominently the ethical responsibilities of language use. Josep Perarnau i Espelt has edited the special treatise devoted to presenting this theory, "*Lo sisè seny, lo qual apel.lam affatus*, de Ramon Llull," *Arxiu de Textos Catalans Antics*, 2 (1983):23-103.

[29]Cicero, *De inventione* 1.15.20.

[30]Ed. D. H. Inguanez and H. M. Willard as *Flores Rhetorici* (Montecassino, 1938), pp. 36-37.

[31]As in the opening remarks of William of Sherwood in his *Introduction to Logic*, trans. Norman Kretzmann (Minneapolis, 1966).

[32]As in Robert of Basevorn's *Forma praedicandi*, ed. Th.-M. Charland in *Artes praedicandi: Contribution à l'Histoire de la Rhetorique au Moyen Age*, Publications de l'Institut d'Études Médiévales d'Ottawa, no. 7 (Paris and Ottawa, 1936), pp. 231-323.

[33]*The "Parisiana Poetria" of John of Garland*, ed. and trans. Traugott Lawler (New Haven, 1974), pp. 110-11.

[34]As in Thomas Aquinas, *Summa Theologiae* 1a.5, 4 ad 1, Blackfriars Edition, 60 vols. (New York and London, 1964-76).

[35]*Libre de contemplació en Deu*, 359.11, ed. Salvador Galmés, 7 vols., in *Obres Originals*, vols. 2-8 (Palma de Mallorca, 1906-14), at 8:536.

[36]Cited in M.-M. Lebreton, "Recherches sur les principaux thèmes théologiques traités dans les sermons du XII siècle," *Recherches de théologie ancienne et médiévale*, 23 (1956):5-18; at p. 7.

Mark D. Johnston

[37]"Volentes igitur, quod ex multo tempore concupivimus, ordinandorum ornatorumque verborum notitiam tradere sermonesque componere secundum artem generalem--sed non valentes propter alia quedam negocia que vitare non possumus, presertim quia ipsi sermones requirant scripture longitudinem cum multum secundum materiam diffundantur--hunc librum sub compendio edidimus in quo componendi disserendique pulchros et naturales sermones ad multas variasque materias servato ordine debito et processu via facilis et perutilis reseratur" (*Rethorica nova*, fols. 95vb).

[38]On these terms, see Allen, *Ethical Poetic*, p. 72 and A. J. Minnis, *Medieval Theory of Authorship: Scholastic literary attitudes in the later Middle Ages* (London, 1982).

[39]Ramon Llull, *Liber de praedicatione*, ed. Abraham Soria Flores, *Raimundi Lulli Opera Latina*, vols. 3-4 (Palma de Mallorca, 1961-63).

[40]"Ut autem huius libri doctrina clarius se legentibus offerat, ipsum librum in partes distinximus ut ordo doctrine pateat, et quod quisque in eo voluerit, possit facilius invenire. Sunt autem partes ipsius quatuor, scilicet [1] ordo, [2] pulcritudo, [3] scientia, atque [4] caritas. Ponitur autem pro tanto ordo pars istius scientie quia in eo traditur doctrina pro loquentibus qua docentur in sermonibus ac verbis quibuslibet observare ordinem debitum deordinationemque vitare, ut ex hoc loquentium ad audientes mutua pax et amicitia procuretur, quam initiant ordinata verba et pulcra, cum iuxta Senece testimonium "principium sit amicitie bene loqui." Pulcritudinem vero similiter partem ponimus quam et diximus huius artis esse subiectum, quia eam tanquam subiectum ipsius rethorice volumus declarare, ut per eam doctrinam tradere valeamus qua per ipsam et cum ipsa unus quisque sua verba ornare valeat et decore congrue venustare. Scientiam autem ponimus huius nostre rethorice partem, ut tradamus doctrinam per quam insinuetur legentibus ipsam, qualiter per illam et cum illa inquiri oporteat speciem ornatumque verborum, qualiterque inveniri debeant verba ornata et pulcra, ut discerni possint pulchra et ordinata ab inordinatis et turpibus, ut pulchra in usum summantur et turpia devitentur. Quartam quoque partem istius artis assignamus et dicimus caritatem, quia hic est tradenda de ipsa doctrina, an in verbis sit aut non, eo quod verba ex caritate prolata tanta ex ipsa pulcritudinis speciositate clarescunt, ut sine caritate finaliter nequeant esse pulchra" (*Rethorica nova*, fols. 95vb-96ra).

[41]Jordi Rubió Balaguer, "La 'Rhetorica nova' de Ramon Llull," *Estudios Lulianos*, 3 (1959):5-20 and 263-74; at p. 17.

[42]Gilles Gerard Meersseman, "Seneca maestro di spiritualità nei suoi opus-

coli apocrifi dal XII al XV secolo," *Italia medioevale e umanistica,* 16 (1973):43-135.

[43]*In Isocrates,* ed. George Norlin, vol. 1 (London, 1928), p. 25.

[44]*Tractatus de arte loquendi et tacendi,* ed. Thor Sundby in *Della Vita e delle Opere di Brunetto Latini* (Florence, 1884), pp. 475-506; at p. 502.

[45]*Li Livres dou Tresor,* ed. Francis J. Carmody, University of California Publications in Modern Philology, no. 22 (Berkeley and Los Angeles, 1948), p. 245.

[46]As in Geoffrey of Vinsauf, *Poetria nova,* ed. Edmond Faral in *Les arts poétiques du XIIe et du XIIIe siècle. Recherches et documents sur la technique littéraire du moyen âge,* Bibliothèque de l'École des Hautes Études, no. 238 (Paris, 1923), pp. 194-262; at p. 251.

[47]Composed perhaps in 1276, ed. Salvador Galmés in *Obres Originals* (Palma de Mallorca, 1935), 18:1-66.

[48]See the still useful review of these doctrines by Jean Rohmer, *La Finalité morale chez les théologiens de Saint Augustin à Duns Scot* (Paris, 1939).

[49]*De doctrina christiana* 1.3.3, ed. William M. Green, Corpus Scriptorum Ecclesiasticorum Latinorum, vol. 80 (Vienna, 1963).

[50]See especially his remarks in *Monologion* 68, *De veritate* 7, and *De libertate arbitrii* 3 and 9, ed. Franciscus S. Schmitt in *Opera omnia,* vol. 1 (Edinburgh, 1946).

[51]*Rethorica nova,* fol. 96^{va-b}.

[52]As in the anonymous twelfth-century Bolognese treatise *Rationes dictandi,* ed. Ludwig Rockinger in *Briefsteller und Formelbücher des elften bis vierzehnten Jahrhunderts* (Munich, 1863; rpt. New York, 1961), pp. 9-28.

[53]John A. Alford, "The Grammatical Metaphor: A Survey of Its Use in the Middle Ages," *Speculum,* 57 (1982):728-60; at pp. 742-43. Llull obviously ignores the suggestion of sexual meanings for grammatical terms; Jan Ziolkowski carefully documents Alan of Lille's techniques in *Alan of Lille's Grammar of Sex: The Meaning of Grammar to a Twelfth-Century Intellectual* (Cambridge, MA, 1985).

Mark D. Johnston

[54] A good example of the little-studied *ars arengandi* is Matteo de' Libri da Bologna, *Dicieri volgari*, ed. Luigi Chiapelli (Pistoia, 1900).

[55] This story evidently derives ultimately from Seneca *De beneficiis* 2.16.1, ed. John W. Basore in *Moral Essays*, vol. 3 (London, 1935). This is *exemplum* #100 in Frederic Tubach, *Index exemplorum: A Handbook of Medieval Religious Tales, Folklore Fellows Communications*, 86.204 (Helsinki, 1969).

[56] *Rethorica nova*, fol. 96rb.

[57] Such as John of Garland in his *Parisiana poetria*, p. 12.

[58] On these see my "The Treatment of Speech in Medieval Ethical and Courtesy Literature," *Rhetorica*, 4 (1986):21-46.

[59] *Rethorica nova*, fol. 97va.

[60] *Rethorica nova*, fol. 97vb.

[61] *Rhetorica ad Herennium* 1.5.8, ed. Harry Caplan (London, 1954) and *De inventione* 1.16.22, ed. H. M. Hubbell (London, 1949).

[62] As in Humbert of Romans, *De eruditione praedicatorum*, p. 399.

[63] On these see Carolyn Walker Bynum, *Docere verbo et exemplo: An Aspect of Twelfth-Century Spirituality*, Harvard Theological Studies, 31 (Missoula, 1979).

[64] Surveyed magisterially by Morton Bloomfield, *The Seven Deadly Sins: An Introduction to the History of a Religious Concept, with Special Reference to Medieval English Literature* (East Lansing, MI, 1952).

[65] *Rethorica nova*, fol. 107ra. The standard account of this definition in Llull's day was Peter of Spain, *Summule logicales*, ed. Lambertus M. De Rijk (Assen, 1972), p. 2.

[66] "Si Deus posuit virtutes in herbis et lapidibus, multo magis in verbis que virtuosa sunt per virtutes morales et theologicales in loquente existentes. Et ideo quando loquens habet verba virtuosa, quorum virtus est subiectum sive materia, colorat formam eorum, propter quam colorationem forma pulcra est. Et ipsam ornatam formam audientes cum delectatione verba suscipiunt, et aures atque cor inclinant benivolas ad auditum" (*Rethorica nova*, fol. 105rb).

[67]As in the text edited by André Wilmart, "Un Répertoire d'exégèse composé en Angleterre vers le début du XIIIe siècle," in *Mémorial Lagrange* (Paris, 1940), pp. 308-46.

[68]*Confessiones* 4.15, in *PL* 32.

[69]Jean Leclercq neatly describes the contemplative function of this spiritual sense in *The Love of Learning and the Desire for God: A Study of Monastic Culture*, trans. Catharine Misrahi (New York, 1982), p. 73. Among the pre-Scholastic authorities known to Llull, Richard of St. Victor frequently mentions the spiritual senses in his *Benjamin maior*, *PL* 196:63-202; especially at cols. 118-19.

[70]*Rethorica nova*, fol. 104[vb].

[71]*Rethorica nova*, fol. 105[ra].

[72]*Rethorica nova*, fol. 105[va].

[73]*Ethics* 1.1 1094a2-3, ed. Jonathan Barnes in *The Complete Works of Aristotle. The Revised Oxford Translation* (Princeton, 1984).

[74]*De doctrina christiana* 1.35.39-1.40.44.

[75]The *locus classicus* is Gregory the Great, *Regula pastoralis*, in *PL* 77:50. A typical Scholastic product is the *Liber exemplorum ad usum praedicantium*, ed. A. G. Little (Aberdeen, 1908).

[76]*Rethorica nova*, fol. 108[va-b].

[77]Allen, *Ethical Poetic*, pp. 87 and 103-04.

[78]As suggested by Allen, *Ethical Poetic*, p. 70 and Sheila Delaney, "Undoing Substantial Connection: The Late Medieval Attack on Analogical Thought," *Mosaic*, 5.4 (Summer 1974):31-52.

[79]Allen, *Ethical Poetic*, p. 205.

[80]*Ethical Poetic*, p. 192.

[81]On the earliest Lullian disciples, see J. N. Hillgarth, *Ramon Lull and Lullism*, pp. 135-49.

[82] Zink, *La prédication en langue romane*, pp. 169-70.

[83] "La Biblioteca de La Real: fuentes posibles de Llull," *Estudios Lulianos*, 7 (1963):5-17.

[84] Zink, *La prédication en langue romane*, pp. 163-69 and 184.

[85] *La prédication en langue romane*, p. 236.

[86] *La prédication en langue romane*, p. 244.

[87] *La prédication en langue romane*, pp. 250 and 288.

[88] As described by C. A. Robson, *Maurice of Sully and the Medieval Vernacular Homily* (Oxford, 1952), p. 35.

[89] *La prédication en langue romane*, p. 279.

[90] *La prédication en langue romane*, p. 285.

[91] *La prédication en langue romane*, p. 308.

[92] *La prédication en langue romane*, p. 471.

[93] *La prédication en langue romane*, p. 478.

[94] "La catéchesme occitane ou catalane de Matfre Ermengaud et de Raymond Lulle," in *La religion populaire en Languedoc du XIIIe siècle à la moitié du XIVe siècle*, ed. M.-H. Vicaire, Cahiers de Fanjeaux 11 (Toulouse, 1976), pp. 217-26; at pp. 221-22.

[95] "La religion populaire au Moyen Age," *Revue d'histoire de l'Église de France*, 63 (1977):79-86.

Preaching the Passion: Late Medieval "Lives of Christ" as Sermon Vehicles

Lawrence F. Hundersmarck

This study examines the passion narratives of two lives of Christ: the Meditationes Vitae Christi *of Pseudo-Bonaventure (c. 1300), and the* Vita Christi *of Ludolf of Saxony (d. 1378). While scholarly speculation has centered on John de Caulibus as author of the* Meditationes Vitae Christi, *we only know him as possibly an Italian Franciscan who lived at the end of the thirteenth century. Long ascribed in manuscipts to St. Bonaventure, the* Meditationes *is now credited to "Pseudo-Bonaventure" by modern scholars. A complete text of the* Meditationes *was edited by A. C. Peltier in the Paris edition [1868] of the* Opera Omnia Bonaventurae *[Vol. 12:509-630]. A critical edition of the Passion narrative of the* Meditationes *was published by M. J. Stallings (Catholic University Press, 1965). A modern critical text of the* Vita Jesu Christi *by the Carthusian Ludolf of Saxony is, unfortunately, lacking. Ludolf, who also penned* Expositio in Psalterium Davidis, *is justly famous for his* Vita, *which appears before 1800 in many manuscripts, editions, and translations. The latest, a folio edition published by Victor Palmé in Paris, 1865, was followed by two octavo editions of four volumes in 1870 and 1878 edited by L. M. Rigollot.*

The Meditationes *and the* Vita, *early attempts to set forth a complete life of Christ, provide a harmonization of the gospels interwoven with numerous patristic and medieval quotations, dogmatic and moral lessons, and apocryphal details. In structure, they both appear as a long series of sermons arranged according to gospel pericopes. Because of their encyclopedic quality, these two works greatly influenced later preachers and spiritual writers. An examination of their homiletic styles and images of the suffering Christ illustrate how these narratives serve as vehicles for preaching the Passion. This study indicates that the* Meditationes *is an emotive, sentimental conceptualization of Scripture which, through an imaginative representation of Christ's life, aims to arouse compassion and sorrow for the Man of Sorrows. The* Vita, *while also highlighting the physical pain of the Passion, tends to be more reserved and less emotional. Its aim is not so much to return to the events of the gospels as to make them relevant for the present by means of prayer, religious practice, allegory, analogy, and pious examples. For the Carthusian, more than the Franciscan, the Passion is a textbook for Christian life and virtue.*

This essay studies the Passion narratives of two important lives of Christ: the *Meditationes Vitae Christi* of Pseudo-Bonaventure (ca. 1300)[1] and the *Vita Christi* of Ludolf of Saxony (d. 1378).[2] These two lives of Christ use the biblical narrative as the occasion for an elaborate sermon and are excellent examples of Passion preaching. With these two texts, we are not dealing with individual sermons preached on specific occasions but, rather, with literary works which preach the Passion. This essay seeks to give some indication of how sermon material can form the basis of texts that are not properly traditional sermons.

The *Meditationes* and the *Vita* have long been recognized as the work of preachers.[3] The unknown author of the *Meditationes* is thought to have been a Franciscan[4] and, as such, would have stood in a rich homiletic tradition.[5] The Carthusian author of the *Vita*, Ludolf of Saxony, would have been unable to preach with his tongue; thus, like many Carthusians of the Middle Ages, he preached with his pen.[6] For both authors, preaching the Passion was of central importance for an understanding of the life of Christ. Both authors stand in a rich and ancient tradition of homiletic and spiritual writings devoted to the Passion,[7] and both saw the Passion as fundamental to an ascetic theology basic to their Franciscan and Carthusian lives. Their works argue that the Passion is the supreme expression of God's love for humankind as well as an inexhaustible source of Christian piety.

These two gospel harmonies, which seek to relate the events of Jesus's life, were immensely popular. One reason for their great success was that through them, the faithful could have access to the gospel narratives in vernacular translations of the original Latin editions. Also, because these two works were in essence elaborate sermons surrounding the gospel text with explanations and pious reflections, Church authorities often considered them to be safer reading than translations of the "naked text."[8] It is well known that later preachers, artists, and religious reformers would find in them a rich source of Christian spirituality and iconography conveniently organized around any given aspect of Christ's life.[9]

Ludolf of Saxony knew the *Meditationes*[10] possibly through the work of Michael of Massa (d. 1337).[11] In terms of direct quotations, the total amount of *Meditationes* material in Ludolf's *Vita* is only about five per cent. Pseudo-Bonaventure is just one of some fifty different authors integrated into the *Vita*'s Passion narrative.[12] Nevertheless, it is fair to say that Ludolf was influenced by his Italian predecessor in the general pattern of presentation although the number of text borrowings remains relatively small.

Both works stand in the tradition of St. Bernard of Clairvaux (1090-1153), whose sermons contained loving meditations on the principal events in the life of Christ. Both works are rooted in the tradition of medieval devotion to the humanity of Christ where the Christian is to remember and imitate that humanity.[13] However, unlike the homilies of Bernard, the *Meditationes* and the *Vita* seek to accustom the reader to a contemplation of the entire earthly life of Jesus according to a chronological order. Indeed, rarely had so extensive a subject been presented all at once. Put in other words, these two works represented almost a new phenomenon in the history of Christian spirituality, a kind of "mystical biography."[14]

Throughout this essay, attention will be given to the basic way in which these two biographies present the events of the Passion as a reality relevant to the individual Christian. To achieve this end, these preachers of the Passion had to consider certain issues. For example: In what manner is the Christian related to the events of Christ's life? Is it a return to the past? If so, what are the dynamics of this return? What are the implications of the Passion throughout the history of salvation? What does the Passion teach regarding the moral life? What is the Christian to feel because of the Passion? This study of the Passion narratives of the *Meditationes* and the *Vita* will examine some of the answers which the two texts give to these issues, in order to set forth their contrasting conceptualizations of Passion preaching.

The preachers of the Passion throughout the history of Christianity most often sought to make the sacrifice of Christ the core of Christian life. Both *Vitae* saw as their purpose to probe the meaning of this sacrifice. Both sought to bring their audience to a closer relationship with the suffering Christ. In this broad way, these medieval harmonies are like the gospels which form their substratum. In this way they also preach the Good News. Pseudo-Bonaventure and Ludolf of Saxony, like the authors of the gospels, had to decide how to represent the past as valuable to the present and as a guide for the future.

In the early Apostolic Church, the preaching of the Passion gave rise to different accounts, each with its own focus and thematic development. Thus, for example, the gospel of Mark presented Jesus as suffering and kingly while Luke tended toward a portrait of him as merciful and innocent. Just as we are accustomed in the context of twentieth-century biblical scholarship to look at the synoptics with an eye to their unique literary and theological characteristics, so also a focus on the emerging genre of late medieval "Lives of Christ" reveals important differences which had wide influence on subsequent ages. A study of these two works illustrates the different paths such preaching can take as it confronts the last hours of Jesus's earthly life.

The *Meditationes Vitae Christi* was penned in a vernacular Latin and addressed to a Poor Clare nun who lived in, or around, the region of Tuscany. Scholars think that the author may have had authority as a spiritual director over her and perhaps her whole convent.[15] As spiritual director, he often encourages her in the virtues of poverty, humility, and charity. His aim, however, is not only to present the virtues of Christ's life, but to picture for her the details of Christ's life in a solid and visual way so as to elicit an affective and imaginative response. In fact, he intends his audience not to be a mere passive receiver of the work but, like a preacher, he calls for and seeks to prompt an active response to his words.

The *Meditationes* presents itself as a work more interested in a sentimental conceptualization of Scripture than an actual reflection on the events of the Passion. It is a work which has the disposition of St. Francis of Assisi (1182-1226), strongly emotive and concrete. Rather than presenting the Passion in a series of ideas, the author of the *Meditationes* paints images.

The *Meditationes* depicts events of the Passion and events of Jesus's life to let the realities of the gospel affect one's whole mind (MVC, 511). It encourages a full re-living of the life of Christ; thus, it recounts all the aspects of that life which will inflame and quicken the heart.[16] We are called to heed all things of the Passion as though we were there (MPVC, 98); in short, to meditate. The events of the Passion are to be food for rumination (MVC, 511). The aim of this meditation is to become eventually like a saint who is always bearing in her heart the gospel of Christ (MVC, 510).

Because the author of the *Meditationes* is a preacher, he wants his reader to experience Christ (MVC, 510); to recall in mind and heart the Passion here and now as it once was there and then. The author gives his audience the following advice for reaping the fruits of these meditations:

> . . . place yourself before these things which are narrated as done or said by the Lord Jesus as if you were hearing them with your own ears and seeing them with your own eyes, with all the powers of your soul, diligently, delightfully and lingering over it, setting aside for the moment all other cares and worries.   (MVC, 511)

To aid in this imaginative reconstruction of the Passion, the author of the *Meditationes* adds apocryphal details to the biblical text. Thus, after the agony in the garden, Jesus washes his blood-stained face in a nearby stream (MPVC, 102). Later, the text points out that he is bound to a stone column for the entire night after his arrest (MPVC, 104). John tells Mary of these events (MPVC, 104), while elsewhere, it is Mary who uses her veil to cover her son's nakedness (MPVC, 112) and tries to protect her dead son from having his legs broken (MPVC, 118).

Pseudo-Bonaventure not only adds extra-Scriptural details to his presentation, he also adds dialogue that cannot be found in the biblical text. There is, for example, an entire conversation between Jesus and the angel Michael in the garden. We are told that the angel has taken the prayers and sweat of blood to the Father, and with the whole heavenly court Michael prayed that the cup of suffering be taken away. The angel then tells Jesus:

> "The Father replied, 'My most beloved Son knows that the redemption of mankind, which we so desire, cannot be accomplished without the shedding of his blood. . . .' Then the Lord Jesus replied to the angel, 'I wish above all the salvation of souls; and therefore I choose to die.'" (MPVC, 101)

On the cross there is another created dialogue between the Father and the Son. As Jesus reaches the point of death, the Father says: "Come, my most beloved Son. You have done everything well. I do not wish you to be further troubled. Come, for I will receive you to my breast and embrace you" (MPVC, 115). Before this scene, on the cross, Jesus makes the following silent prayer to his Father:

> "My Father, see how afflicted my mother is. I ought to be crucified, not she, but she is with me on the cross. It is enough that I, who bears the sins of all the people, am crucified; she does not deserve the same. See how desolate she is, consumed with sadness all day, I recommend her to you, make her sorrow bearable." (MPVC, 114)[17]

The author of the *Meditationes* seeks to create, in the words of one scholar, an "audio-visual reconstruction"[18] where all the senses participate in the formulation of a dynamic image. The author is aware that these extra details are not found in Scripture (MPVC, 96) yet justifies them in that they deepen the piety of the reader (MVC, 511). In any event, it is his view that the evangelists have not described everything (MPVC, 121).[19] Thus, to sharpen our imagination we are told that the distance Christ knelt from his disciples in the garden was a stone's throw, ". . . not as when the arm is violently agitated but as when the stone is thrown without great force" (MPVC, 100). As the reader tries to visualize Christ being led from the garden, the imagination is again assisted with this description: ". . . hands tied behind his back, his mantle removed, his dress is in disorder, head uncovered, bowed by fatigue, and going in great speed" (MPVC, 103).

Imagination is the essential dynamic which characterizes meditation for this preacher. Thus, we are advised to pay diligent attention to the manner of crucifixion (MPVC, 112). Two ladders, which permit the evil-doers to ascend holding nails and hammers, are set on either side of the cross. Another ladder, used by Jesus to ascend the cross without compulsion, is placed in the front. When he reaches the top, Jesus turns around and opens his arms, allowing the crucifiers to drive in the nails.

Immediately following this description, the author of the *Meditationes* adds another paragraph which again indicates his view of the value of imagination, just as long as it ends in a deeper relationship with Christ. He writes:

> There are, however, those who believe that he was not crucified in this manner, but that the cross was laid on the ground and that they then raised it up and fixed it in the ground. If this suits you better, think how they take him contemptuously like the vilest wretch and furiously cast him onto the cross on the ground, taking his arms, violently extending them and most cruelly fixing them to the cross. Also consider his feet which they dragged down as violently as they could. (MPVC, 112-13)

Other passages calling us to actualize our imagination could be cited;[20] however, let us conclude this point on the preacher's use of imagination with the following scene regarding the deposition of Christ from the cross:

> Two ladders are placed on opposite sides of the cross. Joseph ascends the ladder placed on the right side and tries to extract the nail from his hand. But this is difficult, because the long, heavy nail is fixed firmly into the wood; and it does not seem possible to do it without a great pressure on the hand of the Lord. Yet it is not brutal, because he acts faithfully; and the Lord accepts everything. The nail pulled out, John makes a sign to Joseph to extend the nail to him, that the Lady might not see it. Afterwards Nicodemus extracts the other nail from the left hand and similarly gives it to John. . . .
> (MPVC, 120)

This work of Pseudo-Bonaventure would influence late medieval drama.[21] It has a realism which creates a moving, sweeping scene. This unity of drama and homily stands in the tradition of St. Francis, who, after constructing a manger-scene at Greccio, spoke to the people on the tenderness, joy, and humility of this birth.[22] Here the scene and the message are interwoven as in a monastery fresco. This tendency to express ideas in the form of images, to embody in visible forms all holy concepts, would become very characteristic of the late Middle Ages.[23]

Throughout the *Meditationes*, the author seeks to drive home the image of the "Man of Sorrows" (Is 53:3) by repeating again and again the intensity and multiplicity of Christ's pain, torment, and sufferings. Everywhere injury, abuse, and affliction (MPVC, 113) are heaped upon Christ by many tormentors (MPVC, 96). The sufferings of Christ are described in vivid detail. Thus, as Jesus was led from Herod to Pilate, he was struck by a stone (MPVC, 106), while elsewhere, after being stripped, he was left to stand nude (MPVC, 109). Here the emphasis is on what happens to Christ rather than how he meets the Passion. The discussion is on the intensity of the torments which Christ endured. When the scene of the scourging is described, the text highlights his blood which flowed from all parts of his body. In describing this torment, the preacher tells us, lest we forget its intensity: "Again and again, repeatedly, closer and closer, it is done, bruise upon bruise, cut upon cut, until not only the torturers but also the spectators are tired; then he is ordered untied" (MPVC, 106-07). Again, in the description of the Crucifixion, the reader is reminded that Christ tolerated the bitterest pain (MPVC, 113) and ". . . rivers of his most sacred blood flowed from his great wounds" (MPVC, 114). Pain and suffering touched every part of his body (MPVC, 113).

The *Meditationes* notes that the Passion shows the charity of Christ (MPVC, 96) and the Father (MPVC, 99), yet this concept is not developed. With the focus of attention on the attacks heaped upon the afflicted Christ, his response throughout this battle (MPVC, 96) is presented in terms of endurance. Christ is he who bore everything with patience (MPVC, 110) and humility (MPVC, 109). There are a number of passages which develop this theme.[24] This preacher wants his audience not only to imagine these sufferings but also to become actually involved with the event--to step into the scene, so to speak. Thus, when Mary and her companions return home after the burial of Christ, we read:

> ... if it be within your power, you should at least know how to prepare for them and serve them, and to console and comfort her, seeing to it that she should eat a little and encourage the others to eat, for they have not yet broken fast. And then, having received a blessing from our Lady and from each of the others, you may withdraw.
> (MPVC, 126)

The audience is to be emotionally present at every scene of the Passion (MPVC, 98 and MVC, 522).

This Franciscan preacher calls the audience to feel the appropriate emotions of pity and sorrow. Like Joseph of Arimathea and Nicodemus, whose sorrow was so great that for an hour they were unable to speak (MPVC, 119), the audience is to be overcome with sorrow and weeping. Mary Magdalene is placed at the feet of the dead Christ so that once again they may be moistened not with tears of remorse, but with "much more copious tears of sorrow and compassion" (MPVC, 122). In fact, everyone at the foot of the cross wept inconsolably (MPVC, 116), most especially Jesus's mother, whom the author believes was half dead from her sorrows (MPVC, 116). He writes: "It appears to me that one can say not improperly that not only the penal and mortal Crucifixion of the Lord, but also that suffering that went before, is cause for strong compassion, bitterness and stupor" (MPVC, 96). Thus, after the scourging at the pillar, the preacher warns, "Here then, consider him diligently for a long time and if you do not feel compassion at this point, you may count yours a heart of stone" (MPVC, 107). This often-repeated call to suffer with the suffering Christ (MPVC, 106, 109, and 110) was a common theme in the late Middle Ages.[25]

The work of Ludolf of Saxony, the *Vita Jesu Christi*, may have been originally penned for his brother Carthusians. He uses the scene of Jesus's being spat upon to remind the reader that one ought never to despise one's religious superior (VC, 42).[26]

When Peter denies Christ, Ludolf draws the lesson that the priesthood was given to sinful men, not angels, for such men would have compassion on others (VC, 49). Elsewhere the same idea is set forth in a passage which gives a clear description of Carthusian life. Ludolf is perhaps being unconsciously autobiographical when he draws five parallels between the dead Christ and the religious life: first, as a dead body has nothing, so also a religious should own nothing; second, as a dead person takes no pleasure in anything sensible, so the monk should be dead to his flesh; third, as a dead man does not resist when moved, so a monk must not resist the superior who governs him nor murmur when moved from monastery to monastery; fourth, as the dead do not come out of the grave until the final judgment, so the monk should not go out of his cloister without the command of his superior; and finally, the monk ought to be like the dead Christ, for in death the soul is separated from the flesh, thus teaching that in the true religious the soul must never consent to carnal love (VC, 153-54).[27]

Before contrasting the *Meditationes* and the *Vita Christi* with an eye to some of their basic differences in tone and conceptualization of the Passion, I wish to comment on some of the ways the *Vita*'s Passion narrative exhibits characteristics which are not found in the *Meditationes*. The *Vita* is structured differently from the *Meditationes*, with its Carthusian author setting forth the biblical text, drawing a number of lessons from the text, and, finally, calling the reader to conform to it and the points that flow from it, either by a prayer or by some specific action. This structure allows Ludolf to preach by means of prayer, religious practices, allegory, analogies, and pious examples and stories.

For Ludolf, one essential way to approach the Passion is through the vehicle of prayerful recollection, petition, and praise. He often calls the reader to prayer; a prayerful spirit pervades the Passion, and throughout the *Vita* every chapter ends with a prayer.[28] Along with prayer, the reader is advised to perform a number of spiritual practices so as to conform to the Passion event. The reader ought to examine his conscience, reflecting on his many sins (VC, 41) or on how he has injured the image of God in himself (VC, 43 and 63). Like Jesus in the garden, a man ought to fall on his face on the ground, praying earnestly and reflecting that an angel is with him (VC, 20).[29] Elsewhere Ludolf tells his reader to kiss the feet of Christ on the crucifix (VC, 26), and, in imitation of the Crucifixion, the Christian is to extend his arms and all the limbs of his body in the form of a cross, either while standing or lying on the ground (VC, 97). Ludolf does suggest that the reader scourge himself, if not physically, at least mentally (VC, 73); however, he never advocates the extremes of the contemporary movement known as the Flagellants.[30] He also advises that to conform to the scene of Jn 18:20, a person may give himself a slight blow or slap to represent the blow inflicted on Christ by the servant of the high priest (VC, 37).[31] For the author of the *Vita*, the Passion calls for continual self-mortification (VC, 97).

These various practices are necessary because self-satisfaction and love of the world are contrary to true contemplation of the Passion (VC, 4). Thus, to avoid all softness of bed or clothing (VC, 11) and to partake sparingly of food and drink aid in the contemplation of the Passion (VC, 2). Here, again, is the Carthusian world-view. This Carthusian preacher calls the world a whirlwind of temptation (VC, 17), a vale of tears (VC, 18), and a place of poisonous persuasion (VC, 48). Ludolf uses the scene in the garden to have Jesus warn his disciples not to fall victim to the world (VC, 14). Later in the *Vita*, Ludolf notes that Judas sought the support of the worldly emperor and the high priest rather than God (VC, 22). We read: "Morally Judas is the world, which smiles when lavishly bestowing riches, kisses us when giving us pleasures and comforts, embraces us when showering honors on us; but in all these ways deceives us and betrays us to eternal death" (VC, 25).

The author of the *Vita* is fond of using allegory, not only in the many Old Testament types which he sees as prefiguring the Passion,[32] but also in his fondness for symbolism. Thus, the three apostles taken with Jesus to the garden symbolize that we ought to have in our prayer faith, contempt for worldly goods, and grace (VC, 12). Judas hanged himself halfway between heaven and earth, symbolizing that he was not fit for the company of either angels or humans (VC, 53). Elsewhere Ludolf sees Christ crucified between two thieves as a symbol of the Last Judgment with the lambs on the right and the goats on the left (VC, 103). Jesus's white robe signifies innocence and purity (VC, 61), while Peter, before his denial, was numb not with the cold of night, but with the cold of infidelity (VC, 45).

Ludolf is a careful preacher, striving in every way to make his ideas clear. Sometimes he will delineate a number of ideas by listing them, point by point (VC, 15). Other times he tries to make analogies so that there will be no mistaking the issue. Thus, Christ voluntarily undergoes suffering to save humankind as a sick person voluntarily undergoes a bitter treatment to gain health (VC, 15). And, just as a thief who hears a shout flees, so also does the devil when one shouts to God in prayer (VC, 16). The cross is like a professorial chair and the wood like a rostrum, for it is from this place that Christ teaches (VC, 112). Elsewhere, the shedding of Christ's blood is likened to what a good doctor prescribes, that is, blood-letting for the correction of bad humors (VC, 126).

A common sermon technique is to set forth pious examples and stories to deepen the piety of the audience. In the *Vita*, we read of a certain holy woman who desired to know the number of Christ's wounds. In answer to her prayer it is revealed to her that there were 5,490 wounds on Christ's body (VC, 3). We are told of a certain novice at Paris whose mother wanted to draw him away from the religious life, yet he said to her, "Christ did not descend from the cross on his mother's account, so neither will I for thy sake leave the cross of penance" (VC, 108). Another religious, we are told, had such great devotion to the words "Mother, behold thy Son" (Jn 19:26) "that for nearly twenty years he incessantly shed tears in such abundance that he drank many of them" (VC, 118). In the *Vita* we also meet a woman who had a revelation about the intensity of the pain of the Passion (VC, 96), as well as the familiar stories of Longinus (VC, 136),[33] St. Helena (VC, 154), and St. Andrew (VC, 161).[34]

The elements of prayer and ascetic practices found in the *Vita* are not developed in the *Meditationes*, nor are the elements of allegory, analogy, and pious examples. These in themselves constitute important differences in the character of each work's Passion sermon. However, a more basic point of comparison between the *Meditationes* and the *Vita* lies in two issues; first, the way in which each author seeks to unite the reader with the Passion, and, second, the image of the suffering Christ presented in each text. A discussion of these two issues will reveal much about the contrasting aims of each preacher.

To unite the audience with the Passion, the *Meditationes Vitae Christi* presents Christ as the object of meditation. For Pseudo-Bonaventure, the goal of meditation is to make the Gospel story come alive via the imaginative and emotive response of the audience so that it may have a spiritual stigmata, a re-experiencing of the Passion (not necessarily a re-experiencing of the pain of the Passion, but a deep compassion for the "Man of Sorrows"). To accomplish this aim, the *Meditationes* presents a biographical account of Jesus's life, with a great deal of emphasis on creating a realistic scene which is often sentimental, subjective, and anecdotal. In the *Meditationes*, the focus is on the past events of Christ's life--Christ, as he was then, during his earthly Passion. Although the Franciscan preacher believes himself orthodox, presenting only that which will deepen piety, his entire Passion narrative has all the characteristics of a new apocryphal gospel which encourages us to step into the scene with our imagination. Unlike the Gospels, which were written to prompt faith by proclaiming the message of salvation, the *Meditationes* calls its readers to an emotional compassion as it brings them back to the past.

There is an influence on Ludolf from the *Meditationes* regarding the value of imagination in the meditative process.[35] Also, like Pseudo-Bonaventure, Ludolf calls his readers to feel sorrow and compassion when Christ is spat upon (VC, 45), scourged (VC, 72), condemned (VC, 85), and crucified (VC, 127). One ought, we are told in the *Vita*, to consider the Passion with a sadness of heart (VC, 51). Nevertheless, the Carthusian is much less emotional than the Franciscan in his presentation of the Passion. True, Mary does cry at the foot of the cross in the *Vita* (VC, 134), yet the whole focus of the scene is not on his mother's emotion but on what Christ teaches by his death. In fact, there is, in the *Vita*, a more developed soteriology than can be found in the *Meditationes*.[36] Also, the whole of the *Vita* is less imaginative. It is true that we find some extra-biblical dialogue in Ludolf's work, yet it is kept to a minimum (VC, 58 and 134). We never read, for example, of a dialogue between Jesus and the angel Michael, or between Jesus and his Father, as appears in the *Meditationes*.

To achieve a union with the Passion, the *Vita* not only called its readers back to the past but also focused on the present. For Ludolf, Christ is the center and meaning of all history; thus, the Old Testament foreshadows in its types the events of the Passion. This is why the *Vita* constantly links the present with the past. So we read this Carthusian preacher reminding his audience that when it commits a wicked deed it strikes Christ in the face (VC, 44), and he who boasts of his sins attempts to wound Christ as did the soldier who lanced his side (VC, 136). It is our sins that caused the Passion (VC, 72). So that there be no mistake, we read elsewhere: "He who frequents theatres, places of amusement, or taverns, more than churches, drives iron nails into the feet of Christ" (VC, 97). Ludolf also sees in the Eucharist the same God who suffered (VC, 79 and 155). Thus, he draws a parallel between Judas who betrayed Jesus with a kiss and the Christian who receives the Body of Christ in mortal sin (VC, 26). Also we read:

> It may be said that they literally spit in the face of Christ who receive the Holy Eucharist unworthily, for anyone who having a polluted conscience takes the Body of Christ into his mouth, touches, moistens, and dissolves the Blessed Sacrament with saliva tainted by sin, spits in the face of Christ. (VC, 42)

The lines between the past and the present further disappear when Ludolf uses the Passion to explain the customs and traditions of the Liturgy. As a Carthusian, his life would have been close to the liturgical practices of the Church.[37] Thus, he sees in the garments worn by Jesus symbols of the pontifical garments of his own day (VC, 61); in the elevation of the cross, he sees the elevation of the Host (VC, 98); and he sees the proper hour for the Mass being in the middle of the day because that is when

Christ hung on the cross (VC, 85). It is not uncommon to hear this preacher interrelate the past with the present by using contemporary liturgical examples such as the following:

> So the altars are stripped, because Christ, typified by the altar, was forsaken by the Apostles, signified by its adornments. During those three days the night Office is sung aloud, by which the prophecies about our Lord are referred to, but the day Hours are said inaudibly, because the Apostles did not venture to preach, and for the same reason the bells are not rung. (VC, 30)[38]

Turning to the second issue, the image of the suffering Christ which emerges from each work, it may be noted, as discussed above, that for the *Meditationes* the focus is on the intensity of torment and pain heaped upon Christ. In this work, the Passion is described as a battle throughout which Christ bears everything with patience and humility. Christ's response is seen in terms of endurance.

Ludolf's work, like that of Pseudo-Bonaventure, is in harmony with the Gothic tendency to portray Christ's sufferings in a vivid and clear manner. Thus, the *Vita* dwells on Jesus's bruised feet as he was forced to walk barefoot (VC, 64), his scourged body which was dyed crimson red (VC, 71), and the blood which covered his head from the crown of thorns (VC, 77). Elsewhere we are reminded of the physical pain which he endured as he was struck in the face (VC, 43), stripped of his garments (VC, 95), and nailed to the cross (VC, 97). Ludolf, like Pseudo-Bonaventure, believed that for the sake of brevity the evangelists only described the kind, not the number, of insults inflicted upon Jesus (VC, 8). Thus, Ludolf tells us that the wounds inflicted during the scourging were almost countless, and he justifies this claim with the text of Deuteronomy 25:3: ". . . according to the measure of the sin shall the measure also of the stripes be" (VC, 71).

In the Passion of the *Meditationes* we see Christ's patience, humility, and charity. Yet the focus is on admiring these virtues rather than on imitation and implementation. Not that the Franciscan preacher would reject imitation and implementation of these ideals; rather, he rarely draws out the implications of these virtues for contemporary life. He believes that the Christian ought to imitate the virtues and avoid the vices; yet, he fails in his Passion narrative to give any specific direction as to how this might be accomplished.

Ludolf, on the other hand, sees the Passion as a textbook for the Christian life (VC, 4-5) and thus often tries to apply the virtues expressed throughout the Passion to the present Church situation. The *Vita* does not reject the idea that Christ is the object of meditation and admiration, it simply tends to focus on another idea: Christ the example for all humankind.

For the Carthusian preacher, much more than for the Franciscan, piety is to be translated into action. Therefore, throughout the *Vita*, Ludolf takes every occasion to condemn the religious laxity and moral decadence of his day. To his mind, there are many clergy who delight in worldly honors rather than in following the humility of Christ. He uses satire to tell us that the clergy of his day, unlike the naked man in the garden (Mk 14:51), ". . . spread out garments and fold them up in boxes, and have beasts of burden, and different kinds of vehicles to transport them from place to place. . ." (VC, 31). A little earlier, in the garden scene, when Christ forbids the use of arms, we read: ". . . this is little attended to by prelates nowadays who receive from kings royal presents for war, whereas kings ought to receive from them sackcloth for penance" (VC, 27). Jesus is the Good Shepherd in the garden who carefully watches over his flock, "not like many shepherds nowadays who when those under them are watching and in agony, calmly sleep and take their rest" (VC, 22). Elsewhere Ludolf attacks the practice of simony and sees one reason for the ruin of the synagogue in the fact that Ananias and Caiaphas purchased their offices from Herod (VC, 33), while in the seamless coat the Carthusian preacher sees a symbol of the Catholic Church which he warns ought never to be rent by schism (VC, 106).[39]

The Passion narrative of the *Vita Jesu Christi* presents an image of Jesus not only as a patient sufferer, but also as he who actively meets the challenges of the Passion armed with charity. Thus, it is out of loving kindness that he allows his disciples to sleep (VC, 21), protects them from arrest (VC, 24), addresses

Judas as "friend" (VC, 25), and heals the ear of the high priest's servant (VC, 27). Elsewhere the text dwells on Christ's look of mercy to Peter (VC, 50) and the good thief (VC, 115). Often Ludolf interrupts his narrative to call his audience to notice the greatness of divine compassion.[40] Thus, it is appropriate, we are told, that he be crucified at the sixth hour when the heat of the day is greatest so as to symbolize the great fervor of his love (VC, 89); and that in death he bends his head so as to give a kiss to his beloved ones (VC, 130).

The foregoing analysis indicates that when these two late medieval Lives of Christ are contrasted, key differences emerge. The *Meditationes* seeks to bring the reader back to the past via imagination and emotion to relive the events of Good Friday. The *Vita*, while not rejecting this tendency, seeks to present the Passion as continually alive in the monastic and liturgical life of the Church of its day. Both authors see in the Passion the "Man of Sorrows," yet Ludolf more fully develops the lessons of the Passion for the moral life of the Christian. Both authors, in the multiple ways here indicated, seek to use the Gospel narrative as a sermon vehicle designed, in essence, to preach the Passion.

Notes

[1] *Sancti Bonaventurae Opera Omnia*, ed. A. C. Peltier, 12 vols. (Paris, 1868), 12:509-630 (hereafter cited as MVC with page number parenthetically within the text). The following critical edition will be used for the Passion narrative: M. J. Stallings, *Meditaciones de Passione Christi olim Sancto Bonaventurae Attributae* (Washington, 1965) (hereafter cited as MPVC with page number parenthetically within the text). For an English translation of the entire work, see *Meditations on the Life of Christ: An Illustrated Manuscript of the Fourteenth Century: Paris, Bibliotèque Nationale, MS Ital. 115*, ed. and trans. I. Ragusa and R. Green, Princeton Monographs in Art and Archaeology 35 (Princeton, 1961).

[2] Ludolphus Carthusiensis, *Vita Jesu Christi ex Evangelio et approbatis ab Ecclesia Catholica Doctoribus sedule collecta*, ed. L. M. Rigollot, 4 vols. (Paris, 1878) (hereafter cited as VC with page number to vol. 4 parenthetically within the text). For an English translation of the Passion narrative see H. Coleridge, *The Hours of the Passion taken from the Life of Christ by Ludolf the Saxon* (London, 1887).

Late Medieval "Lives of Christ"

[3]J. Longère, *La Prédication Médiévale,* Études Augustiniennes, (Paris, 1983), p. 123. See also M. I. Bodenstedt, *The Vita Christi of Ludolphus the Carthusian* (Washington, 1944), pp. 106-13; and G. R. Owst, *Literature and Pulpit in Medieval England: A Neglected Chapter in the History of English Literature and of the English People* (Cambridge, 1933; 2nd rev. ed. Oxford, 1961), p. 507.

[4]The author often speaks of having professed a life of voluntary poverty, uses the legends of St. Francis and St. Clare, and makes allusions to various Franciscan practices. See Stallings, *Meditaciones,* pp. 4-5.

[5]J. G. Bougerol, "Les Sermons dans les *Studia* des Mendiants," in *Le Scuole degli Ordini Mendicanti (secoli XIII-XIV)* (Milan, 1978), pp. 251-80.

[6]See the rule of the Carthusian order, the *Consuetudines* (*PL* 153:693). On the prohibition against public teaching see M. Laporte, *Ex chartis Capitulorum Generalium. Ab initio usque ad a. 1951* (Grand Chartreuse, 1953), p. 434.

[7]W. Baier, *Untersuchungen zu den Passionsbetrachtungen in der "Vita Christi" des Ludolf von Sachsen. Ein quellenkritischer Beitrag zu Leben und Werk Ludolfs und zur Geschichte der Passionstheologie* (Salzburg, 1977), pp. 391-448; and Stallings, *Meditaciones,* pp. 13-24.

[8]M. Deanesly, "The Gospel Harmony of John de Caulibus or S. Bonaventure," *Collectanea Franciscana,* 10 (1922):10-19; and E. Salter, "Ludolphus of Saxony and his English Translators," *Medium Aevum,* 23 (1964):26-35.

[9]See Bodenstedt, *Vita Christi,* pp. 53-92; and Émile Mâle, *L'Art Religieux de la fin du Moyen Age en France. Étude sur l'iconographie du moyen âge et sur ses sources d'inspiration* (Paris, 1925), pp. 27-51. See also L. Oliger, "Le 'Meditationes Vitae Christi' del Pseudo-Bonaventura," *Studi Francescani,* 8 (1922):24-25; and L. Zarncke, *Die Exercitia spiritualia des Ignatius von Loyola in ihren geistesgeschichtlichen Zusammenhängen,* Schriften des Vereins für Reformationsgeschichte 49 (Leipzig, 1931).

[10]Baier, *Ein quellenkritischer Beitrag,* pp. 334-38.

[11]*Ein quellenkritischer Beitrag,* pp. 344-61.

[12]Bodenstedt, *Vita Christi,* p. 31; and Baier, *Ein quellenkritischer Beitrag,* pp. 197-390.

[13]L. Bouyer, et al., *A History of Christian Spirituality,* 3 vols. (New York, 1968), 2:197-98.

[14]P. Pourrat, *Christian Spirituality,* 4 vols. (Westminster, 1953), 2:185. See also, Bodenstedt, *Vita Christi,* p. 93.

[15]L. Oliger, "Le 'Meditationes Vitae Christi' del Pseudo-Bonaventura," *Studi Francescani,* 7 (1921):149. For a summary of research on the questions of authorship, sources, style, and manuscripts, see Stallings, *Meditaciones,* pp. 3-83.

[16]H. Boehmer, *Loyola und die deutsche Mystik,* Berichte über die Verhandlungen der sächsischen Akademie der Wissenschaften zu Leipzig 73 (Leipzig, 1921), pp. 40-41.

[17]For an overview of the place of Mary in medieval Passion piety, see T. Meier, *Die Gestalt Marias im geistlichen Sphauspiel des deutschen Mittelalters* (Berlin, 1959); and S. Beissel, *Geschichte der Verehrung Marias in Deutschland wahrend des Mittelalters* (Freiburg, 1909).

[18]*Dictionnaire de spiritualité ascétique et mystique,* s.v. "Humanité du Christ (Devotion et Contemplation)," pp. 1085-86.

[19]In this context he is affirming that Jesus's beard was torn, in harmony with Isaiah 50:6.

[20]See MPVC, 98, 103, and 105-16. Words such as: *Aspice, Attende, Intuere, Considera,* and *Conspice* are key terms which the author utilizes to draw the imagination of the reader upon a particular event. For the location of these terms, see "index verborum" of Stallings's *Meditaciones.*

[21]L. Bracaloni, *L'Arte francescana nella Vita e nella storia di settecento anni* (Todi, 1924), pp. 197-205. G. R. Owst writes ". . . the *Meditationes Vitae Christi* attributed to St. Bonaventura would again give every encouragement to ambitious preachers of the day with a liking for *predicatio theatralis*" (*Literature and Pulpit,* p. 538). On the medieval Passion play in general, see J. Sullivan, *A Study of the Themes of the Sacred Passion in the Medieval Cycle Plays* (Washington, 1943); S. Sticca, *The Latin Passion Play: Its Origins and Development* (Albany, 1970); and R. Bergmann, *Studien zu Entstehung und Geschichte der deutschen Passionsspiele des 13. und 14. Jahrhunderts* (Munich, 1972).

Late Medieval "Lives of Christ"

[22]Thomas of Celano, *Vita Prima Sancti Francisci Assisiensis* (Quaracchi, 1926), pp. 89-92.

[23]J. Huizinga, *The Waning of the Middle Ages: A Study of the Forms of Life, Thought and Art in France and the Netherlands in the XIVth and XVth Centuries* (New York, 1954), pp. 136-48.

[24]See MPVC, 97, 103, 106, and 108. On the theme of patient endurance in the face of adversity and its value for late medieval spirituality, see *The Triumph of Patience: Medieval and Renaissance Studies*, ed. G. J. Schiffhorst (Orlando, 1978).

[25]Huizinga, *Waning of the Middle Ages*, pp. 173-74.

[26]See also VC, 130, where the words "Father into thy hands I commend my spirit" occasion a discussion of how the humble monk ought to say the same words to his superior in obedience.

[27]Note the plural form in this passage: "Hic nunc videndum est, qualiter *debemus* cum Christo sepeliri."

[28]See L. Hundersmarck, "A Study of the Spiritual Themes of the Prayers of the *Vita Jesu Christi* of Ludolphus de Saxonia," in *Kartäuserregel und Kartäuserleben* (Salzburg, 1985), pp. 89-121.

[29]As a comment on Jn 18:6, we read that the wicked fall on their backs while the just fall forward on their faces (VC, 23).

[30]See L. Gougaud, *Devotional and Ascetic Practices in the Middle Ages* (London, 1927), pp. 179-204; and R. Kieckhefer, "Radical Tendencies in the Flagellant Movement of the Mid-Fourteenth Century," *Journal of Medieval and Renaissance Studies*, 4 (1974):157-76.

[31]He identifies the high priest's servant as the same one whose ear had been healed in the garden, thus expressing his extreme ingratitude (VC, 36).

[32]See VC, 26, 29, 45, 98, 99, 100, 111, 119, 129, 137, 139-40, and 154-55.

[33]Longinus is mentioned in the *Meditationes* (MPVC, 118), but Ludolf elaborates on the legend.

[34]Some forty-one "exempla" have been discovered throughout the *Vita*, see

Bodenstedt, *Vita Christi*, pp. 108-10. See also J. Welter, *L'exemplum dans la littérature religieuse et didactique du moyen âge* (Paris and Toulouse, 1927).

[35] Bodenstedt, *Vita Christi*, p. 31; and M. Thomas, "Zum religionsgeschtlichen Standort der 'Meditationes Vita Christi,'" *Zeitschrift für Religions- und Geistesgeschichte*, 24 (1972):211-13.

[36] See VC, 8, 29, 107, 110, 129, and 159. Here the themes of redemption from the devil and the overcoming of Adam's fall are emphasized. See also Baier, *Ein quellenkritischer Beitrag*, pp. 458-74.

[37] See Carolus Le Couteulx, *Annales Ordinis Cartusiensis ab anno 1084 ad annum 1429*, 8 vols. (Monstrolii, 1887-90), 2:526; and L. C. Sheppard, "How Carthusians Pray," *Thought*, 4 (June 1929):294-302. See also C. M. Boutrais, *The History of the Grand Chartreuse* (London, 1934), pp. 221-57; and A. Thorold, "Six Months at the Grand Chartreuse," *The Dublin Review*, 110 (April 1892):282-95.

[38] See also VC, 3, 29, 47, 117, 119, 131, 149, and 150.

[39] Ironically, the western Schism began the year of Ludolf's death and ended with the Council of Constance in 1417. There is no explicit mention of the Avignon papacy in the *Vita*. However, one citation may be construed as a veiled reference to this fact. It reads as follows: "Vel, hodie eris mecum, quod est esse in Paradiso, quia ubi est Christus, qui est Paradisus, ibi est et Paradisus; sicut ubicumque est Papa, ibi dicitur esse Romana curia" (VC, 11).

[40] See VC, 11, 21, 97.

New Sermon Evidence for the Spread of Wycliffism

Simon Forde

Philip Repyngdon (d. 1424) was an Augustinian canon of St. Mary's Abbey, Leicester. He studied theology at Oxford University, where in 1382 he preached several sermons that associated him with prominent Wycliffites. As a result, he and his colleague, Nicholas Hereford, were called to the Blackfriars Synod and forced to recant. It appears that Repyngdon returned to Oxford, and his collection of Sermones super evangelia dominicalia *were probably written at this period. In 1393 he was elected abbot of Leicester and was chancellor of Oxford University in 1400-03. He was promoted to the bishopric of Lincoln in 1404, where he was a particularly active bishop until his resignation in 1419, when he was probably in his late seventies. His sermons are extant in twelve manuscripts, though two merely contain short extracts and two represent substantial fifteenth-century reworkings.*

This article examines three unedited writings: the extant sermons of Repyngdon and Hereford and a tract on usury by their contemporary, John Eyton. It shows that what are termed as "sermons" in the later Middle Ages may not necessarily have been preached but were literary compilationes, *intended to be read as a means of disseminating current biblical scholarship in a liturgical format. Furthermore, by identifying the increasingly favored sermon form, that of "ancient" postillation, it shows how derivative* compilationes *can become useful for historical purposes, not by combing them for contemporary allusions but by examining their sources. In this way there can be identified the theological rigorism that was characteristic of these three writers.*

Traditionally, historians have used two models to account for the influence and transmission of Wycliffite theology into the Reformation period. One model has seen it persisting in England through the fifteenth century in a popularized form among pockets of Lollards.[1] The other has seen continuity at an academic level as Wyclif's Latin works were taken to Bohemia, where they influenced Hus, who in turn influenced Luther.[2] But recent scholarship has shown that these models, when applied retrospectively, give a false, polarized picture of Oxford theological debates in the last quarter of the fourteenth century. Some scholars now suggest that these debates were circumscribed not so much by the attempts from 1377 to hereticize Wyclif or his followers as by Archbishop Arundel's *Constitutions* of 1407, which forbade discussion at Oxford of Wyclif's books.[3]

The present study looks at three Oxford theologians working between these dates and aims to present a non-factional (or perhaps multi-factional) picture of theological study in Oxford and to indicate through these theologians some alternative models for the influence of Wycliffite theology beyond "the schools." I would like to begin by examining first and mainly Philip Repyngdon, one of the prominent Wycliffites in 1382--the year when matters came to head--but one who recanted later that year and subsequently became bishop of Lincoln and even a cardinal. Despite this surprising outcome, it is yet possible to see some integrity between these stages in his career by examining his *Sermones super evangelia dominicalia*.[4]

The way not to use a literary text such as this for historical purposes is the method wherein a historian preselects a specific subject and combs through the text for suitable references to it. This error was made recently by the supervisor of another scholar working on Repyngdon's sermons who said "I have always been astonished at how little [social and political issues] appear in sermons. John Archer, for example, found virtually nothing about the Schism in the sermons of Repington."[5] The same approach was taken by Owst, in his seminal work *Literature and Pulpit in Medieval England*, where he cited six passages from Repyngdon's sermons with the implication that they reflected contemporary satire and complaint. At least three of these passages derived from much earlier sources. One was a short but complete passage drawn by Repyngdon from the *Flores*, the collection of sayings of Bernard of Clairvaux.[6] Since Bernard was not one of Repyngdon's central sources, Repyngdon must have made a conscious decision to select it, and this passage may, in this instance, be justifiably said to reflect his point of view.

However, a second passage attributed to Bernard and cited by Owst is in fact derived from the *Sermones dominicales* of Guillaume Peyraud (or Peraldus).[7] The problem here is that Peyraud's sermons were one of four primary works that Repyngdon divided up and reorganized as the basis for his own sermons, and such sources were often quoted in their entirety. In these cases, it may be more revealing to see which passages from these particular works Repyngdon chose to omit rather than those he did in fact cite. Repyngdon clearly found Peyraud's moral tone congenial, and the *Sermones dominicales* provided a great deal of the moral content in Repyngdon's sermons. But this is not to say that Repyngdon agreed entirely with every precise statement in this source, or that some of the specific complaints by Peyraud concerning his contemporaries would have been framed precisely thus if Repyngdon were to compose his own statements on such matters from scratch.

A further passage is cited by Owst as an allusion to contemporary fashion, since a criticism is made of the "bag-sleeves" that were popular at the time.[8] But the manuscript from which Owst worked was in fact a later, fifteenth-century popularization of Repyngdon's sermon cycle, and this passage is not in the original at all. It becomes clear from this that a lot of preparatory work is necessary before we can draw conclusions from such sermons; and to expect such sermons to make contemporary allusions, to the Schism for example, is to misread the type of literary text from which we are working.

So, let us briefly examine the form of these sermons.[9] The sermon form that we associate with the friars and university preaching--consisting of a short *thema*, expanded by means of a protheme and an elaborate series of divisions and verbal *distinctiones*--was denoted by fourteenth-century theorists as "modern" form. It was falling into disrepute, and a number of writers looked back to a more "ancient" form. The most ancient was that of the Fathers, namely a running commentary, or postillation, on all of the successive verses of the lection. This was adopted, for instance, by many sermons in the "standard" Lollard sermon-collection.[10]

Another "ancient" form was one that had continued in use until the fourteenth century. It too expounded the entire pericope or lection. However, it avoided any division on the text by verbal means and did not employ the *exempla* and *curiosa* that were particularly associated with popular preaching in the "modern" form. This form differed from the patristic model in having a simple, initial framing-device to organize the discussion of the scriptural verses. This was the form Wyclif and Repyngdon frequently adopted. At this date too, we find a revival of vernacular preaching in this "ancient" form with the Middle English translations of some sermons by William de Montibus and other late twelfth- or early thirteenth-century authors, such as Odo of Cheriton.[11]

Repyngdon used Latin works from this era by Jean Halgrin d'Abbeville and Grosseteste. However, the main works that he systematically used in his sermons were the gospel commentaries of William of Nottingham[12] and Nicholas de Gorran for the literal or historical analysis of the text, and the *Sermones dominicales* of Jacopo da Varazze and Peyraud for the moral analysis. These works all date from the late thirteenth or early fourteenth centuries. As we have seen, these main authors were cited in turn on each successive verse or group of verses in the lection. Other authorities were cited where there was a problem in interpreting conflicting accounts of an incident in the gospels; Nicholas de Lyre and Augustine were the favored authorities.

More common, but still quite rare, are the instances where Repyngdon was moved by the gospel exegesis to discuss contentious topics. On these occasions he mainly cited canon law, Grosseteste's *Dicta*, and the *Flores* of Bernard of Clairvaux. In addition, during extended discussions of philosophical and theological issues such as Donatism, the sacraments, or almsgiving and temporal wealth, Repyngdon quoted on more than one occasion Aquinas's *Summa theologiae*, Duns Scotus on the *Sen-*

tences, Peter the Chanter's *Verbum abbreviatum*, and several works by Guillaume d'Auvergne, including his *De sacramentis* and *De prebendis*. These "topics" were also a characteristic of the Wycliffite text, the *Glossed gospels*, both of which used Aquinas's *Catena aurea* and patristic commentaries for the basic biblical commentary, but then inserted into the postillation discussion of topics that were uncontroversial, such as "Patience" or "Prayer," or controversial, such as "The Sufficiency of Scripture" or "The Sacrament of the Altar."[13] These topical discussions are structured similarly to those in Repyngdon's sermons. It is in identifying and studying Repyngdon's topical passages that our clearest picture of his views can be obtained.

The "topics" also appear significant if we examine the manuscript tradition. There are eight manuscripts of the "standard" sermon cycle together with four containing later, fifteenth-century redactions[14] of it (see table on next page). But within the central eight manuscripts, two groups can be distinguished, differentiated by slight but significant variations in content. At a simple level, entire extracts may be omitted or inserted in some manuscripts. For instance, on one occasion an extract attributed to Alexander of Hales is inserted into the gospel exegesis in one manuscript.[15] But Alexander is not quoted anywhere else in the sermons, so he was not one of the integral sources when the sermons were first put together. This passage therefore appears to be a fine example of the process whereby material can later be grafted onto the exegesis; a type of organic growth possible in compilations[16] such as this text.

At a larger level, however, there are three anomalous sermons which are not common to all the manuscripts--anomalous, too, because they do not fit into the normal Sunday Gospel format. These are the sermons for Ascension Thursday and the Epistle for the twentieth Sunday after Trinity, together with a ten-folio *excursus* on Donatism inserted within the Trinity Sunday sermon (see table on next page). The interesting feature about the distribution of these three anomalous sermons is that neither the Epistle sermon nor the *excursus* are found in the manuscripts containing the Ascension Day sermon, while the *excursus* is found in all the remaining manuscripts and the Epistle sermon is found in most of them. Hence we can identify two parallel, but mutually exclusive, manuscript traditions. It would be informative to see whether the shorter inserted extracts, like the one from Alexander of Hales, substantiated this pattern, but such an examination is beyond the scope of this essay.

anomalous sermons	Li	B	W	CO	G	L	P	Cc
Ascension Thursday	/	/	/	x	x	x	x	x
Donatist *excursus*	x	x	x	/	/	/	/	/
Epistle for Trinity 20	x	x	-[17]	/	/	/	x	x

Philip Repyngdon, *Sermones super evangelia dominicalia:*
- Li   Oxford, Lincoln College MS lat. 85
- B   Oxford, Bodleian Library, Laud. misc. MS 635
- W   Worcester, Dean and Chapter MS F.121
- Co   Oxford, Corpus Christi College MS 54
- G   Cambridge, Gonville and Caius College MS 246/492
- L   Lincoln, Dean and Chapter MS 10
- P   Cambridge, Pembroke College MS 198
- Cc   Cambridge, Corpus Christi College MS 82

later redactions:
- Br   Oxford, Bodleian Library, Barlow MS 24
- T   Oxford, Trinity College MS 79
- H   London, British Library, Harleian MS 106
- R   Manchester, John Rylands Library, MS lat. 367

We may be sure from an internal analysis of these "anomalous" sermons that they were composed separately from the material common to all the manuscripts. This fact is particularly interesting since they provide more outspoken views than is usual. The Ascension Day sermon is devoted entirely to the subject of preaching, the promotion of which was a central concern for Wyclif and his followers. The Epistle sermon contains an extract decrying prelates who become too identified with the secular power. The *excursus* in the Trinity Sunday sermon is the most useful "topical" discussion of all because it deals directly with the question of whether bad ministers can validly confer the sacraments, which is one of the beliefs for which Wyclif was condemned in 1382.[18]

Before describing what is said in these "topics," we need to be able to date the sermons so that the views in them can be contrasted with Repyngdon's known views at other stages of his career. As there are no direct statements or allusions to datable historical events, the dating has to come from an internal textual analysis. For this analysis two passages are of use. First, during a discussion of tithes (on Lk 18:12; *Co*, fol. 306vb, lines 6-7), Repyngdon quotes William of Nottingham's discussion of the Old Testament precept that lay behind the Christian tithing practice, but adds simply to one point: "ubi notare debetis doctorem de Lira." The significance of this phrase lies in expecting the audience to have access to the works of Nicholas de Lyre in order to follow up the reference. The expectation that the reader will know or wish to verify and check the references is found elsewhere in these sermons.[19]

The second passage occurs at the start of the commentary on the gospel for the first Sunday in Advent, the text narrating Jesus's messianic entry into Jerusalem (Mt 21:1-9). Repyngdon writes:

> This gospel is normally read on two Sundays, namely the first Sunday in Advent and Palm Sunday. On the second it is read according to its historical sense which is literally fulfilled at that time. On the first in Advent it is recited according to its allegorical sense which covers Christ's incarnation. As a result, by the grace of God, I shall briefly expound it for both senses.[20]

That is to say, Repyngdon expects the reader, if he wants to have an exposition suitable for one of these two Sundays, to divide up this extant sermon and extract for himself the material relevant for *either* a literal or allegorical interpretation. This passage explains the absence in every manuscript of a separate Palm Sunday sermon. And again, this phenomenon occurs elsewhere in the collection.[21]

The implications which result from these two passages are that the sermons must be aimed at an educated, probably university, readership, a fact supported by the known ownership of the manuscripts.[22] We can go on to say that the sermons probably therefore postdate Repyngdon's period as a theology student at Oxford. Academic writings from his student days would have consisted mainly of a *Sentences*-commentary and commentaries on single books from the Old and New Testaments, and would not normally allow for such a vast undertaking as this sermon-collection. We know that Repyngdon continued to be resident at Oxford after he gained his doctorate in theology in 1382.[23] Furthermore, the tone of many of his comments in the sermons directed at prelates suggests that he was not yet himself a prelate. This indicates a *terminus ante quem* of 1404, when he became a bishop, or more probably 1393, the year he became abbot of his own house at Leicester. This intervening period, 1382-93, would have probably corresponded for Repyngdon to a period at Oxford as regent master and teacher, and we know for other scholastic writers that this was the stage when their mature literary output was produced.

The "topics" that we have identified provide treatments of the following issues: preaching, the importance of proper knowledge of the Scriptures, the failings of the friars and (to a lesser extent) the monks, and the proposition that the poor are the true people called to preach or evangelize. Repyngdon seems to have a deep concern for the poor and places great emphasis on almsgiving in one lengthy "topic."[24] He strongly opposes the temporal holdings of the Church, which he believes prevent the Church from carrying out its true mission, a failing he blames squarely on the prelates.[25] In another "topic," he shows that he considers the primitive, apostolic Church to be the standard against which all later developments should be judged.[26] In yet another he defends tithes, providing reasons probably calculated to appeal to those who criticize certain shortcomings of the Church and therefore wish to abolish tithes. He makes a case that tithes can in fact assist good standards of preaching and help the poor, since the rector might be moved to show a good example by giving alms out of his assured income, while in an alternative system Repyngdon foresees the danger of preachers having to temper their message by not criticizing their wealthy, secular paymasters.[27]

Just as his justification for tithes places Repyngdon outside a narrow, "Lollard" faction, so too are his topical views on almsgiving and Donatism distinctive. A marginal hand in one manuscript points out that his discussion of Donatism is "a note against the opinions of the Lollards."[28] In the earlier part of the *excursus*, Repyngdon maintains the orthodox position, following Duns Scotus and Aquinas, saying that the validity of conferring sacraments depends not on the merit of the minister but on the prayer of the whole Church. He even calls the opposing (Wycliffite) position "ridiculous."[29] Nevertheless, the latter part of the *excursus* attempts to confront the problem of unsuitable and ill-living ministers conferring sacraments. It does this by exploring existing powers to punish such priests and to exclude them from the sacraments--though Repyngdon recognizes that this did not invalidate their sacraments if they continued to minister even after such sanctions were imposed.

These "topics" therefore cast Repyngdon in the role of a reformer working within the Church, sharing the concerns and priorities of Wyclif, but differing in several important points from the Lollards who began to work outside the existing Church structures. Repyngdon maintained these concerns and attempted to implement many such reforms when he was bishop of Lincoln.[30]

We may now turn to Nicholas Hereford and John Eyton, both of whose writings I am currently editing, to see how Wycliffite ideas may have affected two other Oxford theologians of this date. The sermon *reportatio* of Nicholas Hereford's Ascension Day sermon in 1382 shows how outspoken and insurrectionary this sermon really was and how polarized the two factions were becoming.[31] Repyngdon was one of Hereford's associates at this stage, albeit a more junior partner, while on the other side there was a group of Carmelites and some Benedictines who had become very active and hostile opponents of those they considered to be "Wycliffites." We know too that before 1382 Hereford had been an even more vociferous critic of the monks and friars than Wyclif, and also that he isolated himself within the Theology Faculty, refusing to make his notes and writings available for other scholars to examine.[32] There may be a psychological connection between his being so extreme and yet so withdrawn, and this may account for his stubbornness and his activism at the periphery of the Church. In the years after his excommunication in 1382, he may have been involved with others in the translations for the Wycliffite Bible and also in a commentary on the book of Revelations, the *Opus arduum*, composed, if it is his, during one of the several periods in prison immediately prior to his recantation in 1391.[33] Both these works are thoroughly scholarly, the Bible translation not overtly polemical, the Revelation commentary still largely theoretical and theological in its criticisms of the contemporary Church. Little is known of Hereford after he recanted, but it may be significant in view of his alleged isolationist tendencies that he eventually became a Carthusian.

John Eyton, an Austin canon like Repyngdon, for his part was never tainted by a charge of Wycliffism. But in 1387, while regent master in theology at Oxford, he composed a tractate on usury in which he maintained a rigorist opposition to any form of usury. I have argued elsewhere that what is interesting about the tract is the choice of sources.[34] Allowing for some slight differences due to the different forms and subject matter between a usury tract and a sermon cycle, the sources are almost identical to those used by Repyngdon, whose selection is in turn greatly influenced by the theological and moral conservatism of Wyclif. Thus, someone not connected to Wyclif by the traditional, polarized models can nonetheless be shown, I believe, to have been a part of the new theological movements at Oxford instigated by Wyclif, but developed in new ways in the generation after his death.

Several implications arise from this essay. First, sermons in the late medieval period do not have to be preached, but can be a literary *compilatio*, intended to be read as a means of disseminating current biblical scholarship in a liturgical format. Second, a text of 650,000 words, such as Repyngdon's sermon collection, which is extremely derivative can yet become useful for historical purposes, provided that it is approached sympathetically and not by the "combing" method described at the beginning of this study. Third, in addition to the Lollard and Hussite models by which Wyclif is thought to have influenced

Simon Forde

religious and social change, there is another model in which the new theological rigorism that we have identified here did not operate solely at the margins but exerted influence on the middle ground within the Church. The three distinctive individuals at whom we have looked were all influenced by this new rigorism, but each maintained some personal integrity in reconciling it to a life within the Church.

Notes

This essay was originally delivered as a lecture to the Fellows and Students of the Pontifical Institute of Mediaeval Studies in Toronto in February, 1986.

[1] See, for instance, the series of studies by A. G. Dickens, *Lollards and Protestants in the Diocese of York, 1509-1558* (London, 1959; rpt. London, 1982); J. A. F. Thompson, *The Later Lollards, 1414-1520* (London, 1965); C. Kightly, "The Early Lollards, A Survey of Popular Lollard Activity in England, 1382-1428," Ph.D. diss. (University of York, 1975); and J. F. Davis, *Heresy and Reformation in the South-east of England, 1520-1559*, Royal Historical Society Studies in History, 34 (London, 1983).

[2] See, for instance, the editor's introduction in S. E. Ozment, *The Reformation in Medieval Perspective* (Chicago, 1971), p. 6.

[3] See particualrly J. I. Catto, "The English Manuscripts of Wyclif's Latin Works," in *From Ockham to Wyclif*, ed. A. Hudson and M. Wilks, Studies in Church History, Subsidia, 5 (Oxford, 1987), pp. 353-59; and C. von Nolcken, "An Unremarked Group of Wycliffite Sermons in Latin," *Modern Philology*, 83 (1986):233-49.

[4] See S. N. Forde, "Writings of a Reformer: A Look at Sermon Studies and Bible Studies through Repyngdon's 'Sermones super evangelia dominicalia,'" 2 vols., Ph.D. diss. (University of Birmingham, 1985).

[5] *Medieval Sermon Studies Newsletter*, ed. G. Cigman, no. 17 (Coventry, 1986), p. 10.

[6] G. R. Owst, *Literature and Pulpit in Medieval England: A Neglected Chapter in the History of English Letters and of the English People* (Cambridge, 1933; 2nd rev. ed. Oxford, 1961), p. 277; cf. *Flores*, bk. 4, chap. 6 (e.g., in Oxford, Bodleian Library, Laud misc. MS 385, fols. 64vb-65ra) cited

New Sermon Evidence for the Spread of Wycliffism

by Repyngdon in Oxford, Corpus Christi College MS 54 (*Co*), fol. 228[va], lines 27-40; and see Forde, "Writings," 2:173. But Owst worked instead from the John Rylands Library codex (*R*), which seems to be a later redaction. In this instance, *R* duplicates material found in the central eight manuscripts of Repyngdon's sermons, but for the final seventeen "sermons" in *R*, this is not the case (see Forde, "Writings," 1:137-62).

[7]Owst, *Literature and Pulpit*, p. 304; cf. Peyraud, *Sermones super evangelia dominicalia* (Lyons, 1576), pp. 151[v]-52[r] cited by Repyngdon in *Co*, fol. 228[va], l. 2.

[8]Owst, *Literature and Pulpit*, pp. 409-10 citing *R*, fol. 256 (Owst's source for the two quotations above also).

[9]The following description is given more fully in H. L. Spencer, "English Vernacular Sunday Preaching in the Late Fourteenth and Fifteenth Century, With Illustrative Texts," Ph.D. diss. (Oxford University, 1982), summarized in part in A. Hudson and H. L. Spencer, "Old Author, New Work: The Sermons of MS. Longleat 4," *Medium Aevum*, 53 (1984):220-38.

[10]See *English Wycliffite Sermons*, ed. A. Hudson, 4 vols. (Oxford, 1983-).

[11]See John Wyclif, *Sermones*, ed J. Loserth, Wyclif Society Publications, 7, 4 vols. (London, 1887-90; rpt. New York, 1966); Forde, "Writings," 1: 203-15; and Spencer, "Vernacular Sunday Preaching," 1:233-42.

[12]See B. Smalley, "Which William of Nottingham?" *Medieval and Renaissance Studies*, 3 (1954):200-38.

[13]See H. Hargreaves, "Popularizing Biblical Scholarship: The Role of the Wycliffite *Glossed Gospels*," in *The Bible and Medieval Culture*, ed. W. Lourdaux and D. Verhelst, Mediaevalia Lovanensia, ser. 1, stud. 7 (Leuven, 1979), pp. 171-89.

[14]These are described in Forde, "Writings," 1:109-92. The occurrence of fifteenth-century redactions is commonplace for sermon cycles of this period. See, e.g., Spencer, "Vernacular Sunday Preaching," 1:233-42; and *The Advent and Nativity Sermons From a Fifteenth-century Revision of John Mirk's "Festial,"* ed. S. Powell, Middle English Texts, 13 (Heidelberg, 1981).

[15]In Lincoln, Dean and Chapter MS 10 (*Li*), fol. 66[va], lines 31-38, corresponding to *Co*, fol. 92[va], line 8. The text is ascribed in the margin of *Li* to

"Halys," and reads: "Aliam causam assignat Halis dicens quod vno die et duabus noctibus in sepulchro iacuit, quia lucem, id est graciam sue mortis que tantum in carne erat, tenebris nostre duplicis mortis que in carne et anima erant opponeret et hac ad significandum quod lux sue mortis curauit nostram mortem duplicem." This passage is inserted before the last of the three points raised by Nicholas de Gorran on part of the Quinquagesima Sunday gospel, i.e., Lk 18:32-34. This extract is untraceable in Alexander of Hales's gospel commentaries in Durham, Dean and Chapter MS A.II.22 (cf. F. Stegmüller, *Repertorium bibliam medii aevi,* 11 vols. (Madrid, 1950-80), 1:1151-54, 6:9960, and 8:1151-54). On Alexander, see B. Smalley, "The Gospels in the Paris Schools in the Late 12th and Early 13th Centuries: Peter the Chanter, Hugh of St. Cher, Alexander of Hales, John of La Rochelle," *Franciscan Studies,* 39 (1979):230-54, esp. pp. 251-54. There were, of course, other scholars with the same surname (see, e.g., A. B. Emden, *A Biographical Register of the University of Oxford to A.D. 1500,* 3 vols. [Oxford, 1957-59], 2:850 (hereafter cited as *BRUO*); and A. B. Emden, *A Biographical Register of the University of Cambridge to 1500* [Cambridge, 1963], p. 280), but none seem to have written works which could have produced this passage and which are extant.

[16]See M. B. Parkes, "The Influence of the Concepts of *Ordinatio* and *Compilatio* on the Development of the Book," in *Medieval Learning and Literature: Essays Presented to Richard William Hunt,* ed. J. J. G. Alexander and M. T. Gibson (Oxford, 1976), pp. 115-41.

[17]The sermons after the seventeenth Sunday after Trinity are now lost in *W*, so no judgment is possible whether this Epistle sermon formerly existed there.

[18]See *Concilia Magnae Britanniae et Hiberniae,* ed. D. Wilkins, 4 vols. (London, 1737), 3:61; and see *Fasciculi zizaniorum magistri Johannis Wyclif cum tritico,* ed. W. W. Shirley, Rolls Series, 5 (London, 1858), p. 278.

[19]See Forde, "Writings," 1:224-26 citing, for instance, *Co*, fol. 167[rb], lines 22-29, and fol. 283[va], line 43-fol. 283[vb], line 1.

[20]"euangelium autem istud in duabus Dominicis solet legi, videlicet in prima Dominica Aduentus et in Dominica in Ramis Palmarum. In 2[a] legitur propter sensum historicum qui tunc ad literam implebatur. In prima Aduentus propter sensum allegoricum recitatur, in quo Cristi incarnacio includitur. Ideo ad vtrumque sensum per Dei graciam breuiter hoc exponam" (*Co*, fol. 1[rb], lines 32-40; see also Forde, "Writings," 2:12).

New Sermon Evidence for the Spread of Wycliffism

[21] See Forde, "Writings," 1:220-22 citing, for instance, *Co*, fol 121[rb], line 30-fol 121[va], line 1.

[22] See Forde, "Writings," 1:227.

[23] See Emden, *BRUO*, 3:1566.

[24] Within his sermon for the fourth Sunday after Trinity: *Co*, fol. 225[ra], line 44-fol. 257[va], line 40; and see Forde, "Writings," 1:306-10 and 2:195-97.

[25] See the discussion and references from *Co* in Forde, "Writings," 1:300-03.

[26] Within the Passion Sunday sermon, Repyngdon drew from Bradwardine's *De causa dei* ten signs of God's departure from the Temple after Jesus's death which Repyngdon applied allegorically to the contemporary Christian Church. He did this by contrasting the purity of the apostolic Church (*ecclesia primitiva*) with its current state. See the summary of his argument in Forde, "Writings," 1:311-16.

[27] See *Co*, fol. 285[va], line 44-fol. 285[vb], line 10 in Forde, "Writings," 2:227, discussed there, 1:303.

[28] "Nota contra opiniones lollardorum vbi dic<it> quod eque a malis confertur sacrament<um> sicut a bonis, vt hic dicitur per multas raciones" (*Co*, fol. 211[rb]).

[29] ". . . si dixerint quod merita ecclesie non sufficiunt absque sanctitate sacerdotis hoc ridiculosum est" (*Co*, fol. 212[vb], lines 5-7). The *excursus*'s argument is summarized in Forde, "Writings," 1:316-25.

[30] See *The Register of Bishop Philip Repingdon, 1405-1419*, ed. M. Archer, Publications of the Lincoln Record Society, 57 (1963), 58 (1963) and 74 (1982), esp. 1:xv-li; and M. Archer, "Philip Repingdon, Bishop of Lincoln, and His Cathedral Chapter," *University of Birmingham Historical Journal* (now *Midland History*), 4 (1954):81-97.

[31] Extant in Oxford, Bodleian Library, MS Bodley 240 (S.C.2469), pp. 848[b]-850[b], of which the two columns at p. 848[b] and p. 850[a] are reproduced in *Wyclif and His Followers*, ed. J. I. Chatto, P. Gradon and A. Hudson (Oxford, 1984), pp. 31-32; note also Beryl Smalley's introductory comment on pp. 5-6. My introduction to and edition of this sermon are forthcoming in *Mediaeval Studies*, 51 (1989).

Simon Forde

[32]See J. Crompton, "Fasciculi zizaniorum I and II," *Journal of Ecclesiastical History,* 12 (1961):35-45 and 155-66; and also the documents and their narrative links in *Fasciculi zizaniorum,* passim. For the criticism of Hereford's academic miserliness, see p. 296.

[33]A consensus has not been fully reached concerning the authorship of or the method adopted in the successive translations which constitute the Wycliffite Bible; suffice it to say that the collaborative procedures which have been identified in the production of certain other "Lollard" texts (e.g., A. Hudson, "Some Aspects of Lollard Book Production," *Studies in Church History* 9 [1972]:147-57) argue against an earlier tendency to assign the translations to specific individuals, whether Hereford, Purvey, or Wyclif himself. For the possibility of Hereford's authorship of the *Opus Arduum,* see A. Hudson, "A Neglected Wycliffite Text," *Journal of Ecclesiastical History,* 29 (1978):257-79.

[34]See S. N. Forde, "Theological Sources Cited by Two Canons From Repton: Philip Repyngdon and John Eyton," in *From Ockham to Wyclif,* pp. 419-28.

From Treatise to Sermon: *Johannes Herolt on the* novem peccata aliena

Richard Newhauser

> *Johannes Herolt (d. 1468) was one of the leading figures of a new Dominican spirituality in fifteenth-century Germany which emphasized the practical goals of pastoral work over mystical subtlety. He enjoyed great popularity as an author: his* Liber de eruditione christifidelium, *published in 1416, is extant in at least fifty manuscripts and was printed seven times before the end of the fifteenth century; his* Sermones de tempore, *completed in 1416, can be found in over two hundred manuscripts and forty pre-sixteenth-century printed editions. There are no modern editions of either work. Both of these catechetically-oriented collections contain treatments of the "nine accessary sins" in either tractate or sermon form. My analysis of these treatments is meant to illuminate Herolt's understanding of the fluid boundary between the* sermo *and the related genre of the treatise on vices and virtues, as it also suggests general criteria for distinguishing between these two forms.*
>
> *The* novem peccata aliena *were a common element in catechesis in German-speaking Europe from the mid-thirteenth to the sixteenth century. Treatises and sermons used them to describe ways in which the instigator or supporter of another person's sin is still morally responsible for the evil committed. These treatises and sermons take their place in intellectual history in the later medieval search for groupings of vices and virtues which had a greater degree of scriptural authority and were more psychologically authentic than the traditional Seven Deadly Sins.*

At the close of the Middle Ages, one can note a tendency among the Dominicans in Germany to turn away from the intense mysticism of their fourteenth-century predecessors and to develop instead a theology emphatically more practical in its methods and goals. The speculations of a Meister Eckhart or Heinrich Seuse give way to the more simplified and immediately comprehensible instructions in the moral life assembled by such friars as Johannes Nider and Johannes Herolt. The pastoral literature which testifies to this transition is marked, at times, by mundaneness and generally by a distinct lack of originality, but at least it has the virtue of being responsive to the everyday needs of the congregation. In their preaching as well, the fifteenth-century German Dominicans show a predilection for usefulness rather than subtlety, for that which can easily be grasped rather than what is barely imaginable.[1] Herolt's comment on Isaiah 58:1 (*et annuncia populo meo scelera eorum*) in the third sermon of his Lenten cycle succinctly characterizes their conception of the preacher's duties and at the same time introduces the guidelines Herolt himself followed when rewriting as model sermons material he had originally cast in treatise form:

> Hic dominus instruit predicatores, quid debeant predicare communi populo, . . . id est vtilia et non subtilia, id est decem precepta, articulos fidei, septem peccata mortalia, septem sacramenta, et de penis inferni et gaudijs celi, quia pene retrahunt a peccatis et gaudia celi inflamant ad bonum.[2]

It is clear that Herolt's list of subject matter is not meant to be exhaustive, for it was supplemented in practice by various other educational schemes, including that of the *novem peccata aliena*. But in any case, this late medieval echo of ecclesiastical resolutions extending back to the Fourth Lateran Council (1215) indicates that for Herolt, and for his contemporaries, the office of preacher remained essentially a moral and catechetical one.[3]

Surprisingly, we know very little about Johannes Herolt, who consistently referred to himself only as a humble student (*discipulus*), not a teacher, of Christian morality. He must have been born in the late fourteenth century, judging from the date of publication of his earliest work, the *Liber de eruditione christifidelium* (1416). The evidence of his career is limited almost exclusively to Nürnberg: in 1436 he was confessor for the nuns of St. Catherina there, in 1438 prior of the city's Dominican cloister, and in 1451 *vicarius generalis* of St. Catherina. He died in 1468 on a visit to the Dominican cloister of St. Blasius in Regensburg, where he was also buried.[4] The scantiness of these details is all the more unusual when seen in the light of Herolt's overwhelming popularity as an author. Of the *Liber de eruditione christifidelium* there are at least fifty entire or partial manuscript copies extant; of the *Sermones de tempore* (1418), the other work I will make use of here, well over two hundred.[5] Yet overshadowing even this broad manuscript transmission is Herolt's success in print: the *Liber* went through seven editions in a matter of twenty years (ca. 1476-96), the *Sermones de tempore* were printed first in 1474 and then over forty times before the end of 1500.[6] In both his choice of material and his treatment of it Herolt seems to have been instinctively attuned to the possibilities offered by the new medium.

Nearly everything he wrote was conceived as an aid to the clergy engaged in instructing their congregations in the fundamentals of leading a virtuous life. The nucleus of this educational program consisted of material frequently associated with catechesis at various stages along its historical development but then regularly included in the catechetical and confessional handbooks of the late Middle Ages: the Ten Commandments, Paternoster, Creed, Seven Deadly Sins and Chief Virtues, and the Sacraments.[7] To these major parts of the syllabus many others had been added by the fifteenth century. Herolt's *Liber de eruditione christifidelium* consists of nine tractates on the: (1) Decalogue, (2) *novem peccata aliena,* (3) Capital Vices, (4) Works of Mercy, (5) Paternoster, (6) Ave Maria, (7) Creed, (8) Sacraments, and (9) Gifts of the Holy Ghost. Much of his treatment of these topics served as the foundation for model sermons on the same issues appended later to the *Sermones de tempore*. That the discussion of the Commandments forms the initial, and in many ways most important, treatise in the *Liber* is typical of a fifteenth-century tendency to supplement conventional groupings of the vices and virtues by more subtle classifications and those with a greater degree of scriptural authority.[8] Herolt's emphasis on the *novem peccata aliena* was also motivated by the same search for psychologically authentic schemes of the sins.

Johannes Herolt on the novem peccata aliena

The "nine vicarious [or indirect, or accessary] sins" were of particular importance in the later Middle Ages in German-speaking Europe, where the focal point of their transmission is also to be found. They had been a part of vernacular preaching at least since the activity in the 1260s of the earliest German redactor of Berthold of Regensburg (ca. 1211-72) and remained a familiar element in popular catechesis into the sixteenth century. Yet, they were also important enough by the end of the Middle Ages to influence instruction on moral theology in Latin at the University of Vienna. Thomas Ebendorfer of Haselbach, professor of theology there until 1460, dealt with the nine sins in a long sermon, and Georg Tüdel of Giengen, dean of the arts faculty in Vienna in 1445, 1448, 1455, and 1460, composed a series of sermons on the *novem peccata aliena*.[9] In Latin they had also long been available in summarized form (and were transmitted in numerous manuscripts) as the mnemonic couplet:

> Jussio, consilium, consensus, palpo, recursus,
> Participans, mutus, non obstans, non manifestans.[10]

As a theological construct, they had been developed to demonstrate how, and in how many ways, the instigator or abettor of a sinful act performed by someone else could still be morally liable for the effects of that vice. Thomas Ebendorfer of Haselbach explained in his *Sermo de alienis peccatis* that they were referred to as accessary sins:

> ... non quod non sint propria, quia vt dicit Augustinus in <Libro> de libero arbitrio: Omne peccatum est adeo voluntarium, quod si non esset voluntarium, non esset peccatum ..., sed quia occasione peccati aliene persone homo incidit in peccatum actuale proprium. Adeo dicuntur aliena peccata, hoc est per aliam personam occasionaliter inducta....[11]

The number of these vicarious sins was always nine; though, as will be seen, neither their order nor, in all cases, their precise content was without variation.

In order to provide a more detailed account of the *novem peccata aliena* and the place of Herolt's treatment of them (in tractate form) in the tradition of this concept, I have chosen the most common sequence, that versified in the Latin couplet, of the sins found with the greatest frequency in works from the thirteenth to the late fifteenth century. I present them here with special attention to (a) designations for the vices and (b) the concrete examples used to illustrate those who engage in them. I have employed the following abbreviations when describing the *novem peccata aliena* here:

S 90 = Berthold of Regensburg, sermon 90 in his *Sermones Rusticani de sanctis*, according to the text found in München, Bayerische Staatsbibliothek MS Clm 8739, fols. 161rb-162ra (collated with Clm 7961, fol. 156^{ra-va}). The two German texts which follow are redactions of this sermon.[12]

Berthold 15 = *Sermo 15: Von den fremeden Sünden*, in Berthold von Regensburg, *Vollständige Ausgabe seiner Predigten*, 1, ed. F. Pfeiffer, rpt. with intro. Kurt Ruh (Berlin, 1965), pp. 211-19.

Berthold 16 = sermon 16 of the "Streuüberlieferung" in the German redactions of sermons by Berthold of Regensburg, ed. Richter, *Überlieferung*, pp. 253-59.[13]

Gewissensspiegel = Martin von Amberg, *Der Gewissensspiegel*, ed. S. N. Werbow, Texte des späten Mittelalters 7 (Berlin, 1958). The text was completed before 1382.

Herolt = Johannes Herolt, *Tractatus de nouem peccatis alienis* in *De eruditione christifidelium cum thematibus sermonum dominicalium* (Strasbourg, 1490), H6^{rb}-J3^{ra}.

TE = Thomas Ebendorfer of Haselbach, *Sermo de alienis peccatis* in Wien, Österreichische Nationalbibliothek MS 4886, fols. 236^{r}-312^{v}.

Peicht = "Eine gute peicht" (*Speculum christianitatis*), ed. Weidenhiller, pp. 52-83 (text of the fifteenth century).

Cgm 121 = the catechetical table in München, MS Cgm 121, ed. Weidenhiller, pp. 44-52 (text of the fifteenth century).

Cpg 438 = Heidelberg, Universitätsbibliothek, MS Pal. germ. 438, fols. 85^{r}-95^{v} (an illuminated treatment of the nine sins in a manuscript bound together with seven blockbooks).[14]

Hollen = Gottschalk Hollen, OESA, Sermo de novem peccatis alienis (*Sermo III de dominica III post pascha*) in West Berlin, Staatsbibliothek Stiftung Preussischer Kulturbesitz, MS Theol. lat. fol. 50, fols. 73rb-78va.[15]

Christenspiegel = *Der Christenspiegel des Dietrich Kolde von Münster*, ed. C. Drees, Franziskanische Forschungen 9 (Werl, 1954).[16]

Johannes Herolt on the novem peccata aliena

The nine indirect sins could, then, be committed by:

1. Command

(a) Der die sünde heizet tuon (Berthold 15:212); bose und suntleiche dinck heisen tuwen (Gewissensspiegel, p. 70); so von aines geschäftes wegen dy sund volbracht wirdet (Cgm 121, p. 49); iussio (Herolt, H6rb).

(b) Implicated in this type of sin is not only the lord who orders his *kneht* to steal someone else's grain, hay, or firewood (Berthold 15:212-13; TE, 240v notes "Per iniustum preceptum maculantur seruitores, qui obediunt eidem."[17]), but also women who command others to dance or commit adultery (Berthold 16: 255; Cpg 438, 85r contains an illustration of a mother sending her daughter off to dance, with the devil looking on). In S 90, 161rb, Herod the tetrarch and Pontius Pilate are cited as biblical examples of the malevolent effects of an authoritarian relationship; Herolt, H6va and Hollen, 73va add to these two Nebuchadnezzar and Antiochus; TE, 244r-251v uses many others.

2. Advice

(a) Die sünde des râtes (Berthold 15:213); yemantz hulpe raijt off daijt gijfft sunde tzo doin (Christenspiegel, p. 136); consilium (Herolt, H6va).

(b) Examples of this type of sinner are those who counsel others to dance, drink, gamble, visit the inn, commit robbery and manslaughter, or engage in tournaments, in particular a *trüllerin* or *die ungetriuwen râtgeben* of lords (Berthold 15:213 with the biblical examples of Ahithophel, the Cushite of 2 Sam 18:21ff., and Balaam; S 90, 161rb had cited Caiaphas, Haman, Judas, and Ahithophel), but also those who advise someone to leave his spouse and take another's wife as his own or seek revenge from enemies (Berthold 16:255). To these illustrations a sociologically relevant component is added in Herolt, H6va- J1ra in the form of a lord's advisors who suggest new tallages, the increase of existing ones, or other ordinances which will go to the detriment of the poor (a phenomenon illustrated in Cpg 438, 86r).[18]

3. Consent

(a) Gunst der sünden (Berthold 15:213); mit willen gestaten (Gewissensspiegel, p. 70); das eyn mensche eyne beheglichkeit hot yn ander lewte sunde (Cpg 438, 87ᵛ; see Christenspiegel, pp. 136-37 in position 4); verhengen zu sünden den unttertanen und andern (Peicht, p. 78; cf. also Cgm 121, p. 49); consensus (Herolt, J1ʳᵃ).

(b) This general category includes all those who do not want to perform a sinful deed themselves (murder, manslaughter, robbery, arson, and treason are mentioned in Berthold 15:213) but are pleased when someone else does so. In S 90, 161ʳᵇ, Berthold of Regensburg emphasizes that even if someone has not given a command or advice leading to a sin, he is not exonerated from joint responsibility for it if he is not saddened by the evil which occurs. Herolt, J1ʳᵃ and TE, 240ᵛ point out that by giving one's consent to crimes which would not have been perpetrated without it, one is also made responsible for the crimes. As examples of sinners in this category, Herolt's compilation specifies city fathers who consent to evil out of a desire for temporal gain, to win favor, or because of their fear of reprisals; and those who allow the presence of gamblers in their cities.

4. Praise

(a) Mithellunge (Berthold 15:214; see Berthold 16:255 in postion 3); in den andern lewten lieb chosen (Gewissensspiegel, p. 70); loben den sünder in seiner posshait, das ist zu tutteln (Cgm 121, p. 49; see also Peicht, p. 78; Cpg 438, 88ᵛ); de adulacione, quomodo inducit ad peccandum (TE, 266ʳ; cf. also Herolt, J1ʳᵃ); palpatio siue adulatio (Hollen, 75ʳᵇ).[19]

(b) This type of *peccatum alienum* includes minstrels (*hystriones*) who praise robbers and the proud (S 90, 161ᵛᵃ); *jâherren*, backbiters, deceivers, flatterers and sycophants who encourage their lord in his sins (whether he is merely sexually unchaste or a murderer); maids who support their mistresses in seeking a lover; and servants who help their masters cheat in their daily work (Berthold 15:214). In Herolt, J1ᵛᵃ-J2ʳᵃ, however, most of the discussion deals with the mechanism of adulation by which flatterers give the name of virtues to vices (*dissolutio socialis* ["social wantonness"] being termed *iocunditas* ["merriment"] in one who dances and gambles, *astucia* ["slyness"] named *prudentia* ["sound judgment"] when someone is perfidious in his business dealings, etc.) and disparages someone's virtues in the opposite way.

5. Protection

(a) Beschirmen widerz recht (Berthold 16:256); herberg zu den sünden zu verleichen und also helffen (Cgm 121, p. 49); zuflucht vergungen [!] den übeltättern (Peicht, p. 78); defendere malos (S 90, 161va); recursus (Herolt, J2^{ra}).

(b) These designations are used for sinners who knowingly protect in their castles, towns, or homes someone placed under a ban (see in particular Christenspiegel, pp. 136-37), thieves, and heretics, for in this way they act as the criminals' shields (Berthold 15:215; Herolt, J2^{ra} uses the same image; see also below, 8b). Berthold of Regensburg, S 90, 161va cites as a biblical example of this *peccatum alienum* the tribe of Benjamin, destroyed because of its defense of Gibeah (see Judges 19:16ff.). In Herolt's treatment one also finds mention of innkeepers who serve dissolute guests foods expressly forbidden during Lent or who give lodging to gamblers (see the illustration of this *peccatum alienum* in Cpg 438, 90^r)[20] and the blasphemous, as well as the head of a household who allows a servant and maid to live in sin in his home.

6. Participation

(a) Nutz der sünde (Berthold 15:215; see Berthold 16:256 in position 4); der teilhaftig werden (Gewissensspiegel, p. 70; see Peicht, p. 78 in position 7); participatio (Herolt, J2^{ra}).

(b) Examples of those sinning by participation are judges (ecclesiastical and secular) who profit from the usury of others and for the same reason allow tradesmen to cheat the poor; craftsmen who hire criminal apprentices in order to make use of their crimes; women who gladly eat, drink, and dress well from money given them by sinners; and innkeepers who, though they do not gamble themselves, still increase their revenues indirectly from the gambling on their premises (Berthold 15: 215-17). In Herolt's compilation (J2[ra-b]), one finds a further specification of the first example. Thus, a Christian who receives a gift from Jews which they, in turn, acquired through usury must restore the present to its rightful owner, if known, or else donate it to the poor. Herolt's list also follows Berthold of Regensburg's analysis (S 90, 161va) by including here those wielding public authority who profit from the shortage of bread (or wine, as Herolt adds) which they have allowed to occur, and wives or children who knowingly enjoy, or inherit, goods acquired unjustly.

7. Concealment

(a) Die dâ die sünde verswîgent (Berthold 15:217; see also Peicht, p. 78 in position 6); stvmmen zu den sünden (Berthold 16:257 in position 8); tacere (S 90, 161va); qui tacet, dum contradicere tenetur et ex cuius contradictione malum interciperetur (TE, 240[v]);[21] mutitas (Hollen, 77va).

(b) One who knows, for example, that stolen goods are being kept somewhere and does not reveal it sins indirectly by keeping silent (Berthold 15:217). Other treatments of this type of vice specifically mention the failure to reveal to a bishop or priest that someone is a witch or a heretic (Berthold 16:257; Cgm 121, pp. 49-50). In contrast, S 90, 161[va-b] and Herolt, J2[rb-va] (and see TE, 290[r]-296[v]) make this category, as the next one, dependent on the other side of the authoritarian relationship: it is the duty of a prelate or head of a household to speak openly of his subordinates' (or children's) sins and to correct them. The failure to do so wholeheartedly amounts to concealment. In S 90, 161vb, Berthold of Regensburg likens such prelates to dogs which do not bark when they see a wolf or a thief. It will be noted that the precise boundaries between this and the next two categories of the sins remained somewhat fluid.

8. *Not opposing*

(a) Der die sünde niht wert swâ man sie ze rehte wern sol (Berthold 15:217); die sich nicht seczent wider die sünd (Berthold 16:257 in position 6); eyn mit den wercken moecht sunden hynderen ind en deit des neit (Christenspiegel, pp. 136-38); non obstare (S 90, 161vb); qui non resistit malefacientibus, cum possit et teneatur (TE, 240^v).[22]

(b) For all commentators, this type of sin presupposes someone in a position of authority which, however, he does not exercise to justly punish a crime committed publicly. In S 90, 161vb, those who perform this duty correctly are described as shields of the church (see above, 5b). Berthold 15:217 covers nearly the full spectrum of possibilities drawn on by most later writers: judge (ecclesiastical or secular), abbot, abbess, provost, deacon, priest, mother, or father. Herolt, J2^{va-b} focuses in particular on the adversaries of the poor: prelates and secular rulers who look on complacently while their subordinates curse, beat, injure, mock, and mistreat the *pauperes*. An illustration of this category in Cpg 438, 94^r attributes the frequency of crimes in a country to the laxity of its ruler in punishing them.

9. *Not revealing*

(a) Der die sünde niht offent dâ er sie offenen sol (Berthold 15:217; see Berthold 16:256 in position 7); nicht warnen den sünder oder den, der sich möcht underchomen (Cgm 121, p. 50); qui legitime inquisitus contra malos veritatem non manifestat, presertim si malum eorum est publicum et pluribus, per quos eciam in iudicio probari posset, notum (TE, 240^v).[23]

(b) The common element in the various treatments of this type of sin can be identified as an unwillingness to reveal someone's crime to a person (or group) with the authority to correct it. Frequently this vice is committed in a legal setting: witnesses at a public ecclesiastical hearing do not reveal the truth (Berthold 15:217-18); or at the diocesan court they do not disclose another's incest, adultery (see the illustration of this phenomenon in Cpg 438, 95^r), usury, heresy, or soothsaying (Berthold

16:256-57). Both Berthold 16:256 and Herolt, J3[ra] devote attention to the motives for not revealing the truth (familial ties, desire for profit, fear of retribution), but Herolt also adds an exhortation pointing out that the disclosure of another's sins is similar to warning a blind man of the open pit before his feet--or being responsible for his death when he falls in because he was not warned.[24]

It is probable that Herolt's treatise was inspired by Berthold of Regensburg's sermon on the *novem peccata aliena*, for though Herolt's text is far more detailed than Berthold's, the two works frequently agree in the construction and imagery of their arguments, and there also appear to be a few verbal echoes of Berthold's sermon in the later analysis.[25] In Herolt's depiction of the nine sins, however, catechesis has come to be tailored fully to the needs of an urban environment. This can be seen first of all in his explicit references to towns and, for example, the sins perpetrated within their walls by those in a position of authority (J1[ra], see above, 3b). Likewise, Herolt used the opportunity offered by a discussion of the sin of advice to point out the moral consequences of civic irresponsibility: "Item qui in ciuitatibus dant consilium ad nouas institutiones in damnum pauperum et communitatis, tales rei erunt omnium peccatorum illorum, que ex consilio eorum perpetrata sunt vel perpetrabuntur vsque ad nouissimum diem. . . ."[26] Yet a further indication of how Herolt compiled with an eye to the actual situation of his Nürnberg audience can be found in his employment of types of sinners familiar to town dwellers as illustrations of the vices. If Berthold 15:212-13 had depicted the sin of command by means of the feudal relationship between *herre* and *kneht*, Herolt supplements this by referring to: ". . . mechanici in ciuitatibus, qui iubent suos famulos infideliter laborare sua artificia. Item pannifices, qui iubent pannum nimis excessiue laniare et extrahere. Item caupones, qui iubent famulos suos mensuram cum vino non bene implere."[27] In these clothiers and petty innkeepers, one can observe at least a part of the ultimate recipients of Herolt's instructions for preachers. The precise influence of his text on the composing of sermons by other preachers remains a matter for future study, but one can note here already that there are a number of significant parallels between Herolt's treatise and Gottschalk Hollen's sermon on the *novem peccata aliena* which make it possible that the former directly influenced the latter.[28]

The *tractatus* on the nine sins is marked everywhere by Herolt's endeavor to make his subject matter as clear as possible. Its elements of content and form are, in fact, the necessary constants characterizing the treatise on vices and virtues as a genre in the Middle Ages.[29] Its discursive concentration on a system of moral constructs is carried by a sober, objective tone interrupted only by the infrequent recourse to apostrophe. Yet even this rhetorical figure is employed to guide the clergy in the practical task of communicating the *peccata aliena* to their catechumens, as is clear from the following example taken from Herolt's words on the necessity of revealing another's sins: "Sed aliqui dicunt, cum aliqua iniusta fieri vident: Quid hoc pertinet ad me? Respondeo illis: Ex precepto fraterne charitatis quilibet tenetur preuenire periculum sui proximi corporis et anime, cum hoc commode potest."[30] The structure of the treatise places the members and sub-members of the moral system in hierarchic relationship to each other, something observable in clearest form where Herolt deals with the sin of *adulacio* and distinguishes its two major categories (giving the name of vices to virtues and virtues to vices) and their sixteen further sub-categories (J1va-J2ra). Moreover, that Herolt conceived of the *Tractatus de nouem peccatis alienis* as only one of many parts of a catechetical *summa* is further typical of the history of the treatise on vices and virtues as a genre in the late Middle Ages, when it began to lose its independent identity by being subsumed into more comprehensive handbooks.

The *Tractatus* was not Herolt's final word on the subject of the nine sins, for he himself rewrote the treatise later as sermons 144-45 found among the *Sermones communes* and appended to the *Sermones de tempore*.[31] Frequently, these topical sermons simply follow word for word what he had already composed in his catechetical handbook, but at least in the case of those on the nine sins, one can no longer speak of mere resumés of the earlier treatment.[32] They show well over thirty-one changes, additions, or deletions as compared to the text of the treatise, and, though they were conceived as models of pulpit discourse and were not delivered in this form before a congregation, their reworking affords us an excellent view of Herolt's implicit understanding of the *sermo* genre and how it differs from that of the *tractatus*. How fluid the boundary was between these two forms is clearly documented by Herolt's treatment of the material on the nine sins, for he transformed into a treatise what was originally a sermon, only to recast it as sermons again. It is, at any rate, clear that the generic distinctions he drew here are ultimately a question of functional intent and cannot be reduced to a mere dichotomy between written and oral presentation.[33]

The differences are first of all structural in nature, the sermons developing, at least nominally, a theme which precedes the text (for sermons 144-45 this is Ps 18:14: "Ab alienis parce seruo tuo"). *Sermo* 144 also ends with a long *exemplum* which has no equivalent in the treatise; in his model sermon collections, Herolt preferred a tripartite form (and applied it without exception in the *Sermones de sanctis*), the last section of which nearly always consisted of an exemplary narrative.[34] But beyond these formal elements distinguishing Herolt's sermons from his treatises, one can see that he also took pains to suggest ways in which the preacher could make the doctrine of the *sermones* more immediately and dramatically accessible to his listener than was even the case in the catechetical handbook. Partially, this meant carrying tendencies further which were already noticeable in the *tractatus*. Thus, the sermons give more room to phenomena with which an urban audience would have been familiar, adding, for example, cobblers and fishmongers to the list of tradesmen who sin by ordering their subordinates to work dishonestly (Gg2[va]). References to "the present age" are also found (e.g., Gg3[ra]), without counterpart in the treatise. And in a long addition to one of the sermons which purports to represent actual occurrences, Herolt provided an account which verified his analysis of how the sin of protection is committed during Lent:

Johannes Herolt on the novem peccata aliena

Sermo 144, Gg3[rb-va]

Si es receptor hospitum et recipis in domum tuam homines non bonos et . . . propter lucrum administras eis quicquid desiderant et cibum prohibitum ab ecclesia. Uerbi gratia: Sicut repertum est, quod in quadragesima in vna quarta feria, in qua etiam fuit angaria et cum hoc fuit vigilia Mathie apostoli, quam plures fortes, sani et robusti vsi sunt de lacticinijs, et alias habuissent sufficientiam de cibis quadragesimalibus. In quo non modicum peccant tam commedentes quam etiam illi, qui administrant propter lucrum temporale eis talia fercula.[35]

Liber, J2[ra]

Item si tu es receptor hospitum et recipis in domum tuam homines non timentes deum et . . . propter lucrum amministras eis cibum illicitum, tunc particeps eris illorum peccatorum.

Yet much was also deleted from the analysis of the nine sins on its way from tractate to sermon. The absolute value for Herolt of usefulness over subtlety in the pulpit is demonstrated clearly in his excision from the *sermones* of a long passage in the *tractatus* dealing with adulation which cited patristic sources and Seneca on flatterers' perversion of the order of right reason (J1[rb]). The lengthy use of authorities in the treatise, in particular including exemplary figures from the Old Testament, is also restricted in the sermons. Of those referred to in the earlier work, only one has remained in the rewritten texts (in the discussion of the seventh sin, Gg3[vb]): Eli, the priest who did not correct his sons (1 Sam 2:22ff.). As the intended audience for his sermons, then, Herolt obviously had in mind a congregation more receptive to the illustrative power of its everyday surroundings than to an appeal to written authority. The appearance of the text with a minimum of such appeals may be indicated by the following quotations, taken from Herolt's analyses of the sin of command:

Sermo 144, Gg2[va]

quicquid iussisti, quod est contra charitatem dei et proximi, in isto reus es et damnaberis cum illis, qui hoc perpetrauerunt ex iussu tuo. Unde Sapientie xviij: Simili pena seruus cum domino afflictus est.

Liber, H6[va]

quicquid iussisti, quod est contra charitatem dei et proximi, in istis reus es et damnaberis cum illis, qui hoc ex iussu tuo perpetrauerunt. Unde Sapientie xviij: Simili pena seruus cum domino afflictus est, immo quandoque iubentes plus peccant quam facientes. Herodes enim non decollauit Johannem, tamen ita reus est, tanquam cum propria manu fecisset. Et hoc quare? Quia iussit. Similiter Pilatus, qui non crucifixit Christum propria manu, sed milites sui ex iussu suo. Nabuchodonosor Holifernem predari iussit. Antiochus iussit, quod leges non seruari deberent, quod fuit contra deum; et multi alij, qui hoc iusserunt fieri, quod est contra deum. Et hi omnes et consimiles damnati sunt et damnabuntur.[36]

What remains in the sermons is the often unadorned moral lesson of the *novem peccata aliena*. This concentration on a practical morality rather than subtleties of doctrine and finesse in argumentation is the most characteristic quality, not only of Herolt's pastoral work but of other German Dominicans in the fifteenth century as well and is the single most important factor underlying Johannes Herolt's extraordinary popularity as an author.

Notes

Earlier versions of this essay were read by Prof. Dr. B. Wachinger, Prof. Dr. B. K. Vollmann, and Dr. A. Holtorf. I gratefully acknowledge their suggestions for improving it.

[1] On the theology and preaching of the German Dominicans in the fourteenth and fifteenth centuries, see Johann Baptist Schneyer, *Geschichte der katholischen Predigt* (Freiburg i. Br., 1969), pp. 171-76 and 205-06; Gundolf

Johannes Herolt on the novem peccata aliena

M. Gieraths, *Reichtum des Lebens: Die deutsche Dominikanermystik des 14. Jahrhunderts,* Für Glauben und Leben 6 (Düsseldorf, 1956), pp. 44ff.; Anton Linsenmayer, *Geschichte der Predigt in Deutschland von Karl dem Grossen bis zum Ausgange des vierzehnten Jahrhunderts* (Munich, 1886), pp. 391ff.; and Rudolf Cruel, *Geschichte der deutschen Predigt im Mittelalter* (Detmold, 1879; rpt. Darmstadt, 1966), pp. 370ff.

[2]"Here the Lord instructs preachers in what they should preach to the common people, . . . i.e., useful matters and not subtle ones, that is, the Ten Commandments, the articles of the faith, the seven deadly sins, the seven sacraments, and about the punishments in hell and the joys of heaven, since the punishments keep one from sins and the joys of heaven incite one to do good" (*Sermo tercius in Quadragesimale Discipuli* [Reutlingen: Johannes Otmar, 1489], p. a4^{vb}). Capitalization and punctuation of citations from manuscripts and early printed books are my own; emendations are given in <>.

[3]See also H. Siebert, "Die Heiligenpredigt des ausgehenden Mittelalters," *Zeitschrift für katholische Theologie,* 31 (1906):473.

[4]The earliest competent account of Herolt's life is to be found in Nicolaus Paulus, "Johann Herolt und seine Lehre," *Zeitschrift für katholische Theologie,* 26 (1902):417-25. On the evidence of his epitaph in Regensburg, see G. Anton Weber, "Johann Herolt," *Zeitschrift für katholische Theologie,* 27 (1903):362-66 and Paulus's response in the same issue of the journal, pp. 366-68; and Friedrich Bock, "Das Nürnberger Predigerkloster: Beiträge zu seiner Geschichte," *Mitteilungen des Vereins für Geschichte der Stadt Nürnberg,* 25 (1924):173 and n. 73. See also Bertrand-Georges Guyot, "Hérolt (Jean)," *Dictionnaire de Spiritualité,* 7.1 (1969), p. 344; Thomas Kaeppeli, *Scriptores Ordinis Praedicatorum Medii Aevi,* vol. 2 (Rome, 1975), p. 450; and F. J. Worstbrock, "Herolt, Johannes (Discipulus)," *Die deutsche Literatur des Mittelalters: Verfasserlexikon,* vol. 3, 2nd ed. (Berlin and New York, 1981), p. 1123.

[5]For manuscripts of the *Liber,* see Morton Bloomfield, et al., *Incipits of Latin Works on the Virtues and Vices, 1101-1501 A.D.,* The Mediaeval Academy of America Publication No. 88 (Cambridge, MA, 1979), nos. 3692, 3774, 5445, 5639 (the entry for Sigmaringen 21 must be corrected to show a more complete copy of the work), 5681, 8662, and probably 3455; Kaeppeli, pp. 451-51; and Worstbrock, col. 1125 (Nr. 1). For the *Sermones de tempore,* see Bloomfield, *Incipits,* 0027-28 (not identified here as copies of Herolt's sermons on the *novem peccata aliena*), 3773, 5638, 8876; and Kaeppeli, pp. 451-54; Worstbrock, col. 1125 (Nr. 2).

Richard Newhauser

[6]For the *Liber,* see Ludwig Hain, *Repertorium Bibliographicum* (Stuttgart and Paris, 1831), nos. 8516-22. For the *Sermones de tempore,* see Hain, nos. 8473-8508; W. A. Copinger, *Supplement to Hain's Repertorium Bibliographicum,* vol. 2 (London, 1898), nos. 2921-27; and Frederick R. Goff, *Incunabula in American Libraries* (New York, 1964), nos. H-118, H-123.

[7]On the content of late-medieval catechesis, especially in Germany, see Egino Weidenhiller, *Untersuchungen zur deutschsprachigen katechetischen Literatur des späten Mittelalters,* Municher Texte und Untersuchungen zur deutschen Literatur des Mittelalters 11 (Munich, 1965), pp. 16-25; Josef Andreas Jungmann, *Katechetik: Aufgabe und Methode der religiösen Unterweisung,* 3rd rev. & enlarged ed. (Freiburg, 1965), pp. 12-19; Paul Bahlmann, *Deutschlands katholische Katechismen bis zum Ende des 16. Jahrhunderts* (Münster, 1894); Peter Göbl, *Geschichte der Katechese im Abendlande vom Verfalle des Katechumenats bis zum Ende des Mittelalters* (Kempten, 1880), pp. 121-245; and Johannes Geffcken, *Der Bildercatechismus des funfzehnten Jahrhunderts und die catechetischen Hauptstücke in dieser Zeit bis auf Luther,* vol. 1 (Leipzig, 1855), pp. 20ff.

[8]Lewis W. Spitz, "Further Lines of Inquiry for the Study of 'Reformation and Pedagogy,'" in *The Pursuit of Holiness in Late Medieval and Renaissance Religion,* ed. C. Trinkaus and H. A. Oberman, Studies in Medieval and Reformation Thought 11 (Leiden, 1974), p. 295; and Morton W. Bloomfield, *The Seven Deadly Sins* (East Lansing, MI, 1952; rpt. 1967), pp. 170 and 411 n. 94. See also Joseph A. Slattery, "The Catechetical Use of the Decalogue from the End of the Catechumenate through the Late Medieval Period," Ph.D. diss. (Catholic University of America, 1979), esp. pp. 166ff.

[9]On Ebendorfer, see below, n. 11. For Tüdel (d. 1466), see *Die Akten der Theologischen Fakultät der Universität Wien (1396-1508),* ed. P. Uiblein, vol. 2 (Wien, 1978), pp. 645-46; Schneyer, *Geschichte,* p. 192; and Joseph Aschbach, *Geschichte der Wiener Universität im ersten Jahrhunderte ihres Bestehens,* vol. 1 (Wien, 1865), pp. 526-27. His treatment of the nine sins has been preserved in Wien, Österreichische Nationalbibliothek MS 4256, fol. 1ra-74rb (incipit: "Abiciamus opera tenebrarum et induamur arma. . . . Vas eleccionis et sidus appostolicum predicator veritatis et doctor gencium beatus Paulus appostolus capitulo 13 ad Romanos monet et hortatur tamquam fidelissimus pater . . ."; explicit: ". . . ut in die extremi iudicii mereamur cum beatis omnibus recipi ad eternum beatitudinis regnum per dominum nostrum Iesum Christum qui cum Deo patre in unitate Spiritus sancti vivit et regnat Deus in seculorum secula. Amen" [information supplied by Dr. Franz Lackner, Austrian Academy of Sciences, whose assistance is gratefully acknowledged]).

Johannes Herolt on the novem peccata aliena

See *Tabulae codicum manu scriptorum . . . in Bibliotheca Palatina Vindobonensi asservatorum,* vol. 3 (Wien, 1869), p. 219. The text is not found in Bloomfield, *Incipits.*

[10]"Command, advice, consent, praise, retreat, / Participating, keeping silent, not opposing, not revealing." For the transmission of the couplet, see Hans Walther, *Initia carminum ac versuum medii aevi posterioris latinorum, Carmina medii aevi posterioris latina,* vol. 1 (Göttingen, 1959); Walther, *Ergänzungen und Berichtigungen, Carmina medii aevi posterioris latina,* vol. 1 (Göttingen, 1969), part 1, no. 9990; and Bloomfield, *Incipits,* 2877, and see 3454. To the manuscripts they have listed can be added West Berlin, Staatsbibliothek Stiftung Preussischer Kulturbesitz, MS Germ. qu. 1976; ibid., MS Theol. lat. oct. 16 (Rose 255), fol. 206^v; ibid., MS Theol. lat. fol. 51 (Rose 574), fol. 73va; Eger (Hungary), Egyházmegyei Könyvtár, MS Aa 1x 38, fol. 95^v (and see Richard Newhauser, "Latin Texts with Material on the Virtues and Vices in Manuscripts in Hungary: Catalogue II," forthcoming in *Manuscripta,* text no. 66); Giessen, Universitätsbibliothek, MS 687, fol. 253^r; Hamburg, Staats- und Universitätsbibliothek, Petri MSS, MS 55, fol. 46^v; Klagenfurt, Studienbibliothek, MS Pap. 83, fol. 132^r-133^v; Klosterneuburg, Stiftsbibliothek, MS 902; Koblenz, Landeshauptarchiv, Bestand 701 MS 198, fol. 202vb; Munich, Bayerische Staatsbibliothek, MS Cgm 324, fol. 3vb (and see Weidenhiller, pp. 101ff.); ibid., MS Clm 8738, fol. 137^v; Wien, Österreichische Nationalbibliothek, MS 4886, fol. 240^v; ibid, MS 4913, fol. 205^v; and Wien, Schottenkloster MS 449 (561), fol. 257^v. The list is far from being complete. Walther prints *retrorsus* for *recursus*; in text 16 of the "Streuüberlieferung" among the German redactions of Berthold of Regensburg's sermons the word appears as *recusans* (*Von den neun fremden Sünden,* ed. D. Richter in Richter, *Die deutsche Überlieferung der Predigten Bertholds von Regensburg,* Municher Texte und Untersuchungen zur deutschen Literatur des Mittelalters 21 [Munich, 1969], p. 255); in the Giessen manuscript it is found as *receptans*; in Clm 8738 it appears as *susurro*. Berlin, MS Theol. lat. oct. 16 glosses all of the terms for the sins and adds the following verse after the couplet: "Tot tu participas peccatis, que fecit alter" ["You have a share in so many sins which another person has committed"].

[11]". . . not because they do not properly belong to the individual, since as Augustine says in *On the Free Will*: 'Every sin is voluntary, because if it were not voluntary, it would not be a sin . . . ,' but since it is on the occasion of another person's sin that a man falls into his own active sin. For that reason they are called 'accessary sins,' that is, brought about circumstantially by another person . . ." (Wien, ÖNB, MS 4886, fol. 240^v). Various parts of this work are dated 1445-51 in the Vienna manuscript which, according to Al-

phons Lhotsky (*Thomas Ebendorfer*, Schriften der Monumenta Germaniae Historica 15 [Stuttgart, 1957], p. 82, no. 94), is Ebendorfer's autograph text. See also Alois Madre, *Nikolaus von Dinkelsbühl: Leben und Schriften*, Beiträge zur Geschichte der Philosophie und Theologie des Mittelalters 40, 4 (Münster, 1965), pp. 328-29; Bloomfield, *Incipits,* 0279. The matter of individual responsibility is also at the center of the more simplified explanation for the term "frömd sünd" found in a catechetical table from the fifteenth century in Munich, Bayerische Staatsbibliothek, MS Cgm 121 (ed. Weidenhiller, p. 50): "wann wie wol wir sy in aygner person nicht tuen, so mügen wir ir aber dennoch schuldig werdenn...."

[12] On the Latin sermon and its relation to the German texts, see Richter, *Überlieferung,* p. 188; Anton E. Schönbach, *Studien zur Geschichte der altdeutschen Predigt, VI: Die Überlieferung der Werke Bertholds von Regensburg, III,* Sitzungsberichte der Kais. Akademie der Wissenschaften in Wien, Phil.-hist. Kl. 153, 4 (Wien, 1906; rpt. Hildesheim, 1968), p. 66; Georg Jakob, *Die lateinischen Reden des seligen Berthold von Regensburg* (Regensburg, 1880), pp. 69 and 166. See also Johannes Baptist Schneyer, *Repertorium der lateinischen Sermones des Mittelalters,* vol. 1, *Beiträge zur Geschichte der Philosophie und Theologie des Mittelalters,* 43/1 (Münster, 1969), 484, no. 154. Clm 8739 is of the thirteenth century and belonged to the Franciscans in Munich; Clm 7961 is of the fourteenth century, from the Cistercian monastery in Kraisheim: see Laurentius Casutt, *Die Handschriften mit lateinischen Predigten Bertholds von Regensburg* (Freiburg/CH, 1961), pp. 29-30. Manuscripts containing the sermon are legion, and the evidence provided by these two codices must be used carefully.

[13] The German texts of these sermons are not by Berthold himself, but both represent reworkings of his authentic Latin sermon, S 90. Berthold 15 was prepared, according to Richter, *Überlieferung,* pp. 69-70 and 73-78, in Augsburg in 1264, and Berthold 16 is presumably the work of the same redactor (see Richter, *Überlieferung,* p. 188). On Berthold 15, see also Göbl, p. 204. For digests of recent work on Berthold, see Volker Mertens in *Lexikon des Mittelalters,* vol. 1 (1980), pp. 2035-36; F. G. Banta in *Die deutsche Literatur des Mittelalters: Verfasserlexikon,* vol. 1, 2nd ed. (Berlin and New York, 1978), pp. 817-23; and Banta, "Berthold von Regensburg: Investigations Past and Present," *Traditio,* 25 (1969):472-79.

[14] The codex and blockbooks which follow it are found on paper manufactured ca. 1455-58; they were probably produced in eastern Central Germany and may have been owned by the prince elector Ludwig IV (1424-79) or his guardian, the count palatine Otto von Mosbach (1391-1461). On the

Johannes Herolt on the novem peccata aliena

manuscript, see Wilfried Werner's commentary in *Die Zehn Gebote: Faksimile eines Blockbuchs von 1455/1458 aus dem Codex Palatinus Germanicus 438 der Universitätsbibliothek Heidelberg* (Dietikon-Zürich, 1971), pp. 15-22; Werner, *Cimelia Heidelbergensia* (Wiesbaden, 1975), pp. 51-53; Hans Wegener, *Beschreibendes Verzeichnis der deutschen Bilder-Handschriften des späten Mittelalters in der Heidelberger Universitäts-Bibliothek* (Leipzig, 1927), pp. vii and 49-52; Karl Bartsch, *Die altdeutschen Handschriften der Universitäts-Bibliothek in Heidelberg, Katalog der Handschriften der Universitäts-Bibliothek in Heidelberg,* vol. 1 (Heidelberg, 1887), pp. 137-38, no. 240; and Geffcken, *Beilagen,* cols. 1-19.

[15]The sermon forms a part of Hollen's *Sermonum opus* which he completed in 1471 and which was printed at Hagenau in the early sixteenth century, though with an incomplete version of the sermon on the nine sins. This *sermo* may be an abbreviated form of the treatise on the nine sins he is reported to have written but which is no longer extant. On the sermon and its author (b. 1411, d. 1481), see Willigis Eckermann, *Gottschalk Hollen OESA,* Cassiciacum 22 (Würzburg, 1967), esp. pp. 141-43; Eckermann, in *Die deutsche Literatur des Mittelalters: Verfasserlexikon,* vol. 4, 2nd ed. (Berlin and New York, 1983), pp. 109-16; and Kaspar Elm, "Mendikantenstudium, Laienbildung und Klerikerschulung im spätmittelalterlichen Westfalen," in *Studien zum städtischen Bildungswesen des späten Mittelalters und der frühen Neuzeit,* ed. B. Moeller et al., Abhandlungen der Akademie der Wissenschaften in Göttingen, Phil.-hist. Kl. 3, Folge, 137 (Göttingen, 1983), esp. pp. 595-615. Eckermann's monograph includes on p. 143 a list of many of the authorities which Hollen cites in his sermon. As will be illustrated below, this work on the nine sins also shows many parallels with Herolt's treatise on the same topic.

[16]The text was composed 1476-79; see also H. Brück, "Der religiöse Jugendunterricht in Deutschland in der zweiten Hälfte des fünfzehnten Jahrhunderts," *Der Katholik,* 56/1 (1876):378.

[17]"By an unjust command the servants are defiled who are obedient to it" (TE, 240^v).

[18]Herolt's criticism of antisocial behavior is obviously not unique in German preaching. For the views of Berthold of Regensburg (and his redactors) on the estates, their duties, and their failures, see Helmuth Stahleder, "Das Weltbild Bertholds von Regensburg," *Zeitschrift für bayerische Landesgeschichte,* 37/3 (1974):762-76; Stahleder, *Arbeit in der mittelalterlichen Gesellschaft,* Miscellanea Bavarica Monacensia 42 (Munich, 1972), pp. 169ff.; and the recent materialist analysis by Irmela von der Lühe and Werner

Röcke, "Ständekritische Predigt des Spätmittelalters am Beispiel Bertholds von Regensburg," in *Literaturwissenschaft und Sozialwissenschaften*, 5, ed. D. Richter (Stuttgart, 1975), pp. 41-82.

[19]"On fawning and how it leads to sinning" (TE, 266[r]); "Flattering or fawning" (Hollen, 75rb).

[20]The illumination has been reproduced in Wegener, p. 51.

[21]"Whoever keeps silent when he is bound to speak out against evil, and by whose objection the evil could have been impeded" (TE, 240[v]).

[22]"Whoever does not oppose evil-doers, although he is able and bound to do so" (TE, 240[v]).

[23]"Whoever has been legitimately interrogated and does not reveal the truth about those who are evil, especially if their evil is public and known to many by whom it can also be proven in a court of justice" (TE, 240[v]).

[24]As detailed as this presentation of the nine vices has been, it should be supplemented by a reference to at least one of the less common types of sins included in a sermon which treats the topic. Thus, the last of the *peccata aliena* appears in Berthold 16:257 as "sünd lieben vnd day recht laiden." For other additions to the most common list, see Weidenhiller, p. 22.

[25]It will, of course, remain impossible to say how much Herolt's argument is based on a direct knowledge of Berthold's text until one finally has a critical edition of the latter's sermons. One illustration of the textual parallels must suffice. It is taken from the examples found in the analysis of the sin of participation:

S 90, 161[va]
Item iudices, qui permittunt panem et huiusmodi minorari pro pecunia. Tales omnes cum vxoribus et filiis, qui scientes sic iniusta participant, dampnantur. Exemplum in Daniele, vbi legitur, quod sacerdotes Bel cum vxoribus suis et filiis sunt combusti.

Herolt, J2[rb]
Item iudices et reipublice prouidentes, qui permittunt panem vel vinum minorari pro pecunia et alij quamplurimi, qui participant quocumque modo scienter in lucro peccati, vt vxores et pueri iniusta scienter hereditantes. Vnde tam vxores quam filij sacerdotum Belis simul a rege combusti sunt, vt legitur in Danielis capitulo xiiij.

Johannes Herolt on the novem peccata aliena

[S 90: "Likewise judges who for money allow bread and similar things to grow scarce. All such people are damned with their wives and children who knowingly participate in such injustices. An example in Daniel, where one reads that the priests of Bel were burned with their wives and children."]

[Herolt: "Likewise judges and those who provide for society who for money allow bread and wine to grow scarce and very many others who participate in the wages of sin in whatsoever way, as wives and children who knowingly inherit unjust goods. For this reason both the wives and the children of the priests of Bel were burned at the same time by the king, as one reads in Daniel, chapter 14."]

[26]"Likewise, those in the cities who give counsel in favor of new institutions to the detriment of the poor and the community, they will be answerable for all of the sins which have been committed by their advice, or will be committed, until doomsday. . ." (*Tractatus,* H6^{vb}; see above, 2b).

[27]". . . artisans in the cities who order their workers to carry out their craft in a dishonest way. Likewise, clothiers who order cloth to be shorn and stretched quite excessively. Likewise, innkeepers who order their help not to pour out a full measure of wine" (*Tractatus,* H6^{va}).

[28]Hollen's sermon parallels Herolt's treatise especially in certain portions of the analysis of the first, second, and fourth sins. The following texts may be used to indicate these similarities. They are taken from the description, in the fourth sin, of those who give flattering praise to the misdeeds of some and denigrate the good done by others:

Herolt, J1^{rb}	*Hollen,* 75^{rb-va}
Et ideo tales participes sunt omnium malorum istorum [i.e., peccatorum], nam peruertunt ordinem recte rationis in hoc quod laudant illud, quod reprehensibile et illicitum est et vituperant et subsannant illud, quod salubre et laudabile est. Et propterea tales adulatores sunt maledicti. Ideo habetur Esaie v: Ue qui dicitis bonum malum et malum bonum, ponentes tenebras in lucem, amarum in dulce, dulce in amarum. Quare putatis, quod iam tam femine quam	Tales peruertunt ordinem recte racionis, quia laudant illud, quod est reprehensibile et subsanant illud, quod est salubre et laudabile. Contra quos dicitur Ysaie 5: Ve qui dicitis bonum malum et malum bonum, amarum dulce, lucem tenebras. Ergo tam viri quam femine non cognoscunt se esse peccatores, quia laudantur in malicijs eorum.

viri tot iam habeant peccata, etiam
nescienter, quia laudantur in his, que
faciunt et ideo non cognoscunt se
esse peccatores: sicut coram Deo
sunt et ita decipiuntur.

[Herolt: "And hence such people are partners in all their [i.e., the sinners'] evils, for they pervert the order of right reason insofar as they praise what is hateful and illicit and censure and deride what is wholesome and laudable. And therefore such flatterers are damned. Hence one has in Isaiah 5<:20>: 'Woe to you who call good evil and evil good, putting darkness for light, bitter for sweet, sweet for bitter.' Why else do you suppose that now at this time both women and men commit so many sins, indeed without knowing it, since they are praised in what they do and hence do not recognize that they are sinners: they are, then, in the presence of God and are so deceived."]

[Hollen: "Such people pervert the order of right reason, since they praise what is hateful and deride what is wholesome and laudable. It is said against them in Isaiah 5<:20>: 'Woe to you who call good evil and evil good, bitter sweet, light darkness.' Therefore both men and women do not recognize that they are sinners, since they are praised in their wicked deeds."]

That Hollen's sermon parallels (and perhaps was influenced by) Herolt's treatise and not his sermons is shown below in n. 36.

[29] The history of this genre still remains to be written. For questions involved in the definition of related genres, but with a direct bearing on the treatise on vices and virtues as well, see Bertrand-Georges Guyot, "Quelques aspects de la typologie des commentaires sur le *Credo* et le *Décalogue*," in *Les genres littéraires dans les sources théologiques et philosophiques médiévales,* Université Catholique de Louvain, Publications de l'Institut d'Études Médiévales 2/5 (Turnhout, 1982), pp. 244-48; and, in the same collection, Louis-Jacques Bataillon, "Intermédiaires entre les traités de morale pratique et les sermons: les distinctiones bibliques alphabétiques," pp. 213-26.

[30] "But some, when they see injustices occur, say: 'What does this have to do with me?' I answer them: 'Everyone is bound by the precept of brotherly love to anticipate physical and spiritual danger to one's fellow man, whenever this can be done appropriately'" (*Tractatus,* J3[ra]).

[31] I have used the following edition of the sermons on the nine sins: Johannes Herolt, *Sermones de tempore et sanctis cum promptuario exemplorum et de B. Virgine* (Basel, [1486]), pp. Gg2[va]-Gg4[rb].

Johannes Herolt on the novem peccata aliena

[32]Compare Paulus, p. 420; Guyot, "Hérolt," col. 344. Herolt was also active as a preacher himself, in the vernacular. There is still extant an Advent cycle of German sermons which he held in 1436 at St. Catherina in Nürnberg. See Karin Morvay and Dagmar Grube, *Bibliographie der deutschen Predigt des Mittelalters*, Munich Texte und Untersuchungen zur deutschen Literatur des Mittelalters 47 (Munich, 1974), p. 159; and Dietrich Schmidtke, *Studien zur dingallegorischen Erbauungsliteratur des Spätmittelalters,* Hermaea, N. F. 43 (Tübingen, 1982), pp. 23-24, 103-06 and 448-54.

[33]See Schneyer, *Repertorium,* 1:9-10; Schmidtke, p. 275; and Paul-Gerhard Völker, "Die Überlieferungsformen mittelalterlicher deutscher Predigten," *Zeitschrift für deutsches Altertum und deutsche Literatur,* 92 (1963):212-27. On the importance of model sermon collections for the study of preaching, see David d'Avray, *The Preaching of the Friars: Sermons Diffused from Paris before 1300* (Oxford, 1985), pp. 78-79 and 105.

[34]See Cruel, pp. 480-81.

[35]*Sermo*: "If you are one who takes in guests and you take into your home people who are evil and . . . in order to make a profit you bring them whatever they desire, even food prohibited by the church. An example: it was, thus, discovered that during Lent on a Wednesday on which there was even the quarter-yearly period of fasting and when this was the vigil of the apostle Matthew, many strong, healthy and robust people ate foods prepared with milk, though otherwise they could have had their fill of Lenten food. Both the ones eating as well as those who serve them such dishes in order to make a profit commit a not inconsiderable sin."

Liber: "Likewise, if you are one who takes in guests and you take into your home people who have no fear of God and . . . in order to make a profit you serve them forbidden food, then you will share in their sins."

For *angaria* in the meaning of "Quatemberfasten," see Laurentius Diefenbach, *Glossarium latino-germanicum mediae et infimae aetatis* (Frankfurt a. Main, 1857), p. 34.

[36]*Sermo*: ". . . whatever you have commanded which is against the love of God and one's fellow man, for this you are answerable, and you will be damned with those who have carried out the deed by your command. Hence Wisdom 18<:11>: 'Master and slave were punished together with the same penalty.'"

Liber: ". . . whatever you have commanded which is against the love of God and one's fellow man, for these things you are answerable, and you will be damned with those who have carried out the deed by your command. Hence Wisdom 18<:11>: 'Master and slave were punished together with the same penalty;' or rather, at times those issuing the commands sin more than those carrying them out. For Herod did not decapitate John, nevertheless he was just as responsible as if he had done it with his own hands. And why is this so? Because he commanded it to be done. Similarly, Pontius Pilate, who did not crucify Jesus with his own hands, but rather his soldiers acting on his orders. Nebuchadnezzar ordered Holophernes to engage in plunder. Antiochus commanded that the laws not be adhered to, which was against God; and many others who commanded that something be done which is against God. And all of them, and those similar to them, were damned and will be damned."

A comparison of these two passages with the following section from Hollen, 73[va], shows clearly that the parallels in his work are to Herolt's tractate on the nine sins, not to the sermons: "Exemplum huius [i.e., primi peccati alieni] patet in Pylato, qui non legitur dominum proprijs manibus crucifixisse aut violenter percussisse vel traxisse, tamen dampnatus est, quia iussu suo vvlneratus est. Sic Herodes, qui Iohannem Baptistam iussit decollari, et Herodes pueros interfici, sic Anthiochus leges non seruar<i>. Sic iussit Nabugadonosor Holofernem spoliare. Sic multi nobiles perierunt in isto peccato alieno, de quibus dicitur Sapiencie: Simili pena seruus cum domino est afflictus" ["An example of this [i.e., the first accessary sin] is evident in Pontius Pilate who, as one reads, had not crucified or violently beaten or dragged Jesus along by his own hands, but nevertheless was damned because Jesus was wounded on his orders. In the same way Herod, who ordered John the Baptist to be decapitated; and Herod that the children be murdered, likewise Antiochus that the laws not be adhered to. In the same way, Nebuchadnezzar ordered Holophernes to commit plunder. In this way many noblemen perish, about whom it is said in Wisdom: 'Master and slave were punished together with the same penalty'"].

Pyres of Vanities: Mendicant Preaching on the Vanity of Women and Its Lay Audience

Thomas M. Izbicki

Late medieval friars preached a harsh and strict moralism in their Lenten sermons, using the season of preparation for Easter to focus on sin and repentance. Such sermons tapped a vein of social and moral anxiety in fifteenth-century Italian towns. They were very popular, despite the fact that they denounced all classes, all occupations, and both sexes for their characteristic sins and vices. Women were singled out in these sermons for vanity of appearance in such things as dress, ornament, and use of cosmetics. Popular preachers such as Bernardino of Siena (1380-1444), a Franciscan Observant whose sermons are edited in S. Bernardini Senensis . . . Opera Omnia, ed. Collegium S. Bonaventurae (Quaracchi, 1948-63), could often cap a successful preaching campaign by holding a burning of the vanities of both sexes in a public square, and bringing about enactments of sumptuary legislation. The friars tried shifting the grounds of their attack from the vanities to denying absolution to the women who wore them or the artisans who made them. Such actions resulted in disputes in which canonists tried to moderate the zeal of the friars, as in the case which produced the De ornatu mulierum *of* Antonino of Florence (1389-1459).

Eloquent preaching only partly explains the popularity of the Lenten sermons and the lay audience's willingness to burn vanities and enact new sumptuary laws. Another crucial element came from the anxiety of laymen trying to play a status game, in which appearance both denoted and reinforced status, with resources from increasingly fragile patrimonies. Ambivalence about playing this game produced both laws limiting women's ownership of the dress and ornament purchased to advance family status, and a willingness to respond to the preachers' attacks on these vanities. The actions and attitudes of the lay audience of the Lenten sermons came as much from their own concerns as from the very real eloquence of a Bernardino of Siena.

Mendicant Preaching on the Vanity of Women

One of the most famous and powerful preachers of the fifteenth century was the Franciscan observant Bernardino of Siena (1380-1444). During Lent in 1425, Bernardino returned to his native city to preach to the populace. Speaking in his mother tongue, he denounced the Sienese for such sins as usury and sodomy.[1] If these were the sins of men, Bernardino lashed women in his audience for the vanity of their dress. This was no new theme in Bernardino's sermons. Only the previous year, preaching at Santa Croce in Florence, he had incited his auditors to build and burn a pyre of vanities.[2]

The Lenten sermon took on peculiar aspects in late medieval preaching. The liturgical calendar, the preacher, and the audience combined to produce a charged atmosphere in which eloquence devoted to the moral themes of a penitential season could reduce a lay audience to tears and could bring them to temporary amendment of public or private life, or even to violence against the Jews, the perpetual outsiders in Christendom.[3] The most usual preachers of these Lenten sermons, which could be delivered daily throughout the Lenten season, were members of the mendicant orders. The bishop was the traditional teacher of the flock, but few bishops did much preaching. Likewise, most of the parish clergy, even when the nominal pastor was resident in his benefice, were ill equipped to speak effectively on any theme. Consequently, despite occasional confrontations with bishops and rectors, the orders of mendicant friars, especially the Dominicans and Franciscans, became the most popular preachers of their age. Their education, their tradition of pulpit oratory, and the availability of written aids for preaching made their sermons the best possible for that time. Their mission to work for the salvation of souls and their need for the alms of the laity made them always ready to occupy the pulpit, even to the point of preaching when the parochial Mass was being celebrated, in violation of papal mandates.[4]

The ordinary lay audience of these sermons contained a majority of unlearned men and women who were more easily moved by the spoken than the written word. Even the more learned auditors, lay or clerical, would not be immune to the persuasive power of a trained and inspired preacher such as

Bernardino of Siena.[5] The preacher's art left its impact on the urban fabric of Renaissance Italy. The emblem of the Holy Name of Jesus, Bernardino's popular and occasionally controversial sign of devotion, can be found blazoned on the facade of the Palazzo Publico in Siena and on an outdoor pulpit in Viterbo. The latter is a sign of the preacher's popularity, which drew audiences too large even for the mendicants' "preaching barns"; but it also shows the desire of the populace, lay and cleric, high and low, to find divine protection from the world's woes.[6]

Lenten sermons, because of the penitential nature of the season, served as natural occasions for the castigation of sinners. No class, no age group, and neither gender escaped the preacher's lash. This emphasis on sin received further strength from the papal charge given the mendicants, especially the Franciscans, to concentrate on moral exhortation and to leave doctrinal exposition to the bishops.[7] The Lenten preacher functioned very much like the modern evangelist. One of the usual ways of moving the audience to penitence was the threat of punishment after death, whether in the eternal fires of Hell or in the temporary agony of Purgatory. Speculations about the more spiritual agonies awaiting the soul were confined to the scholar's study.[8] The punishments presented by preachers, however, were all too graphically real. It would be too easy to see, as have critics both past and present of the friars, the preaching of infernal and purgatorial pains as a device to stir up useless emotion or to secure the sale of indulgences.[9] In fact, the preachers themselves, if we take their literature into account, feared that even the best among them might suffer in Purgatory, if only for venial sins.[10]

Preaching to the Sienese in 1425, Bernardino followed this Lenten sermon tradition and launched his principal attack against vanity of dress in a sermon on the psalm text *Odisti obseruantes uanitates superuacue* (Ps 31:6). Men, but more particularly women, were castigated for offending God through the three sins of curiosity, vanity, and superfluity. Curiosity was Bernardino's general heading for fashion, the rush to follow the mode in choice, cut, and ornamentation of dress. Bernardino pointed to prostitutes as the trend-setters in fashion. The woman who followed their example was denounced for advertising to the public that she was discontented with her husband and in the market for a lover.[11]

Superfluity, despite being listed third, formed the next topic in Bernardino's sermon. As the empty-headed followed fashion, they heaped up expenditures on fancy garments which overflowed coffers and burdened clothes poles, while the poor went naked. Bernardino took the magistrates of Siena to task for failing to take effective measures against this folly. Women were denounced for offending God through their attempts to improve on creation by using cosmetics, dyes, padded busts, and like deceits. Bernardino suggested that women should dress up at home to please their husbands and hide their charms when out in public.[12]

Bernardino was unimpressed by beauty and equally unimpressed by custom. Beauty he described as a great misfortune, which could impede the quest for eternal life. God cared neither for looks nor for social status. Custom, if it led to sinful excess, should be ignored. Bernardino's only concession to appearances permitted a woman to take care in dressing her hair if it was in danger of falling out. Otherwise, a woman was advised to content herself with the looks God had given her, just as "the ass doesn't envy the nightingale for his song or the canary either."[13] The woman who indulged in superfluity of ornament was accused of being like the harlot not only in appearance but in the power to entrap souls. The preacher described such evils as vexing the guardian angels of both women and men.[14] The woman risked her soul in other ways, since vanity leads to bitterness, envy, anger, and even gluttony.[15] Mothers were accused of acting as procuresses when they dressed up their daughters on the pretense of finding them husbands.[16] The girl's trousseau was also used as bait to catch a husband and was condemned for expressing the bride's vanity, just as it might also arouse the groom's cupidity.[17]

According to Bernardino, all Siena suffered from the vanity of its women. Money went for gowns and jewels rather than profitable investments.[18] Men, if they could not secure rich dowries, put off marriage and became prone to the vice of sodomy. This, in turn, reduced the population of the city. Bernardino concluded by drawing a connection between the common good of citizens in this life and their salvation in the next. Both were best served by curbing the vanity of women.[19]

In August of 1427, Bernardino returned once more to his native Siena and preached once again on the vanity of women. Perhaps worn down by a hearing into his orthodoxy held in Rome before Pope Martin V, the preacher snapped at the women in his audience for chatting before a sermon during the Mass. Twice he reprehended them for going to Mass only to show themselves to men and to show off to each other.[20] As before, Bernardino devoted one entire sermon to the sin of vanity, particularly the vanity of women's dress. Bernardino adapted his text, *Visitabo super habentes uestem peregrinam*, from Sophoniah 1:8. The promised visitation was that of God's cudgels, which would beat people for their sins. The cudgel would measure the lengths of trains on gowns and would punish the wearers of these garments. The whole city was threatened with woe from this visitation.[21]

This sermon echoed themes from the sermon of 1425. The preacher once more urged the magistrates to act against the vanity of dress by banishing all sinful novelty.[22] The nubile maiden and the newly-wed bride were both threatened with the fires of hell for the vanity of their dress. Bernardino said that the girl would go in first, then her mother, and then the tailor who made the garments. The entire mercantile apparatus of the city was described as tied in with the making of sinful vanities.[23] Hair styles also received particular attention for making a woman's head a tower from which demons fought for the damnation of souls: those of the women themselves; those of men lured into dalliance; and those of men driven into sodomy. Women were urged instead to wear the sign of Tau, the cross of Christ, to fight off the devil who sought such strongholds in the midst of urban life.[24]

Late in life, Bernardino recast his vernacular sermons into Latin texts to which he added references to patristic, legal, and theological authorities. One cycle of Lenten sermons, intended for the first week of Passiontide, contains several sermons concerned with the vanity of women's dress and ornament. Sermon Forty-four contains echoes of the sermon given in Siena in 1425.[25] A key theme of this sermon is that the expenditure required to keep wife and children fashionably clad could drive the head of the household to contract debts at ruinous rates of interest.[26] In sermon Forty-six, Bernardino denounced parents for sending their daughters to perdition by encouraging them to paint and bedeck themselves.[27] The woman who so ornamented herself was compared to a hungry she-wolf, and merchants and artisans were berated for serving her appetites.[28] The same she-wolf, insatiable in her desire for vanities, was described by the preacher as spilling the blood of the poor.[29] At the beginning of this sermon and again at the end, Bernardino held up before his audience the example of the converted Magdalene, a sign that a woman who repented from her vanities could be saved.[30]

In sermon Forty-seven, the preacher warned that vanity offends God, one's neighbor, and the vain person's own self.[31] In an attempt to shame women who dragged about long trains of costly material, Bernardino compared them to monsters with grotesque tails. In a more practical vein, he warned women that trains raised dust which harmed lungs and eyes, and he presented the image of a woman who so befouled her lungs that her spitting defiled her house.[32] Bernardino also compared women with their trains to vain and stupid peacocks.[33]

Going from tail to head, Bernardino denounced once more the vanity of hair styles, which he called demons' towers and banners raised in derision of Christ.[34] In concluding this sermon, the preacher denounced women who labored to present a certain appearance only to incur divine judgment. Good women were urged to burn false hair, to give up trains and sleeves, to pour cosmetics in the privies, and to break looking glasses. The true Christian woman he described as modest and honest in conduct, a woman worthy of eternal life.[35]

As early as a sermon delivered in Florence in 1424, Bernardino had held up the example of the Magdalene to the women in his audience to contrast her former vanity of dress and conduct with her later humility and penitence.[36] In sermon Forty-six of a second set of Lenten sermons, the preacher expounded at length on this model penitent's lessons for the women in his audience. The Magdalene was described as kissing Christ's feet while bewailing her past vanity of mind and dress. Her hair, once an ornament, became a towel for Jesus's feet.[37]

Bernardino's attacks on the vanity of women's dress and ornament complemented his wider vision of person and home as austere, even parsimonious, in ornament. "True parsimony" could save the soul from hell. Bernardino was willing to admit a distinction between the dress of a noble's wife, that of a citizen's wife, and that of a rustic's wife. Nonetheless, he continued to warn against vanity, which could entrap even the most noble of birth and status into ruin.[38]

Bernardino's sermons denouncing vanity drew upon a long tradition within Christian moral teaching. Patristic texts from Tertullian's time onward had attacked luxury of dress and ornament as pleasing to the devil. Jerome's works were among the authorities most often cited by medieval writers and preachers in their denunciations of vanity.[39] Medieval moralists, among them members of the mendicant orders, had attacked vanity as Satan's snare for women and as a tower of the devil's fortress, language Bernardino repeated in his sermons. Vanity was often depicted in art and word as a woman in an embroidered robe gazing raptly into a mirror.[40] The mendicant idea of education stressed modesty and dismissed all superfluous dress, ornament, or artifice as foolish.[41] Nor were preachers slow to expound on this topic. Whether the preacher was a secular cleric such as Jacques de Vitry or a mendicant such as the Franciscan Guibert de Tournai, the vanity of women served as a standard topic for sermons.[42]

Bernardino had burned vanities at Florence in 1434. In 1493 a namesake among the Franciscan observants, Bernardino da Feltre, revived the practice on the occasion of a meeting at Florence of the Minorite general chapter. These and other burnings provided a release for the displays of emotion which could follow the preaching of a master pulpit orator, and moralized the traditional bonfires of carnival.[43] Such moralism was politicized in the career of the Dominican observant Girolamo Savonarola. Late in 1494, less than two years after Bernardino da Feltre had conducted his burning of vanities, the Dominican firebrand preached his sermons on the psalms and Haggai. In these sermons Savonarola contrasted, as had Bernardino, the beautiful but modest woman with the woman whose beauty had been degraded by sin and fashion until it resembled the painted image of a prostitute.[44] The preacher urged women to give up their vanities, while urging their husbands and fathers to constrain them to give up the accursed thing which ruins households.[45] In the same vein as Bernardino, Savonarola warned against the diabolical snare of vanity which incurs divine wrath.[46] In one sermon, Savonarola urged his hearers to give up poems, games, taverns, sumptuous garments, and other things harmful to their souls.[47]

In 1496, Savonarola had sufficient political power to send bands of youths through the city to collect vanities. Reports vary as to whether these youths were courteous or threatening when they approached a woman dressed in too fine a fashion. Whatever the approach, the vanities collected that year were sold to provide money for charities.[48] In 1497, Savonarola had a pyre of vanities burned at the beginning of Lent and repeated the action the following year. Although scholars have concentrated on the works of art destroyed, most of the material consumed in these last public shows of the friar's sway over Florence was of a more humble sort--cosmetics, veils, playing cards, and the like.[49]

Savonarola's ability to convert a symbolic gesture into a political act suggests that moral doctrines could have practical consequences. We should inquire whether the impact could be felt in more ordinary circumstances, especially in the confessional. Bernardino's threat that a tailor might be damned for making garments which appealed to the vain is relevant in this context. Medieval moralists were comparatively lenient with craftsmen, reserving their most severe censures for merchants. The artisan might be guilty of cheats and deceptions, but the merchant's very place in Christendom, as trafficker, banker, or industrialist, was suspect. In Florence and other Italian cities, vanity of dress derived from the industrial base, most notably in the manufacture of fine woolens and silks.[50]

At least one tailor found himself classed as a practitioner of a suspect art, the manufacture of vanities. The Franciscan observants became interested, at least by 1438, in using the confessional as a means of curbing the luxury trades. In that year, John Capistran, a leading light of the movement, was sent to Bologna to consult Pope Eugenius IV, who was awaiting the arrival of the Greeks to attend the council of union at Ferrara. The topic of the consultation was a supposed decree of John XXII entitled *Cupientes,* which denied absolution to women who wore false hair.[51] The pope made a verbal response (*uiue uocis oraculum*) urging the friar to be lenient in his dealings with women accused of vanity of dress and ornament.[52] Despite this reply, the Franciscan observants at San Paolo in Monte, near Bologna, took the opposite tack. One of their priests denied absolution to a tailor who catered to the luxury trade. Apparently the tailor took exception to this refusal, which caused the Franciscans to send two of their leaders, Franciscus de Platea and Iacobus de Primatitiis, to Florence, the new seat of the council of union, to consult the pope again.

Pope Eugenius was asked once more to rule on the applicability of *Cupientes* in cases involving vanity of dress and ornament. The pope was vague about the nature of his reply to Capistran; but he established a commission, effectively led by Antonino, the founder of the Dominican house of observants at San Marco in Florence, later the seat of Savonarola's prophetic ministry, to look into the question. The commissioners looked with disfavor on *Cupientes,* the main authority cited by the Franciscans in defense of their denial of absolution to the tailor. They urged instead that penitents guilty of wearing vain clothing or guilty of manufacturing such things be treated mildly.[53] At least once more in his career, Iacobus de Primatitiis would ask the same question and receive the same reply.[54]

The Franciscans were not the only religious to be troubled by the text *Cupientes*. Even earlier, in 1437, the Venetian canon Paolo Maffei had asked Pope Eugenius whether the text was genuine. On the pope's behalf, his cousin Ludovico Barbo, bishop of Treviso, expressed skepticism about *Cupientes* and ordered that absolution be given to any penitent woman who had confessed to wearing false hair.[55] The pope, however, seemed to have forgotten his cousin's reply when dealing with the Franciscans. In 1439, Dominic of Catalonia, a Dominican active in the region of Pavia, had inquired of Antonino of Florence about the same matter and received the same answer.[56]

Having once been consulted in 1439 and now consulted again by the pope himself in 1440, Antonino prepared a *consilium*, his *De ornatu mulierum,* for the commission's response to the inquiry of the Franciscan observants. This work was widely circulated in three forms--by itself, as an appendix to the second recension of his *Confessionale "Defecerunt,"* and as part of his *Summa moralis*.[57] Antonino's *consilium* on female dress and ornament was thought by Morçay to be the first from his pen, but Creytens, noting the lack of any reference in the tract to Antonino's reply to Dominic of Catalonia's question about the applicability of *Cupientes*, has argued that the *De ornatu* cannot be dated earlier than 1439.[58] The text of Franciscus de Platea's report on his mission to Florence makes it clear that the *De ornatu mulierum* was composed in 1440 to guide the commission appointed by Eugenius IV.[59]

The judicious tone of Antonino's *De ornatu* contrasts starkly with the fiery tone and astringent doctrine of Bernardino's sermons. Antonino's *consilium* has the structure of a scholastic disputation in which the original question about absolution of the tailor is subordinated to the larger question of whether women are permitted to wear gowns, false hair, and jewels. The culpability of the manufacturer was said to depend on the sinfulness of using his products. Thus Antonino began by asking whether ornament worn according to the custom of the country was permissible. The negative argument turned on an attempt to prove that ornamentation of the female form displeased God, an argument similar to that of Bernardino's sermons.[60] Several texts from Scripture and canon law were cited as proof of this contention, most notably the list in the third chapter of Isaiah of the baubles to be taken away from the daughter of Zion.[61]

The affirmative arguments turned on the contention that ornament violated no law except when it was carried to excess.[62] The Scriptural example of Esther dressing up to please Ahasuerus and thus to win safety for her people was used to argue that ornament could be used to a good end. Bernardino, by contrast, had dismissed any contention that a woman might dress to please her husband.[63] Antonino cited the authority of Thomas Aquinas and that of Alexander of Hales to the same end.[64] The supposed authority of *Cupientes* was dismissed because it did not appear in any collection of papal decretals.[65]

Antonino's solution to this question turned on two distinctions: between good and bad intentions in dressing up; and between dress which did or did not conform to local custom. Antonino denounced women who sinned against love of neighbor by trying to make themselves alluring, drawing men into carnality.[66] He also upbraided women who ornamented themselves out of vainglory, though that might be, according to Thomas Aquinas, a venial sin.[67] A woman, if married, was permitted to dress in a manner pleasing to her husband, while a marriageable girl might dress up to attract a potential mate. This argument contrasted sharply with Bernardino's threat that the girl, her mother, and her tailor would burn in hell. The girl was permitted to follow local custom, even if it demanded a high degree of ornamentation, to avoid bringing scorn down on herself. Any of these better motives permitted a woman to display herself to best advantage with little peril to her soul.[68]

As was noted above, Antonino used Saint Thomas's authority to prove that custom was a legitimate criterion for determining whether a woman dressed properly. We should note, however, that Antonino did not place custom above divine law.[69] Nor was custom egalitarian. Antonino was careful to mention, in addition to the custom of the land or city, the woman's status in life. We have already mentioned the concessions made to a marriageable girl. Now another criterion, social status, also applied. What custom permitted the well-born it forbade to others, a distinction that even Bernardino had admitted.[70] Nonetheless, excess in dress remained a real possibility which could be measured in terms of money, a sin of prodigality, as well as in terms of evil intent.[71] In cases of mortal sin arising from prodigality or ill intent, the confessor could withhold absolution until the woman promised to amend her life. Absolution, however, could not be denied in cases of venial sin. The mere use of ornament was, in itself, no reason to withhold absolution.[72] Antonino urged both preachers and confessors to warn the faithful against excess in dress to wean them away from vanity, but he sagely warned against treating all ornament, even that which followed custom, as an automatic occasion of sin.[73]

Antonino drew a second set of conclusions from these arguments when he declared that an artisan could not be denied absolution simply because he made vanities. This denial was permissable only if the artisan carried on his trade in a positively sinful way, clearly intending to lead women to ruin by promoting lascivious conduct. Absolution could be refused, even in such a case, only if the artisan made no promise to amend his life.[74]

Antonino's advice to respect custom and to not treat the problem of vanity of dress in a simplistic way was not wholly original. He made good, if somewhat free, use of Aquinas's discussion of this matter, although Aquinas never specifically made a concession to the marriageable girl.[75] Nor was Antonino's the only voice raised in favor of moderation.

Among the mendicant observants, the Franciscan Bartolomaeus de Chaimis in his *Confessionale* added to considerations of custom and social status a similar concession based on maintaining the dignity of any public office which the woman's husband might hold.[76] The prominent jurist Antonio Roselli, a layman, wrote an opinion on the same subject in 1447 while teaching at Padua. Roselli also used Scripture, law, and the authority of Saint Thomas to grant custom a place in the regulation of women's dress. This jurist also defended the validity of sumptuary laws which required a husband to restrain his wife's taste in ornament.[77]

This moderation was unpopular with many religious zealots. Most Franciscan observants took a different tack. Franciscus de Platea replied to Antonino's *De ornatu* by arguing that evanescent fashion never could obtain the status of custom, which required a forty-year duration. The curial commissioners replied that Aquinas and Alexander of Hales had meant by custom not the legal term but the current way of living in a particular city.[78]

They also reminded the friar that confessor should bring penitent to amendment of life, which could not be done by denying absolution to those guilty of venial sins.[79] Another Franciscan, Orpheus de Cancellariis, took an even harder line, refusing to make any concessions to unmarried women and criticizing the Thomistic argument on ornamentation. Like Bernardino, however, Orpheus did make one concession, permitting a rich woman to spend more than a poor one did without being thought extravagant.[80]

The Franciscans continued preaching against vanity in the tradition of Bernardino long after his death. John Capistran, followed by Giacomo della Marca and Alberto da Satreano, urged that respectable women be denied trains, and would permit them only to prostitutes.[81] Giacomo in particular preached against women's vanity over many years in terms derived from Bernardino's sermons. Trains were denounced as the devil's bed and as public notices that women were for sale, since women dressed in this fashion to go out but did not bother to do so at home. Giacomo added an anti-Semitic turn to this message, as did many of his colleagues, by arguing that women's vanity drove their men to borrow from the Jews at usurious rates.[82] Giacomo also repeated Bernardino's accusation that women's demands for bridal gifts of finery caused men to abstain from marriage out of fear that a bride's dowry would not support the burdens of marriage. This, in turn, was supposed to drive men into sodomy.[83] Like Bernardino, Giacomo held up before women the example of the penitent Magdalene, the woman saved from the sins of the flesh and from vanity of dress and ornament.[84]

How are we to understand the enduring popularity of Franciscan preachers such as Bernardino who denounced the vanity of women's dress and ornament in such fiery, not to say Old Testament, language? As in the case of Savonarola, part of their appeal was based on eloquence and force of personality. We must also remember that the fifteenth century was an age of social, political, and economic uncertainty. To that first answer we must add the need of audiences to hear a reaffirmation of the traditional pieties. Such reaffirmations gave them a sense of security in a turbulent age when the commune was giving way to aristocratic regimes in which the old nobility of birth and the new patriciate of wealth gradually ceased to be distinguishable.[85]

Even accepting this answer, we must inquire which pieties the audiences were interested in having reaffirmed. Perhaps the more religious were concerned about the sinfulness of vain dress and ornament, but this does not entirely explain the electric effect of these sermons. After all, some of these sermons were followed not only by pyres of vanities but also by the enactment of new sumptuary laws.[86] Sumptuary laws were important manifestations of the ambiguities toward women's dress and ornament in the minds of men in the preachers' audiences. The many rationales for these laws included morality, the fear of excessive expenditure, and the desire to curb the old aristocracy whose dress had distinguished them from citizens of lesser birth. All of these motives had a place in the communal milieu in which republican values were all the more loudly proclaimed as republican institutions crumbled. Social distinction in dress, which was admitted in the lifetimes of Bernardino and Antonino, gave way later to conspicuous display of wealth as a denotation of status.[87]

Historiography often has contained acknowledgements that the men who passed sumptuary laws also violated them. Sometimes the blame for this contradiction has been laid at the feet of women.[88] In fact, the real problem lay with the Italian sense of social status which was shared by both sexes. Women were aware of this problem. Nicholosa Sanuti said as much in protest of the sumptuary laws imposed on Bologna by Cardinal Bessarion, arguing that ornament and apparel were women's "insignia of worth"; other women were quick to claim dispensation given by Church or state exempting them from obedience to sumptuary laws.[89] Men may have been less willing to admit this openly and cloaked their motives with the rhetoric of religion and statecraft. Nonetheless, they made sure that their weddings were celebrated with sufficient pomp, with trousseaus conveyed through the streets in painted *cassoni* and brides receiving gifts of gowns and jewels in addition to the key ceremony of the groom's placing a ring on the bride's finger.[90] The wife was expected to dress down to her husband's status if her father were of higher rank. Thus she would maintain her husband's status instead of outshining him.[91] Custom and sumptuary law allowed a nubile daughter more leeway in dress than a matron, perhaps to attract a suitor.[92] This was the reasoning that Bernardino denounced but which Antonino acknowledged as valid.

A husband would expect to receive use of the dowry which came with his bride; otherwise, he might postpone marriage. He, in turn, was expected to buy his wife rich presents of garments and ornaments. These would be used only in the few years between marriage and her adoption of the matron's black dress, but the immediate cash outlay could be substantial. It was this type of expenditure which Bernardino and Giacomo della Marca denounced as an incentive for men to fall into the vice of sodomy.[93] The lawyers, at least, acknowledged the real reason for these expenditures, which was not to please the bride but rather to advertise the social status of the groom. These "vanities" never really belonged to the wife; instead, they were the property of the husband's family. Any widow who tried to keep such goods was soon disabused by law of any illusions that they had been bought for her. As part of the family patrimony, the garments and ornaments passed on to the male heir.[94]

The *Quattrocento* was an age of fragile patrimonies. Many families found themselves unable to keep up proper appearances and spent themselves into the class of the noble poor.[95] Consciousness of status could push a family into a financially risky "sumptuary war" with its rivals.[96] Small wonder sumptuary laws which increasingly concentrated on women's dress and ornament in an attempt to defend patrimony against the risks of the status game were enacted again and again. Needless to say, these attempted safeguards failed. The narrowing circle of the ruling class supported the burdens of status, and status helped to feed the luxury industries of the day.[97]

The same men who bought bridal gifts worried about the costs of these tokens of status. This anxiety, if anything, explains the willingness of men of the cities to hear the preaching of Bernardino of Siena against the vanity of women. These same men later would buy gowns and ornaments for their wives and daughters and would even buy the much denounced cosmetics and false tresses. For a time, the sermons could make them feel virtuous and help them despise the vanities they burned or outlawed before they went on to order the manufacture of still more vanities to uphold the dignity and status of their families.

Notes

This article incorporates the author's paper, "Dress and Social Status According to Antoninus of Florence," given at a meeting of the American Catholic Historical Association in Los Angeles in December of 1981. Several suggestions of Professor Julius Kirschner, University of Chicago, have been incorporated in the revision.

[1] For an introduction to Bernardino's life and preaching, see I. Origo, *The World of San Bernardino* (New York, 1962).

[2] R. C. Trexler, *Public Life in Renaissance Florence* (New York, 1980), p. 381.

[3] Origo, *San Bernardino*, pp. 150-52 and 233-34; and D. d'Avray, *The Preaching of the Friars: Sermons Diffused from Paris before 1300* (Oxford, 1985), p. 70, n. 3.

[4] d'Avray, pp. 13-28.

[5] d'Avray, pp. 29-43. Occasions of crisis might make the audience's attitude volatile, even allowing for the usual mixture of skeptics and believers, whether learned or unlearned; see Trexler, *Public Life*, pp. 353-54.

[6] Origo, *San Bernardino*, pp. 117-29, recounting charges that Bernardino's use of this symbol was heretical, which were lodged with Martin V, Eugenius IV, and the Council of Basel.

[7] J. Moorman, *A History of the Franciscan Order from Its Origins to the Year 1527* (Oxford, 1968), pp. 272-77. The Dominican tradition had a greater emphasis on doctrine as a means of recalling the erring to the true faith; see H. Caplan, *Of Eloquence: Studies in Ancient and Medieval Rhetoric*, ed. A. King and H. North (Ithaca, NY, 1970), p. 53.

[8]A. Bernstein, "Esoteric Theology: William of Auvergne on the Fires of Hell and Purgatory," *Speculum*, 57 (1982):509-31.

[9]J. Le Goff, *The Birth of Purgatory*, trans. A. Goldhammer (Chicago, 1981), pp. 330-33.

[10]*The Birth of Purgatory*, pp. 316-18.

[11]*The Renaissance*, ed. E. Cochrane and J. Kirschner, trans. L. Cochrane (Chicago, 1986), pp. 119-20.

[12]*The Renaissance*, pp. 120-22.

[13]*The Renaissance*, pp. 122-23.

[14]*The Renaissance*, pp. 123-24.

[15]*The Renaissance*, pp. 124-25.

[16]*The Renaissance*, p. 125.

[17]*The Renaissance*, pp. 125-27.

[18]*The Renaissance*, p. 127.

[19]*The Renaissance*, p. 128; and D. Herlihy, "Santa Caterina and San Bernardino: Their Teachings on the Family," in *Atti del simposio internazionale Cateriniano-Bernardiniano, Siena, 17-20 aprile 1980*, ed. D. Maffei and P. Nardi (Siena, 1982), p. 931.

[20]M. Bretagna, "Gli aspetti sacri di Siena nelle 'Preche Volgari' di San Bernardino," in *Atti del simposio internazionale*, pp. 360 and 367-69.

[21]This text is printed in I. Magli, *Gli uomini della penitenza* (Milan, 1977), pp. 147-52; see especially pp. 147-48.

[22]*Gli uomini della penitenza*, pp. 148-49.

[23]*Gli uomini della penitenza*, p. 149.

[24]*Gli uomini della penitenza*, pp. 149-52.

[25] S. *Bernardini Senensis ordinis fratrum minorum opera omnia* . . . , ed. Collegium S. Bonaventurae, vol. 2, *Quadragesimale de christiana religione, Sermones XLI-LXVI* (Quaracchi, 1950), p. 45.

[26] S. *Bernardini*, 2:47.

[27] S. *Bernardini*, 2:74-75.

[28] S. *Bernardini*, 2:75-76.

[29] S. *Bernardini*, 2:81.

[30] S. *Bernardini*, 2:73 and 86.

[31] S. *Bernardini*, 2:87-88.

[32] S. *Bernardini*, 2:90.

[33] S. *Bernardini*, 2:91.

[34] S. *Bernardini*, 2:93.

[35] S. *Bernardini*, 2:99.

[36] L. Delcorno, "L'ars praedicandi di Bernardino da Siena," in *Atti del simposio internazionale*, pp. 444-45.

[37] S. *Bernardini Senensis ordinis fratrum minorum opera omnia* . . . , vol. 4, *Quadragesimale de evangelio aeterno, Sermones XXVII-LIII* (Quaracchi, 1956), pp. 425-26.

[38] S. *Bernardini Senensis ordinis fratrum minorum opera omnia* . . . , vol. 6, *Tractatus "De vita Christiana"--"De b. virgine"--"De Spiritu sancto" et "De inspirationibus"--"De beatitudinis evangelicis"* (Quaracchi, 1959), pp. 6-7.

[39] D. Bornstein, *The Lady in the Tower: Medieval Courtesy Literature for Women* (Hamden, CT, 1983), pp. 15-16 and 19.

[40] M. L. Bloomfield, *The Seven Deadly Sins* (East Lansing, MI, 1952), pp. 92 and 104.

[41] A. L. Gabriel, *The Education Ideas of Vincent of Beauvais* (Notre Dame, IN, 1962), p. 41.

[42] D. d'Avray and M. Tausche, "Marriage Sermons in the *ad status* Collections of the Central Middle Ages," *Archives d'Histoire Doctrinale et Littéraire du Moyen Age,* 47 (1980):86 and 102-03.

[43] Trexler, *Public Life,* pp. 475 and 477.

[44] Girolamo Savonarola, *Prediche . . . sopra aliquanti salmi e sopra Aggeo profeta . . .* (n.p., 1544), fol. 22[r].

[45] Savonarola, fol. 26[r].

[46] Savonarola, fol. 52[r-v].

[47] Savonarola, fol. 96[v]. See also R. M. Steinberg, *Fra Girolamo Savonarola, Florentine Art, and Renaissance Historiography* (Athens, OH, 1977), p. 33.

[48] Trexler, *Public Life,* pp. 475-78; and E. Garin, *Portraits from the Renaissance,* trans. V. A. and E. Velen (New York, 1972), pp. 229-30.

[49] Steinberg, *Fra Girolamo Savonarola,* pp. 6-7. Because Pope Alexander VI had silenced Savonarola, sermons on these occasions were preached by his disciples; see P. van Paasen, *A Crown of Fire: The Life and Times of Girolamo Savonarola* (New York, 1960), pp. 229 and 231-32.

[50] A. De Roover, *San Bernardino of Siena and Sant'Antonio of Florence: The Two Great Economic Thinkers of the Middle Ages* (Boston, 1967), pp. 9-16.

[51] For copies of this text, see Vatican City, Biblioteca Apostolica, MS Vat. lat. 9399, fol. 2[v]; and Pavia, Biblioteca Aldini, MS 139, fol. 198[rb-va]. The Aldini copy is followed, at fol. 198[va], by another text on the same subject, entitled *Quod aut huiusmodi*. Dr. Jacqueline Tarrant has suggested that this may be a decretal of John XXIII, not of John XXII, but it is more likely to be a forgery.

[52] Vat. lat. 9399, fols. 2[v]-3[r]. For a legal note on *uiue uocis oracula,* see Milan, Biblioteca Ambrosiana, MS D 10 sup. fol. 84[rb]; and Aldini MS 139, fol. 274[va-b].

[53] A full record of this mission, written by Franciscus de Platea, appears in University of Chicago MS 689, fols. 38^r-39^v. A condensed version appears in Vat. Patetta MS 69, fols. 55^r-56^r.

[54] Vat. lat. 9399, fol. 1^r.

[55] L. Pesce, *Ludovico Barbo, vescovo di Treviso (1437-1443)*, vol. 2 (Padua, 1969), p. 7.

[56] R. Creytens, "Le cas de conscience soumis à S. Antonin de Florence par Dominique de Catalogne," *Archivum Fratrum Praedicatorum*, 28 (1958):166 and n. 63. The mendicants had the practice of consulting eminent confreres to obtain guidance in doubtful matters; see Creytens, "Les *consilia* de S. Antonin de Florence O.P.," *Archivum Fratrum Praedicatorum*, 37 (1967):263-342; and J. Kirschner, "An Opinion of Raphael de Pornaixo O.P. on the Market in Genoese *lire de paghe*," in *Xenia Medii Aevi historiam illustrantia oblata Thomae Kaeppeli O.P.*, vol. 3 (Rome, 1978), pp. 507-17.

[57] T. Kaeppeli, *Scriptores Ordinis Praedicatorum Medii Aevi*, vol. 1 (Rome, 1970), no. 249, pp. 87-88 and no. 256B, pp. 92-96; and Antoninus de Florentia, *Summa theologica*, 2 vols. (Verona, 1740; rpt. Graz, 1959), 2: 594-601: in tit. *De inanigloria*.

[58] R. Morçay, *Saint Antonin, fondateur du convent de Saint-Marc, archêveque de Florence (1389-1459)* (Tours, 1914), p. 407; and Creytens, "Le cas de conscience," p. 209.

[59] ". . . qui fecerunt infrascripta consilium, qui incipit, 'Quaeritur utrum ornatus mulierum secundum morem patrie etc.'" (University of Chicago MS 689, fol. 38^v). This clause is omitted in the Patetta MS.

[60] All references to the text of *De ornatu mulierum* will be taken from the University of Chicago MS 689, fols. 32^v-38^v; see fols. 32^v-33^v for this argument.

[61] University of Chicago MS 689, fol. 33^r. An extensive exposition of Isaiah 3:16-26 follows the *De ornatu* in Vat. Ottobon lat. 715, fols. 118^v-120^v. This conclusion to a *Summa de confessione*, which incorporates several intact works of Antonino, is based on Thomas Aquinas, *Expositio super Isaiam, Opera omnia*, vol. 28 (Rome, 1974), pp. 29-34.

[62] University of Chicago MS 689, fols. 33^v-34^v.

[63]University of Chicago MS 689, fol. 34^r; and see fol. 34^v for the example of Judith.

[64]University of Chicago MS 689, fols. 33^v-34^r. Cf. Thomas Aquinas, *Summa theologiae, Opera omnia,* vol. 6 (Rome, 1899), pp. 329-30: IIa IIae q. 163 ar. 2.

[65]"Et si dicatur quod in antiqua compillatione decretalium prohibetur indistincte portare uestium incisarum uel simpatarum, satis est quod in nova compillatione non habetur; ne membranas occupet frustras. Non autem antiqua sed noua compillatio in usu habetur et ligat; ergo [non est peccatum mortale huius ornatus mulierum]" (University of Chicago MS 689, fol. 33^v). University of Chicago MS 689, fol. 33^v reads "ergo etc."; the final passage has been restored from Cornell University MS BX B52, fol. 79ra.

[66]"Nam si mulier se ornat in hac intentione, ut trahat homines ad sue concupiscentiam, certum est ibi peccatum mortale esse, quia agitur contra caritatem [proximi, intendens mortem anime eius, etiam si non sequitur ruina alicuius per concupiscentiam . . .]" (University of Chicago MS 689, fol. 34^v). University of Chicago MS 689, fol. 34^v reads "caritatem Christi"; the passage has been emended from Cornell University MS BX B52, fol. 79va.

[67]University of Chicago MS 689, fols. 34^v-35^r.

[68]"Si mulier sic intenderet ex hoc uitare oprobrium hominum, ne scilicet ommisso ornamento secundum morem patrie despitiatur a ceteris aut ut coniugo tradetur, nullum uidetur aut lege peccatum" (University of Chicago MS 689, fol. 35^r). "Demum intendit precise placere uiro suo, ne huiusmodi obmittendo, ei reddatur ei odiosa, et sic inclinetur ad aliam concupiscendum, uel quia imperatur hoc sibi a uiro, peccatum siquidem nullus erit; quia ymo meritum, si sit in statu merendi, quia actus uirtutis modestie est, nisi excessum faciat in ipsa quantitate uel qualitate ornatus . . ." (University of Chicago MS 689, fol. 35^r).

[69]W. T. Gaughan, *Social Theories of Saint Antoninus from his Summa theologica* (Washington, D.C., 1950), p. 50.

[70]University of Chicago MS 689, fol. 35^{r-v}.

[71]University of Chicago MS 689, fol. 35^v. Antonino advised confessors to seek the advice of *boni uiri* when deciding the limits set by custom on dress.

[72]University of Chicago MS 689, fol. 36[r].

[73]"Fateor tamen apud praedicatores in praedicationibus et confessores in confessionibus audiendis debent talia detestari et reprehendere et persuadere ad dimittendum cum fuit nimia excessiua, ut communiter accidit; non tamen ita indistincte asserat esse mortalis . . ." (University of Chicago MS 689, fol. 36[r]).

[74]University of Chicago MS 689, fols. 37[v]-38[r].

[75]N. Denholm-Young and H. Kantorowicz, "*De ornatu mulierum:* A *Consilium* of Antonius de Rosselis With an Introduction on Fifteenth-century Sumptuary Legislation," *La Bibliofilia,* 35 (1933):328.

[76]Bartolomaeus de Chaimis, *Confessionale,* Holy Name College MS 26, Franciscan Institute, Saint Bonaventure University, fol. 84[v].

[77]Denholm-Young and Kantorowicz, "*De ornatu mulierum,*" pp. 327-28.

[78]"Tunc argui quod consuetudo roboratur spatio 40 annorum, sed iste uanitatates quotidie uariunt; ergo potius debent dici abusiones. Et ibi responderent quod Thomas et Alexander de Ales non intelligunt de consuetudine proprie dicta sed pro modo uiuendi in civitate" (University of Chicago MS 689, fol. 39[v]).

[79]University of Chicago MS 689, fol. 39[v].

[80]Denholm-Young and Kantorowicz, "*De ornatu mulierum,*" pp. 328-29.

[81]D. O. Hughes, "Distinguishing Signs: Ear-rings, Jews and Franciscan Rhetoric in the Italian Renaissance City," *Past and Present,* no. 112 (1986): 25-26 and 58.

[82]Hughes, pp. 24-25 and 28.

[83]Hughes, p. 37.

[84]Hughes, pp. 32 and 54.

[85]J. Kirschner, "Reading Bernardino's Sermon on the Public Debt," *Atti del simposio internazionale,* p. 591.

[86] Hughes, "Distinguishing Signs," pp. 27-28. These renewed sumptuary laws were often accompanied by others restricting money-lending by Jews; see Hughes, p. 38.

[87] Hughes, "Distinguishing Signs," pp. 11, 44-46 and 50-51; E. Brucker, *The Society of Renaissance Florence* (New York, 1971), pp. 179-81; W. B. Scaiffe, *Florentine Life during the Renaissance* (Baltimore, 1893), pp. 80-82; E. Polidori Calamandrei, *Le veste delle donne fiorentine nel Quattrocento* (Florence, 1924), pp. 515-32; and L. Martines, *The Social World of the Florentine Humanists 1390-1460* (Princeton, 1963), pp. 23, 36, 228 and 290.

[88] E.g., Polidori Calamandrei, *Le veste delle donne,* p. 28.

[89] D. O. Hughes, "Sumptuary Laws and Social Relations in Renaissance Italy," in *Disputes and Settlements: Law and Human Relations in the West,* ed. J. Bossy (Cambridge, 1983), pp. 81 and 86-87.

[90] D. O. Hughes, "Representing the Family: Portraits and Purposes in Early Modern Italy," *Journal of Interdisciplinary History,* 17 (1986):11; and B. Witthoft, "Marriage Rituals and Marriage Chests in Quattrocento Florence," *Artibus et Historia,* 5 (1982):47. The worth of the trousseau was evaluated by a professional estimator; see "Marriage Rituals and Marriage Chests," p. 52.

[91] Hughes, "Representing the Family," p. 30.

[92] Hughes, "Representing the Family," pp. 30-31.

[93] C. Klapisch-Zuber, "The Griselda Complex: Dowry and Marriage Gifts in the Quattrocento," in *Women, Family and Ritual in Renaissance Italy,* trans. L. Cochrane (Chicago, 1985), pp. 218-24. For Lucca Landucci's list of the bride goods he bought in 1466, see *The Renaissance,* ed. Cochrane and Kirschner, pp. 147-49.

[94] M. Bellomo, *Ricerche sui patrimoniali tra coniugi* (Milan, 1961), pp. 208-22; T. M. Izbicki, "'*Ista quaestio est antiqua:*' Two *consilia* on Widows' Rights," *Bulletin of Medieval Canon Law,* 8 (1979):47-50; and J. Kirschner and J. Pluss, "Two Fourteenth-Century Opinions on Dowries, Paraphenalia and Non-dotal goods," *Bulletin of Medieval Canon Law,* 9 (1979):65-77.

[95] R. Trexler, "Charity and the Defense of Urban Elites in the Italian Communes," in *The Rich, the Well Born and the Powerful: Elites and Upper Classes in History,* ed. F. C. Jaher (Urbana, IL, 1973), pp. 64-109.

[96]Hughes, "Representing the Family," p. 29.

[97]R. Goldthwaite, *The Building of Renaissance Florence* (Baltimore, 1980), pp. 42-43, 53-54 and 59-66.

Egidio da Viterbo's Defense of Pope Julius II, 1509 and 1511

Ingrid D. Rowland

> *Egidio Antonini of Viterbo (Giles of Viterbo, 1469-1532), Prior General of the Augustinian Mendicants from 1507, was perhaps the most influential public preacher of his day, though few of his orations were ever published. Individual discourses have been edited in recent years, but no substantial publication of his sermons or larger manuscript works yet exists. The existence of multiple copies of these latter writings demonstrates their influence in Egidio's own time. An ardent proponent of church reform, Egidio was also passionately interested in neoplatonism and Cabala. His style reflects both his theological austerity and his preoccupation with the most elaborately convoluted classical rhetoric. The result, in the hands of a man whose administrative skills were sought as frequently as his eloquence, was, in his own word, "tumultuous." But Egidio's years of preaching to the townspeople of central Italy also seem to indicate an ability to speak effectively in a practical vein. Though in many respects their oratory differs radically, Bernardino of Siena and Egidio Antonini come from the same world and address its merchants, city-states, and clerics from a similar standpoint.*
>
> *The sermons delivered by Egidio Antonini and reworked for publication are transformed into elaborate discourses, addressed to kings, emperors, and popes; their rhetoric rises to these lofty and learned occasions. Egidio's words to an entirely different audience, the merchant community of Siena, have been recorded by an eyewitness, the parish priest Sigismondo Tizio. In the city of Bernardino and within memory of Savonarola, Egidio speaks to inspire political action. The sophistication with which he undertakes his task is as remarkable as his appreciative audience of Christians and Jews.*

In 1528, the Italian city of Siena lost one of its most interesting residents, a priest from the hinterlands of Arezzo named Sigismondo Tizio. He left behind a six-volume manuscript entitled *Historia Senensium*, a project apparently begun some ten to fifteen years earlier, which traced the story of Siena from its foundation by the Etruscans up to the year of its author's death. Preserved in the Vatican Library, Tizio's *Historia* remains unpublished, as it departs radically from the classically-inspired canons of Renaissance historiography, the work of Guicciardini or Machiavelli.[1] To these deservedly famous Florentines, proper history treated statesmen, while Tizio saw it as something much more encyclopedic: in this city of bankers, he came to see the extent to which his world was governed by the intrigues of the merchant class and wrote as if these men of secondary social rank held popes and politicians in their thrall.

Like the *Annals* of Tacitus, Tizio's history also relates portentous occurrences: the parrot who pecked the host at an outdoor Mass in 1511, and monstrous births, like the famous omen found in Bologna in that same year.[2] When a meteorite fell on Ensisheim, Alsace in 1492, Tizio obtained a full report of the phenomenon, complete with watercolor illustrations and a descriptive poem in Latin by Sebastian Brant, author of *The Ship of Fools*.[3] Through the pages of his chronicle, we see the small-town amusements by which he and his friends honed their wits: dancing bears, visiting cardinals, itinerant preachers, swordplay, vendetta, poetry, Hanno the elephant (sent from King Manuel of Portugal to Pope Leo X in 1514), and, not least among Tizio's limitless concerns, classical antiquity--preservation of a series of genuine Etruscan inscriptions, copied faithfully enough to be intelligible today.[4] The compendious chronicle is equally filled with political matters: tales of Moroccan conquests, crusades, and the machinations of kings. If such events are faithfully seen from the vantage of Siena, nonetheless his microcosm allows Sigismondo Tizio, like Miss Marple, to observe the world outside with universal insight.

Siena in the early sixteenth century operated primarily within the orbit of papal Rome, a response to inveterate Sienese hatred of nearby Florence, which since the fourteenth century had overtaken Siena as chief city in Tuscany.[5] Sienese bankers formed one of the most powerful blocs in Vatican finance, and many of these merchant families also sent sons to the Apostolic Court to train as lawyers or humanists.[6] It is not surprising that Tizio reports frequently and accurately on doings in Rome; events there had direct bearing on the financial soundness of the Sienese republic as a whole.[7]

Papal politics, perhaps by definition, also involved theology. For this reason, preachers and sermons are one of Tizio's most indicative sources for news about Rome's intentions in early sixteenth-century Italy's treacherous political terrain. Of these preachers, the most significant to Tizio, and with good reason, was Egidio Antonini da Viterbo (Giles of Viterbo), who in 1507 became Prior General of the Augustinian Mendicants, the largest religious order of the day.[8] Before his elevation to that post, Egidio traveled extensively throughout Italy, making a reputation for himself as a popular preacher and an outspoken champion of church reform.[9] Siena, given its position on the important Via Francigena and its proximity to the Augustinian hermitage of Lecceto, remained a frequent stop in Egidio's wanderings.[10] Tizio appears to have attended Egidio's public sermons faithfully, usually reporting that they were "brilliant" (*luculentem*), though on one occasion at least the good scribe confirms the Augustinian preacher's notorious long-windedness.[11] Through Tizio's notes on these sermons, we can reconstruct both their contents and context, which add significantly to our understanding of Egidio da Viterbo's immense political influence.

Through recent publication of his un-edited works, Egidio da Viterbo has been shown to be a seminal figure for the sixteenth-century papacy, above all for the reigns of Popes Julius II and Leo X.[12] Though Egidio himself appears to have believed that Leo would usher in the Christian Golden Age, his own real ascendancy was due instead to the dynamic Julius, whose pugnacious defense of the papacy inspired Egidio to compose his masterwork, the *Sententiae ad Mentem Platonis*, a neoplatonic reworking of Peter Lombard's standard theological text.[13] But Egidio's inspiration also took a more actively political turn. From the Augustinian's own correspondence, it is clear that he consulted with Julius in the latter's aggressive plans to liberate Italy from foreign invaders.[14] Egidio's theological rhetoric gave eloquent voice to Julius's dogged pursuit of this objective. More than this, Julius's plans seem to have been formulated under inspiration by Egidio's distinctive vision: the Pope, too impatient to be a great lover of sermons, listened to the Augustinian's two-hour discourses with rare attention.[15]

On Pentecost of 1509, Sigismondo Tizio reports that:

> On the twenty-seventh of May . . . in the papal chapel Julius II announced that now that Venice was subdued [by the League of Cambrai] an expedition would be mounted against the Turks, those enemies of the faith . . . and furthermore on the next day . . . a procession traversed all Rome. Then, indeed, Egidio da Viterbo, a churchman and a renowned orator, gave a brilliant sermon about how this expedition, which he called a crusade, must be victorious.[16]

"And," Tizio continues with the characteristic phrase by which he introduces choice gossip, "there were those who said that Julius had made this move deliberately at this particular time in order to divert Emperor Maximilian and King Louis of France . . . away from the rest of Italy and from himself."[17]

The Pope's real concern, as Tizio knew, was the threat of foreign invasion. France had been making incursions into Italian territory since 1494 and had obtained control of Milan in 1499. Shortly before the two Roman sermons of May 1509, Louis XII of France had joined with the Hapsburg emperor Maximilian to form the League of Cambrai, which now applied pressure on Venice in hope of further weakening Italy.[18] This military menace served Julius's purpose by breaking Venetian domination of the Adriatic. It also presented the Pope with an equally vexing problem: the vulnerability of Venice increased the vulnerability of the papal state.[19] As Tizio correctly perceived, the pentecostal talk of crusade was a smoke-screen from Rome: pope and preacher were suggesting allusively that the papacy was prepared to join battle, if necessary, to defend its local turf.

As the year 1509 progressed, Julius made it increasingly clear that his real intent was to drive the French from Italian soil.[20] To this end, he mounted a two-pronged military attack on two states which had become increasingly susceptible to French influence: his native Genoa to the west and, to the east, the papacy's nominal vassal state of Ferrara.[21] The decision to attack Ferrara was determined in part by its geography, for it neighbored both Milan and Venice, and also by its relative smallness. Julius's will to proceed was sharpened by the advice of two influential acquaintances, one of them Egidio da Viterbo. In July of 1510, a letter from Egidio shows that pope and prelate had discussed the theological justifications for heading Ferrara back into the papacy's political fold. Egidio pointed out that the temporal power of the church sustained Christ's vicarage on earth.[22] This was a sentiment to which the pope shared a visceral attachment, as his reconquest of a similarly recalcitrant Bologna in 1506 had already shown.[23]

Egidio's letter of July 1510, written from his beloved hermitage above Soriano in Cimino, also laments that continued political consultations might soon put an end to his sylvan retreat: "What pains me now," he writes on 29 July, "is that I expect to be called back to Rome at any moment, commanded to undertake a journey and a task full of danger."[24] If the letter reflects a somewhat melodramatic self-consciousness, characteristic of the private correspondence of this highly public personage, Julius's summons, when it finally came, was no less theatrical:

> The eighth day of August. A messenger who had left Rome with incredible speed approaches Egidio and hands over a letter from the Pope which ordered him to come immediately to Rome, that same day, changing horses along the way. He obeys. The Pope reveals that the Genoese enterprise has not succeeded, but that nonetheless he hopes that something may yet turn out; in any case, though he is an old man and it is the middle of the August heat, he is setting out on the Via Flaminia to lay siege to Ferrara. In the meantime a Spanish victory is announced in Africa, with the capture of the city of Tripolitania by Pedro Navarro. The Pope orders Egidio to preach the next day at San Lorenzo in Damaso. . . .
>
> The eighteenth day of August 1510 after [Egidio] had preached before the people for a long time, and then went on to discuss for five or six hours, he fell into an extremely dangerous fever. . . .[25]

When Egidio fell ill in Soriano after the turmoil of the previous few weeks, his last overexertion almost certainly reached an audience composed of more than humble townspeople of a summer resort. The mountains of Cimino hosted some of Rome's most influential figures during the months when the city itself became dangerously malarial, including, of course, Egidio himself but also such cardinals as Raffaele Rairio, Julius's powerful cousin and head of the Apostolic Chamber, and Alessandro Farnese, eventually a pope himself. Moreover, toward the end of that particular summer, another visitor had made a leisurely stop in the environs of Soriano in Cimino: the man sometimes given credit for originally inspiring Julius's Ferrara campaign.[26]

Julius's other important confidante before the Ferrara campaign had accompanied the pope when he attacked Bologna in 1506, even apparently attending the pontifical sickbed.[27] Agostino Chigi had reportedly used these private audiences to good advantage, as Tizio reported at the time; in any case, Chigi was known for his enterprising--some said opportunistic--ways. By 1510, this Sienese merchant-banker could claim to be the richest man in Italy, quite possibly in all Europe.[28] Before Julius II became pope, Agostino Chigi had made his fortune in Rome by exploiting various leases managed by the Apostolic Chamber.[29] To this shrewd and ruthless capitalist, Ferrara presented an economic threat, for Ferrarese salt undersold the salt produced by the papal state. Though in 1510 Chigi did not himself hold the papal salt lease, his understanding of Vatican finances was unsurpassed, the result of his own variety of genius combined with close friendship with the pontiff. Significantly, Chigi spent the winter of 1510-11 with the papal entourage in Bologna, observing the fate of the Ferrara campaign at first hand.[30]

The superficial differences between Egidio da Viterbo and Agostino Chigi belie one crucial similarity: they both presided over institutions which were themselves the size of small city-states. The Austin Hermits numbered some fifteen thousand in the early sixteenth century, Christianity's largest religious order, while Agostino Chigi once estimated the number of his employees as twenty thousand.[31] Furthermore, their circles of acquaintance overlapped to a considerable extent, including merchants, humanists, ecclesiastics, and statesmen. When Pope Julius received their counsel in preparing his Ferrara campaign, he was thus advised by two of the most gifted administrators of his time.

From Tizio we learn that in Autumn of 1510, Siena's *Balia*, or city council, had named a committee of nine to accept monetary pledges for a campaign to "keep alive [Pope] Julius's rage at Ferrara."[32] In this record of an early political lobby, Tizio acknowledged the role of the merchant class in determining the actions of statesmen. Sixteenth-century Europe, of course, was knit together by the trade networks of her merchants, whose successful financial practices sustained Renaissance culture and paid the price of Renaissance extravagance. Accordingly, the merchants were first to have any news of crops, ships, or statesmen and used their monetary clout to influence the news in order to improve their profits. Siena's close connection with Vatican finance only increased with Agostino Chigi's pivotal position in the Julian papacy, and it was further strengthened by Chigi's movements and actions in succeeding months.

The papal troops set out for Ferrara in the autumn of 1510 with Pope Julius at their head. From a headquarters in Bologna, he supervised the military campaign in person. Foul weather, disease, and Ferrarese gunpowder took their toll. In the winter of 1510-11, racked with gout and, allegedly, syphilis, and barely recovered from a fever which had almost cost him his life, Julius supervised the successful siege of Mirandola. With his strapping physique, an enormous fur hat, and the indomitable temper which had driven him from his sickbed and into the fray, the old man still cut a fearsome figure. Yet for all its dramatics, the capture of one frigid citadel only provided a distraction from the pope's failure to obtain his critical objective.

In the next months, Julius's situation changed from bad to nearly desperate. In an attempt to attack Ferrara from another side, on 11 February 1511, Julius had sidled into Ravenna, where in a show of wilfulness he named eight new cardinals.[33] This action, like so many others taken by this *papa terrible*, served a multiple purpose. It thanked his allies for further infusions of money and replaced a group of renegade cardinals who, with French support, had defied the orders of the irascible pope ever since he had first announced his march on Ferrara. Finally, fearful of falling prisoner to the French, Julius realized that he needed to return to the safety of Rome. Leaving Bologna to face the French, he withdrew toward Rimini on 15 May. On the following day, the rebellious cardinals proclaimed an ecumenical council to be held in Pisa on September 1, where they promised to depose Pope Julius and replace him, presumably with one of their own number.[34]

Siena, in the meantime, through her *Signore* Pandolfo Petrucci, had poured even more money into the papal coffers: some eleven thousand ducats, according to Tizio.[35] Thus, Pandolfo's son Alfonso, a spoiled adolescent obsessed with hunting dogs, had received a cardinal's hat in Ravenna at the age of twenty-two, an event for which Tizio reviles father, son, and supreme pontiff alike.[36] While Julius marched toward Rome, the Sienese watched in apprehension as Bologna fell to the French-backed troops of her former rulers, the Bentivogli, deposed by Julius in 1506 and itching for a comeback.[37] Now only Florence stood between Siena and the foreigner. Furthermore, Pisa, the proposed site of the pro-French schismatic council, was so near that some of the renegade cardinals made their homes in Siena until the conclave actually began. Besides, Siena's violently opposed civic factions furnished a haven for every political persuasion.[38] The Florentines, for their part, began seeking ways to appease France, sending Machiavelli as envoy to Louis XII and taking advantage of Sienese trepidation to push for territorial concessions from their wary southern neighbor.[39] Pandolfo Petrucci, though courageous, was even more wily and prepared for the moment to accede to the Florentine demands.

Pandolfo may simply have been buying time. Though Pope Julius had left the north of Italy in the spring of 1511, Agostino Chigi, who always acted as a Sienese agent, had proceeded on to Venice. There, from February to August of 1511, he undertook an intricate negotiation with the Venetian government to obtain its support for the papacy in return for extensive business concessions.[40] Chigi's presence in the north carried with it some explicit if unknown Sienese orders, for he was eventually paid a small stipend for his efforts by the commune of Siena.[41] He also extracted a Venetian promise of alliance with the papal state to resist the League of Cambrai. When he sailed for Rome in August 1511, Agostino Chigi carried a tangible guarantee of Venetian fealty: thirty thousand ducats in jewels from the state treasury.[42]

How much Pandolfo Petrucci knew of Chigi's machinations is difficult to judge, though Tizio's chronicle indicates that by August news had spread quickly of the Sienese banker's coup.[43] Immediately, Siena reversed her attitude to Florence and resumed her customary defiance. While Chigi labored in Venice, Pope Julius sought other remedies for his dangerous isolation. Successfully, if reluctantly, he appealed for help to Ferdinand of Spain, excommunicated and deposed the schismatic cardinals, and at the same time called his own ecumenical council for the spring of 1512.[44] Felled again by a relapse of his illness, the dauntless old man recovered in September 1511 and in early October proclaimed a Holy League consisting of the papal state, Spain, England, and Venice, against Louis XII and Maximilian. Appropriately enough, one of the signatories to the League's declaration was Agostino Chigi.[45] The Julian papacy had weathered its worst crisis.

As Julius now set his will to regaining his Italian flock, he turned once again to Egidio da Viterbo. On Wednesday and Thursday, 10 and 11 November 1511, Sigismondo Tizio reports that:

> Pope Julius, perhaps hearing of Pandolfo's hesitation and of the Florentine's obstinacy, sent Egidio da Viterbo, a distinguished Augustinian preacher . . . to Siena so that he might sustain [the Sienese] lest they waver in their faith and so that he might admonish the Florentines.[46]

The previous week, on 5 November, the schismatic Council of Pisa had finally held its initial meeting. Granted official recognition by the Florentine government, it was poorly attended and resoundingly unpopular with the citizens themselves.[47] The pope chose Egidio's moment, and his target, with inspired acuity. And, on this occasion at least, Egidio seems to have responded with equal inspiration. In his preaching, Tizio reports, Egidio "imitated Mariano da Genazzano, of the same [Augustinian] order, by his manner of speaking, his beard, and his gestures. He drew both the common people and the civic leaders with his eloquence." Tizio says, "demulcebat aures"--the preacher literally "caressed their ears" with his oratory.[48]

Tizio is an excellent critic. While his usual adjective for Egidio's sermons is *luculentem*, (brilliant), he also recognizes the drawbacks of the Augustinian's preaching style. A discourse of 1503, which Tizio's chronicle records as similarly *luculentem* but also *etsi longum* (a little long), warranted the more accurate marginal comment: "actually, it was so long that it affected the entire audience with boredom and annoyance from such rusty repetition of one of the psalms; while he spoke it seemed that a month went by."[49] On the present occasion, however, the margin reads "a delicious sermon by Egidio," and the discourse of 12 November is recorded in remarkable detail.[50]

The first of these hortatory sermons was delivered in the church of S. Agostino on 10 November 1511. The huge crowd was drawn both by Egidio's reputation and by the practical purpose of his pastoral visit, namely, to justify Julius's unsatisfactory return on the Sienese merchants' substantial contribution to the papacy one year before. How did Egidio approach his delicate and daunting task? Tizio tells us that:

> having proposed some terms of arithmetic, he then [postulated] a circular line, which he referred to God; he moved along through a brief sermon, genuinely enticing the people, promising them that on the next day he would announce some matters more specifically pertinent to the Sienese.[51]

The dazzling abstraction of Tizio's account--a community pressed by an apparently unsuccessful war, the targeted audience a cadre of hardheaded businessmen directed to bear the poor dividend on a cash investment by contemplating a circular God!--is clarified by Egidio's treatment of the same notion in his *Sententiae ad mentem Platonis*, a work composed, moreover, during this same period and in response to the same events.[52] From the *Sententiae* it is clear that Egidio's oration must have adapted a passage of Plato's *Seventh Letter*, a text whose succinct account of divine inspiration was a favorite of Renaissance humanists. In this period of Egidio's intense political involvement, Plato's juxtaposition in the *Letter* of worldly intrigue and philosophical absolutes must have had even more relevance. For both men, political action had been the natural consequence of their having come to apprehend the nature of the world order; absolute reality, however incompletely perceived by the frail human senses, demanded active human response. Plato outlines one of the ways in which human senses may apprehend reality:

> Each thing which exists has three qualities by which it is necessary that knowledge come about. . . . First there is the name of the thing, secondly its definition, third its image, fourth the knowledge of it. Now in order to understand what has been said so far, take one example, and reason in the same way for every other instance. There is something called a circle, for which this ["circle"] which we have just pronounced, is the name. Its definition is comprised of nouns and verbs, for "that which is everywhere equidistant from its margin to its center" would be a definition of that thing for which "roundel" and "ring" are names--and "circle." Thirdly there is the thing which is drawn or forged or turned on the lathe, or even destroyed--but the circle in these things remains unchanged and undergoes no alteration because it is other than all of these. Fourthly there is knowledge, a notion and a true judgment about matters circular; one idea should be adopted, not perceived in terms of words or tangible designs, but a concept held within the soul, and it ought to be clear by now that this circle is different in its nature from the three we have spoken of hitherto . . . fifthly each circle which is drawn or turned on a lathe in actual practice is full of its opposite quality, for it absorbed straightness everywhere, but we say that the circle itself remains the same, and in its own nature it contains no more and no less of its opposite.[53]

Egidio uses this passage early in his *Sententiae* to address the problem of Christianity's trinitarian God: as a good Augustinian, he remained profoundly committed to a subject to which Augustine had dedicated his magisterial attention, and predictably the *De Trinitate* also figures prominently in this section of the *Sententiae*:

> If God is utterly simple and clearly one, how can so many things and such an infinite number of forms and perfections be attributed to him, to whom, as Parmenides affirms, no number can be imputed, and no multitude? Three things must be discussed: first, what the reasoning is [sc. whereby God's multiplicity may be understood]. . . . As for the first matter [of the three things], Plato in his *Seventh Letter* enumerates five stages: name, definition, image, judgment, understanding, and he numbers these stages in an order derived not from investigating for oneself, but as if one had learned it from one's teachers. For first a name is proposed for the thing which is to be put under discussion, as when one says "circle." Then comes its definition, which is nothing but the definition, or explanation, or likeness which the intellect comes to form in response to that particular name, whether it be a definition of the thing or of its name, or the soul's simple conjuring of a circle to mind. Plato applies the word "image" to a circle in gold, or in wood, or created in any other material; knowledge of judgment is what is immediately caused by the image. Understanding, though, is that knowledge which derives no longer from a material image, but from the essence of the thing: the idea, the essence in intangible form reaches the soul. . . .[54]

Later, Egidio evokes the same Platonic passage in a different way, and through the mediation of Plotinus.[55]

Even in the context of purely private musing (which the *Sententiae* were designed to be), Egidio, an experienced public speaker and teacher, has remarked the didactic turn of Plato's account, its clearly numbered stages, and the suggestive example which is to serve as a paradigm for all related contemplations. The whole discourse, as given in the *Seventh Letter* and in the idiosyncratic coded language of Egidio's personal creed, remains strikingly cerebral. The problem is that somehow these abstract considerations were offered up as an explanation to the burghers of Siena for some urgently temporal concerns.

On the day following the sermon on God and the circle, in the words of Tizio, "an immense crowd of people" flocked to S. Agostino's spacious nave for the preacher's second installment.[56] Whatever Egidio said about a circular God, it must have been effective. Exactly how the Christian neoplatonist transformed platonic doctrines can only be hypothesized. Since the basic task of the Christian homily had been to translate an apparently remote scriptural text into prescriptions for action in the here and now, Egidio's audience would have been prepared for exactly such a leap of reasoning from scripture to Plato. The deceptively homely sermons delivered in Siena nearly a century earlier by Bernardino actually show a homiletic technique, and a degree of abstraction, similar to those of Egidio.[57]

The geometric vision of God brought forth in Egidio's sermon of 1511 appealed to the Sienese precisely because their own mental lives were so regulated by mathematics: the arithmetic of monetary exchanges, the geometry of bushels, casks, and quarts. Number and proportion comprised the world of the Sienese businessman, whose task it was to reduce the vagaries of nature and of human society to their effects on the marketplace and to measured and measurable fluctuations in the supply or demand of profitable commodities. His wife applied the same skills to a household which was usually synonymous with the family firm. The difficulty of these arts is demonstrated by the legions of *fallimenti*, bankruptcies which accompany every stage of Italian mercantile history, and by the social toll of broken lives which accompanied these repeated instances of monetary ruin. The *libri di abaco*, by which children were educated in this exacting trade, pose problems of astounding complexity for which correct answers always involve odd but wholly realistic fractions. In a world in which close estimates of impossible amounts were the norm, God's simply circular perfection would indeed have stood out in all its clarity.[58]

Egidio conveyed his ideas stage by stage, frequently resorting to lists or numbers. By this means his hearers could be brought gradually into the genuinely abstruse features of his spiritual world. Again, Bernardino provides a clear precedent with his lists of notions to be committed to memory: three remarkable qualities of the Virgin Mary (one of which is her intelligence!), four gates of Siena, twelve types of prudence: "learn these twelve prudences, and take them four by four. . . ."[59] In remarking that Plato's *Seventh Letter* itself presents the process of learning in a didactic manner, Egidio demonstrates his recognition that learning by lists was already current in the ancient world--one, we name; two, we define; three, we distinguish;

four, we know; five, we understand--in Plato's terms as in those of his Augustinian admirer.[60]

Egidio departs from Bernardino--and typifies his contemporaries (especially those with experience preaching to the Roman Curia)--in his interweaving of classical texts with biblical references.[61] For the Augustinian preacher, this choice is much more than the mere pursuit of Ciceronian eloquence. As his writings convey with vehement insistence, he regarded classical authors as genuinely possessed of divine intuitions which had prepared the world for the perfect revelation of the Messiah.[62] Thus in successive orations he could subject first a platonic text and then a biblical passage to the scrutiny of his Sienese audience in 1511. Nonetheless, for Egidio as for all his Christian contemporaries, scripture remained the most fundamental writing of all; from the preacher's own statement on November 10 that he would relate more momentous matters on the morrow as from Tizio's three-page transcript of Egidio's words on that occasion, it is clear that the weightier discourse was that of Thursday, November 11:

> Before a huge crowd of expectant people [Egidio] posed a question, that is, whether the city of Siena was able to anticipate or to become more certain that she was loved by God, adducing the authority of our father St. Augustine in the middle of his book *On the Trinity*, where he says that the love which I bear my brother is more certain to me than is that very brother whom I love (*De Trinitate* 8.8). And because it is useless to love my brother except through the grace of God, and to that extent I myself am loved, because my love for my neighbor also exists with such certainty, [it is clear] that God's love for me must also exist, without which I could not love my neighbor. Here in fact [Tizio explains] Egidio reverses what is said on Solomon's authority in the ninth chapter of Ecclesiastes, which goes something like this: "The righteous and the wise and their works are in the hand of God: no man knoweth either love or hatred by all that is before them" (Eccl 9:1). In order to reconcile these two authorities Egidio said that Augustine was speaking of habitual love, while Solomon spoke of immediate love; he himself had meant [certainly] of the former and so he should be understood. He concluded that the city of Siena did not have certainty of God's immediate love, and yet he was able to recognize that such certainty was possible through

experience in signs and prodigies or miracles. . . . Then shifting his attention to the more ancient matters which are described in the thirty-second chapter of Genesis, he recounted for us the story of when Jacob wrestled with the angel. . . . For when the angel announced that he would leave Jacob at dawn, that patriarch answered that he would not let the angel go until he received a blessing, and the angel decreed in blessing him that Jacob should now change his name to Israel. Jacob was to be interpreted as a supplanter, a lame man who represented the crippled and hobbling old law, while he interpreted Israel as the new law, which has seen God made man with her own fleshy eyes. And thus when Jacob bore twelve sons, from whom are descended the twelve tribes of Israel, each of these received his own place in the promised land by the decree of Joshua, indeed by Jacob himself on his deathbed, when he called his sons to him in the forty-ninth chapter of Genesis and said: "Gather yourselves together that I may tell you that which shall befall you in the last days. Gather yourselves together and hear, ye sons of Jacob, that is sons of the old lame law. Hearken unto Israel your father and hear the new Law which your God will grant you to see and which shall be accepted in the city of Rome and in Italy her throne, the new promised land which is named in the prophecy of Daniel and which shall be given over to us." Soon his sons had gathered, and Jacob, beginning his blessing, said "Reuben, thou art my first born, my might, and he shall receive the firstfruits, that is blessed Campania, which has received the most plentiful gifts from her neighbor Rome. Simeon and Levi are brethren: instruments of cruelty are in their habitations. For in their anger they slew a man and in their selfwill they digged down a wall. Cursed be their anger, for it was fierce, and their wrath, for it was cruel, because my soul is not revered in their shameless council: these two wretches are Bologna and Ferrara, disobeyers of the Church and of the pontifical will, even rushing the gates of the city with the Bentivogli in order to kill him. They are instruments of cruelty and receptacles of strife against the Roman faith; they digged down a wall, that is, the citadel of Bologna and turned away to the schismatic council of those who joined Ippolito, Cardinal of Ferrara. For the antipopes who have gone into council against Jesus were, so to speak, the tribe of Levi, and for the most part the pharisee cardinals of the tribe of Simeon are from the ranks of the pharisee philosophers from Ferrara and Bologna, which have universities of philosophy. . . ."[63]

Tizio's list continues faithfully through the remaining tribes, of which the last is Benjamin:

> "Benjamin shall ravin as a wolf. In the morning he shall devour the prey and in the evening he shall divide the spoil." This is Siena, whose insignia is a wolf. And Egidio interpreted the words "in the morning he shall devour the prey and in the evening shall divide the spoil" in the following way: because Christ said in the Gospel, "The Kingdom of Heaven already suffers and is ravaged by violent men," following Paul the Apostle [Egidio] accepts these words as meaning that the church, which is of the tribe of Benjamin, snatched many souls from the demons. And in the same way he predicted that the city of Siena would do the same so long as she followed the pope and adored Judah, which is the church, and she would be a wolf in snatching up this Heaven which already suffered and would find salvation in the midst of present troubles. And Benjamin, standing at his father's right hand, should be interpreted as Siena, which stands with her whole territory at the right hand of the city of Rome and of the church. "You Sienese," [Egidio] said, "made to stand at the right hand, persevere at the right hand and preserve yourselves as my own, just as surely as you are here in my presence, and you shall be saved."[64]

"Thus," concludes the astute Tizio,

> it was clear that, along with the Pope who sent him, this preacher distrusted the Sienese. At any rate, his sermon was thought to be well-done, nor did it depart from its sources, for it did not displease some educated Jews who had been standing next to me throughout.[65]

On this occasion, also, then, the preacher had held his canny audience. Siena stayed loyal, a position greatly facilitated by Agostino Chigi's vast fortune and astute use of power, not to mention the inimitable banker's close friendship with the pope.

By 1512, the French were out of Italy, though it is hard to see any rational reason why. Instead, the propulsive force which spurred Julius's domestic crusade must be seen as rhetorical. The pope's campaigns were won, not by the papal *condottieri* who failed to face down the Ferrarese guns, but rather by the verbal arsenal of Egidio, with his crusades, his celestial geometry, and his biblical exegesis. These troops, and their orator, served Julius well. Pope and preacher could hardly have known that, in the pressing political events of 1510-11, another Augustinian would visit Rome and form his own impressions of that bellicose papacy, a preacher no less explosively apt than Egidio himself: the young Martin Luther. In due time, Sigismondo Tizio would record each one of Luther's theses, harbingers of an end to the world created by Egidio's rhetoric, Julius's energy, and Agostino Chigi's wealth.

Notes

[1] There is now an Italian project to publish Tizio's work, in which the present author is also involved. The *Historia* is preserved as Biblioteca Apostolica Vaticana, Codd. Chigi G.1.31-G.2.40. Subsequent references in the present essay refer to Cod. Chigi G.2.37, the volume dealing with the years 1505-15.

[2] Tizio, G.2.37, fols. 138^v and 178^r.

[3] Tizio, G.2.36, fols. 199^r-200^v.

[4] For the Etruscan inscriptions, see O. A. Danielsson, *Etruskische Inschriften aus Handschriftlicher Ueberlieferung* (Uppsala, 1928); and I. D. Rowland, "'New' Etruscan Inscriptions from a Sixteenth-Century (A.D.) Manuscript," forthcoming in *Opuscula Romana*.

[5] For the shift in Sienese politics toward alliance with the papacy, see D. Hicks, "The Education of a Prince: Lodovico il Moro and the Rise of Pandolfo Petrucci," *Studies in the Renaissance*, 8 (1968):88-102. For Sienese relations with Florence, see, W. Langton Douglas, *A History of Siena* (London, 1902); Judith Hook, *Siena: A City and its History* (London, 1979); William Bowsky, *A Medieval Italian Commune: Siena Under the Nine, 1287-1355* (Berkeley, 1981); and Lando Bortolotti, *Siena* (Rome and Bari, 1983).

[6] The Sienese consortium at the papal court is discussed by Felix Gilbert, *The Pope, His Banker, and Venice* (Cambridge, MA and London, 1980), pp. 64-77. See also I. D. Rowland, *The Correspondence of Agostino Chigi in Vatican Cod. Chigi R.V.c, fols. 1-122: An Annotated Edition* (Vatican City, in press).

Egidio da Viterbo's Defense of Julius II

[7]The acute awareness of political events necessary for merchant bankers' success is detailed by Iris Origo, *The Merchant of Prato* (New York, 1957); Federigo Melis, *L'economia fiorentina del Rinascimento* (Prato, 1984); and Gino Luzzatto, *Breve storia dell'Italia medioevale* (Turin, 1958).

[8]For Egidio da Viterbo, see Giuseppe Signorelli, *Il Cardinale Egidio da Viterbo: Agostiniano, umanista e riformatore (1469-1532)* (Florence, 1929); John W. O'Malley, *Giles of Viterbo on Church and Reform* (Leiden, 1968); François Secret, "Egidio da Viterbo et quelques-uns de ses contemporains," *Augustiniana*, 16 (1966):371-85; F. X. Martin, "The Writings of Egidio da Viterbo," *Augustiniana*, 29 (1979):141-93; the anthologies *Egidio da Viterbo, O.S.A., e il suo tempo, Studia Augustiniana Historica*, 9 (Rome, 1938); and the issue of the periodical published by the Biblioteca Comunale di Viterbo dedicated to Egidio and his work, *Biblioteca e Societa*, 4.1-2 (30 June 1982).

[9]This is evident from the Augustinian's correspondence, esp. Rome, Biblioteca Angelica, Codd. Lat. 688, 1001; and Siena, Biblioteca Comunale degli Intronati, Cod. G.X.26.

[10]For Siena's location, see Bowsky, *A Medieval Italian Commune*, pp. 1-19 and 198-202. Egidio da Viterbo's connection with Lecceto is detailed in F. X. Martin, "Giles of Viterbo and the Monastery of Lecceto: the Makings of a Reformer," *Analecta Augustiniana*, 25 (1962):225-53.

[11]See below, n. 49.

[12]See, e.g., John W. O'Malley, "Fulfillment of the Christian Golden Age under Julius II: Text of a Discourse of Giles of Viterbo, 1507," *Traditio*, 25 (1969):265-38; Heinrich Pfeiffer, "Die Predigt des Egidio da Viterbo ueber das goldene Zeitalter und die Stanza della Segnatura," in *Festschrift Luitpold Dussler* (Munich and Berlin, 1972), pp. 237-54; F. X. Martin, "Egidio da Viterbo, Martin Luther, and Girolamo Seripando," *Biblioteca e Societa*, 4:1-2 (1982):5-9; and Charles Stinger, *The Renaissance in Rome* (Bloomington, 1985).

[13]Domenico Gnoli, "Secolo di Leon X?" in Gnoli, *La Roma di Leon X* (Milan, 1938), makes the important point that much of the intellectual ferment under the pontificate of Leo X was actually stimulated by Julius II. Egidio's expectations of Leo X are expressed in *Historia XX Saeculorum*, Rome, Biblioteca Angelica, Cod. Lat. 351, but this work conspicuously lacks the intellectual energy of the immediately previous *Sententiae ad mentem Platonis*. In general, Egidio's increasing preoccupation with the Hebrew lan-

guage after 1512 leads to a curious passivity in his thinking, which stance may also reflect the difference in personality between Julius and Leo. On this issue of intellectual passivity, see John D'Amico, *Renaissance Humanism in Papal Rome* (Baltimore, 1982), pp. 115-43. For the *Sententiae* and their date, see O'Malley, *Giles of Viterbo,* pp. 15-16; and Martin, "The Writings of Egidio da Viterbo," pp. 169-70.

[14]See I. D. Rowland, "A Summer Outing in 1510: Religion and Economics in the Papal War with Ferrara," *Viator,* 18 (1987):347-59.

[15]See O'Malley, "Fulfillment of the Christian Golden Age," pp. 269 and 277; and O'Malley, *Praise and Blame in Renaissance Rome: Rhetoric, Doctrine, and Reform in the Sacred Orators of the Papal Court, c. 1450-1521* (Durham, NC, 1979), pp. 27-28.

[16]"Maij vero die vigesima septima in qua festum pentecostes christiani celebrabant Iulius secundus pontificali in cappella expeditionem domitis iam Venetis in turchos fidei hostes pronuntiavit vexilla quoque plura et ad id issuerat parari quam plurima. Et preterea die et sequenti duabus his causis Roma urbs processione lustrata clericorum Egidius vero viterbiensis concionator insignis sermonem superendem expeditione quam vocat Cruciatam luculentem habuit" (Tizio, G.2.37, fol. 95^r).

[17]"Nec defuere qui dicerent pontificem hanc rem consulto tunc fecisse ut Maxmilianum Ludovicumque Francorum Regem quem multa victoria superbum et quem multa efflagitantem ab italie residuo et a se diverteret" (Tizio, G.2.37, fol. 95^r).

[18]For the War of the League of Cambrai, see Gilbert, *The Pope*; Ludwig Freiherr von Pastor, *History of the Popes*, trans. Frederick Ignatius Antrobus (London, 1950), vol. 6; Marin Sanuto, *I Diario di Marino Sanuto, 1496-1533,* ed. R. Fulin et al., 58 vols. (Venice, 1879-1903), vols. 7-16; and Francesco Guicciardini, *Storia d'Italia,* ed. A. Gherardi, 4 vols. (Florence, 1919), books 8-9.

[19]Discussions between the Venetian envoy Alvise Pisani and the pope about navigation rights in the Adriatic had not been fruitful: Pastor, 6: 309-12; Sanuto, vol. 8, cols. 6-26 (where he identifies the envoy as Zorzi Pisani), 383-93, 133-34 and 139-40; and Guicciardini, bk. 8.4 and 8.12.

[20]See e.g., Pastor, 6:322-32 and 653.

Egidio da Viterbo's Defense of Julius II

[21] The Genoese campaign is discussed in Tizio G.2.37, fols. 124^r, 125^r and 136^v-37^r; Guicciardini, bk. 9.6 and 9.9; Sanuto, vol. 20; and Pastor, 6:327-29.

[22] The letter, written 29 July 1510, is preserved in Siena, Biblioteca Comunale degli Intronati, Cod. G.10.26, fol. 173. Its implications are discussed in Rowland, "A Summer Outing."

[23] Luigi Frati, *Le due spedizioni militari di Giulio II tratti dal diario di Paride Grassi Bolognese* (Bologna, 1886), publishes extracts from the diary of Julius's master of ceremonies detailing the campaigns of 1506 and of 1510.

[24] "Quod me nunc angit est: quod in horas expecto in urbem revocari: iter iussus laboremque plenum periculo ibiturus" (Siena, Biblioteca Comunale degli Intronati, Cod. G.10.26, fol. 173^r).

[25] Biographical notes accompany a manuscript collection of some of Egidio's letters: "Die 8 Augusti. Nuntius ex urbe profectus incredibili celeritate Aegidium adit, litteras pontificis defert, quibus iubebat ut statim mutatis equis eodem die Romam veniret. Paret. Exponit pontifex genuense regentium non successisse, sperare tamen ut quidque succedat, se quumque senem et ardente Augusto, iturum in Flaminiam ad Ferrariae expugnationem. Interea nunciata victoria hispanorum in Africa capta Tripolitania urbe duce Pedro Navarro iubet Pontifex Aegidium ad S. Laurenti in Damaso postridie orationem haberi . . ." (Florence, Biblioteca Laurenziana, Cod. Ashburnhamensis 287, fol. 22^v). See also "Die 18 Aug. 1510 in Cyminiis cum ad populum diu orasset, deinde per quinque aut sex horas disputandi causa subsedisset in periculosissimam febrim incidit . . . " (Florence, Biblioteca Laurenziana, Cod. Ashburnhamensis 287, fol. 22^v). Further examples of Egidio's political preaching are collected by Clare O'Reilly, "'Maximus Caesar et Pontifex Maximum': Giles of Viterbo Proclaims the Alliance between Emperor Maxmilian I and Pope Julius II," *Augustiniana,* 22 (1972):80-117, esp. 82 and 95.

[26] See Rowland, "A Summer Outing."

[27] Tizio, G.2.37, fol. 26^v.

[28] For Chigi, see Gilbert, *The Pope*; I. D. Rowland, "Render Unto Caesar the Things which are Caesar's: Humanism and the Arts in the Patronage of Agostino Chigi," *Renaissance Quarterly,* 38 (1986):673-730; and Rowland, *The Correspondence of Agostino Chigi.*

[29] Gilbert, *The Pope,* pp. 70-85; Rowland, "Render Unto Caesar," pp. 676-80; and Rowland, *Correspondence of Agostino Chigi.*

[30] Rowland, "A Summer Outing."

[31] The Banco Chigi numbered over twenty thousand employees according to Agostino's own estimate; see Giuseppe Bugnoni, *Agostino Chigi il Magnifico* (Rome, 1878), p. 17 (a publication of the *Chisiae Familiae Commentarij* of Fabio Chigi, later Pope Alexander VII, Vat. Cod. Chigi a.1.1). Though context suggests that Agostino may have been exaggerating, a look at his bank records indicates an immense operation. Aside from the bank, Chigi maintained a private port and managed the alum mines of Tolfa with their two workers' settlements of Tolfa and Allumiere. Furthermore, Agostino's mercantile network stretched from London to Constantinople, and his count of employees explicitly includes *procuratores* or agents delegated to handle his business abroad. The number of the Augustinians is given in F. X. Martin, "Egidio da Viterbo, Martin Luther, and Girolamo Seripando," p. 7.

[32] Tizio, G.2.37, fol. 121^{r-v}.

[33] Frati, *Le due spedizioni*, p. 243; and Pastor, 6:331-56. Pastor's discussion refers to the most important contemporary sources preserving information about the Julian military campaigns; therefore subsequent notes point up only Tizio's own awareness of these events.

[34] Pastor, 6:331-56.

[35] Tizio, G.2.37, fols. 138^r-139^v.

[36] Tizio, G.2.37, fols. 138^r-139^v, esp. fol. 138^r: "huiusmodi enim homines . . . iulius fovebat, quamvis prius habuisse exosos."

[37] Pastor, 6:348-65.

[38] The factionalism of Siena was legendary, with its five conflicting *monti*: see Ann K. Chiancone Isaacs, "Popolo e monti nella Siena del primo cinquecento," *Rivista Storica Italiana*, 82.1 (1970):32-80; and the succinct analysis by P. Craveri in the *Dizionario Biografico degli Italiani*, s.v. "Bellanti, Leonardo."

[39] Tizio, G.2.37, fol. 141^r.

[40] This is the subject of Gilbert's study, *The Pope*.

[41] Archivio di Stato di Siena, Balìa 57, c. 30^r.

[42]Gilbert, *The Pope,* p. 94.

[43]Tizio, G.2.37, fol. 140^r.

[44]Tizio, G.2.37, fol. 142^r.

[45]Gilbert, *The Pope,* p. 94.

[46]"Iulius interea pontifex maximus forsitan pandulphi tergiversationibus tum obstinationibus florentinorum. Egidium viterbiensem ex divi augustini sectatoribus continatorem eximium . . . ad senenses direxit ut illos manuteret in fide ne deficerent et florentinos proposita religione premoneret" (Tizio, G.2.37, fol. 163^v).

[47]Pastor, 6:348-65.

[48]"Egidium viterbiensem ex divi augustini sectatoribus continatorem eximium qui Mariani Genazanensis ordinis eiusdem predicando imitator erat, cantilenis barba et gesticulationibus et popellum atque urbium ad se trahebat primores, atque demulcebat aures" (Tizio, G.2.37, fol. 163^v).

[49]The main text describes the sermon as "etsi longum, luculentem tamen," but the marginalium reports: "Verum ita longum ut universum populum tedio afficeret atque fastidio ex tam rugidantici psalmi repetitione dum inquit fecit lunam in tempore suo" (Tizio, G.2.36, fol. 370^v).

[50]"Predicatio Egidii delectabilis" (Tizio, G.2.37, fol. 163^v). The transcript extends from fol. 163^v to fol. 165^r.

[51]". . . cum Sene applicuisset [Egidius] decima novembris dies, in divi augustini templo sermonem ad populum habuit: convenerat enim multitudo ingens propositis autem arithmetice terminis quibusdam, tum circularis linee quam referebat in deum: brevi se expedivit predicatione populum vero alliciens die postera nunciaturum se magis ad senenses pertinentia est pollicitus" (Tizio G.2.37, fol. 163^v).

[52]Daniela Gionta, "'Augustinus dux meus': la teologia poetica 'ad mentem Platonis' di Egido da Viterbo, O.S.A.," *Atti del Congresso internazionale zu S. Agostino nel XVI centenario della conversione, Roma, 15-20 settembre 1986* (Rome, 1987), 3:189-201 dates the composition of the *Sententiae* from about 1507 to 1513, a slightly longer timespan than stated explicitly by O'Malley, *Giles of Viterbo,* pp. 15-16, though his loose *terminus ante quem*

of "at least 1512" easily accomodates Gionta's dating. Egidio's purpose in composing the massive treatise is made explicit: "haec contemplandi studio nobis solis scripsimus" (BAV, Cod. Vat. Lat. 6325, fol. 172ʳ).

[53] Egidio, unconcerned by debate about the authenticity of the *Seventh Letter*, cites it as readily as he does the genuine dialogues. The translation of *Seventh Letter* 342a-c and 343a is my own, taking "definition" to be the force of the infinitely flexible *logos,* the second step toward understanding. Egidio himself translates *logos* as *ratio*; see n. 54 below. Similarly, "roundel" and "ring" are used as one-word synonyms for "circle," though not literal translations of Plato's own choices--"rounded thing" is an awkward circumlocution in English as it is not in Greek, and Plato himself employs awkward circumlocutions.

[54] Egidio's translation of Platonic *logos* by *ratio* cannot be followed into English with the same facility; no one word conveys the wealth of nuances possessed by terms which denote a process of selective reasoning in accordance with a set of principles. In the context of Plato's *Letter* and Egidio's evocation of it, "definition" is the most useful English translation; Egidio himself substitutes the literal translation *ratio* with the specification *definitio*. The present translation therefore seems to repeat itself by defining "definition" as "definition"; in fact, Egidio's Latin is not repetitive at this point: "Si et simplicissimus est Deus, et plane unus, quomodo tam multa, et infinitus formarum, atque perfectionum numerus ei attribuentur? in quo ut Parmenides probat, nullus investiri potest numerus, et nulla multitudo. Dicenda tria sunt: primo quid sit ratio.... De primo, Pla[to] epistula septima, numerat quinque, nomen, rationem, simulacrum, sententiam, intellectum, et haec in eo doctrinae ordine, quae non per se vestigando: sed a preceptoribus docendo suscipitur: Primo enim nomen rei proponitur, qua de disserendi fuerit, ut cum dicitur circulus: Deinde est eius ratio, quae aliquid profecto non est, quam definitio, vel declamatio, vel similitudo, quam de eo nomine postea concipit intellectus, sive sit definitio rei sive nominis, sive simplex animi de circulo cogitatio: Simulacrum vocat Plato circulum in auro, vel in ligno, aut quamvis in materia ductum: Scientiam, sive opinionem quae de simulacro per cogitationem, quae non amplius a simulacro materiali, sed ab immateriali forma essentia, idea, in animam proficiscatur..." (BAV, Cod. Vat. Lat. 6325, fol. 16ʳ).

[55] BAV, Cod. Vat. Lat. 6325, fol. 49ʳ.

[56] "Ingenti hominum turbe" (Tizio, G.2.37, fol. 163ᵛ).

[57] O'Malley, *Praise and Blame,* pp. 36-70, emphasizes the differences be-

Egidio da Viterbo's Defense of Julius II

tween the preaching of Bernardino and Egidio Antonini in his acute discussion of "The New Rhetoric."

[58] This position has been strongly outlined by Michael Baxandall, *Painting and Experience in Fifteenth-Century Italy: a Primer in the Social History of a Pictorial Style* (Oxford, 1972).

[59] The gates of Siena and the attributes of the Virgin are enumerated in Bernardino's sermon in the Sienese Campo, 15 August 1427; the twelve prudences belong to the same series of sermons: "Impara queste duodice prudentie e pigliale a quattro a quattro" (Florence, Biblioteca Laurenziana, Cod. Ashburnhamensis 323, fol. 16ʳ).

[60] The ancient mnemonic techniques outlined by Frances Yates, *The Art of Memory* (London, 1966), are clearly involved in the didactic methods of Plato and of Egidio, both of whom come under Yates's brilliant scrutiny.

[61] O'Malley, *Praise and Blame*, pp. 36-70.

[62] See note 12 above.

[63] "Igitur die undecima cui iovis nomen inerat ingenti hominum turbe prestolanti dubium proposuit Utrum videlicet Sena urbs precipere valerat certior ve fieri a deo optimo maximoque diligi: quod autem eius rei certitudinem amoris habere valeret divi Augustini patris auctoritatem de libro trinitatis in medium adduxit: ubi inquit quod amorem quo fratrem prosequor meum magis certum apud me esse quam ipse frater meus quem diligo: Cum autem nullus valeat fratrem diligere nisi in gratia dei sit et adeo ipse diligatur, stante amoris erga proximum certitudine, certus quoque erga me dei amor esse convincitur sine quo non valeo proximum diligere: Verum Egidium in partem contrariam declinans Salomonis auctoritate nono capite ecclesiastici illam firmabat que huiusmodi est "Sunt visi atque sapientes et opera eorum in manu dei: et tamen nescit homo utrum amore an odio dignus sit:" Ad concordiam autem auctoritatis deducens inquit de amore habituali loqui Augustinum de actuali vero Salomonem: de quo primo suus fuerat propositus et/164r Habendus erat, conclusitque Senam urbem amoris divini certitudinem non habere actualem: hoc tamen experientia signis atque prodigiis seu miraculis illam valere comprehendere. . . . Mox ad vestustiora transiliens que capite geneseos secundo atque trigesimo describuntur in medium afferebat recensebatque angeli cum Iacob luctitationis historiam. ex qua Iacob nervus emarcuit et claudus effectus est: cum autem angelus dimicti efflagitaret a Iacob cum esset aurora, non facturum se nisi benediceretur patriarcha respondit cui benedicens

angelus mutato nomine Iacob Israhelem appellari decrevit: Iacob enim supplantator interpretabatur qui claudus veterem legem mancham et claudicantem representans significaverat Israhel autem videns deum legem novam que deum hominem factum oculis carneis conspexit: Cum vero duodecim filios genuisse Iacob a quibus duodecim tribus emanavere quibus singulis primissionis terre loca per Iosue divisa sunt. Cum igitur ipsi Iacobo dormitionis tempus imineret et geneseos capite nono et quadragesimo vocavit omnes filios ad se Dicitur enim in eodem capite Vocavit autem Iacob filios suis et ait Congregamini ut annuntiem que ventura sunt in novissimis diebus. Congre/164v gamini et audite filij Iacob id est filij veteris legis claude. Ibique subiungite audite Israhel patrem vestrum et audite novem legem que videre deus vobis dabit et in urbe Roma et in Italia sedem suam acceptura est novamque promissionis terram ut in Danielis vaticinio continetur es nobis traditura. Mox congregatis filijs incipiens Iacob benedicere ita loquebatur Ruben primogenitus meus et sequitur Prior in donis hec est felix campania que Rome vicine dona plurima consequuta est: Simeon et Levi fratres vasa iniquitatis vasa bellantia quia in furore suo occiderunt virum et in voluntate sua suffoderunt murum maledictus furor eorum quia pertinax et indignatio eorum quia dura in concilium eorum non veniat anima mea Ista est Bononia et Ferraria inobedientes ecclesie et pontifici voluntate pontificem occidentes cum Bentivlo contra illum ad portas usque cucurrerint: suntque vasa bellantia et receptacula bellorum contra romanam fidem suffoderunt murum id est arcem Bononie in concilium scismaticorum diverterent quibus cum Hippolitus Cardinalis Ferrariensis sentiebat Nam pontifices qui contra Iesum concilium inierunt erant de tribu Levi ut dici possunt Cardinales pharisei autem pro magna parte de tribu Simeonis ex Phariseis philosophie sunt Ferrarienses et Bononienses qui philosphie gimnasia habent. . ." (Tizio, G.2.37, fols. 163ᵛ-64ᵛ).

⁶⁴"Beniamin lupus rapax nam commedet predam et vespere dividet spolia. Hec est Sena vetus cuius insignia Lupa est et est lupus rapax commedens predam et spolia dividens hec verba interpretatus est Egidius: Nam cum in evangelio Christus diserit Regnum celorum iam patitur et violenti rapiunt illud, et pro Paulo apostolo huiusmodi verba accipiat ecclesia qui fuit ex tribu Beniamin rapuitque multas animas a demonum manibus. Itaque Senam urbem predixit esse facturum cum partes pontificis sequatur et ecclesie adoretque Iudam, ertique lupus ad rapiendum celum quod iam patitur et in his tribulationibus/ 165r salvabitur. Adens Beniamin dextere filium interpretati: Sena vero cum agro omni ad urbis Rome et ecclesie dexteram consistere. Vos inquit Senenses ad dexteram constituti estis perseverate ad dexteram et vos mea conservate, quam bene statis in presentia et salvabimini" (Tizio, G.2.37, fol. 165ʳ).

[65] "Visus itaque est Concionator iste de Senensibus una cum pontifice mictente diffidere: eius namque predicatio inconcinna non est visa nec a verbis veteris aliena: nam et Iudeis peritis qui iuxta nos aderant non displicuit: Egidius subinde Florentiam concessit" (Tizio, G.2.37, fol. 165^r). This glimpse of comfortable relations between Christians and Jews in Siena just before the Reformation and the Counter-Reformation is of particular interest.

Index

Admonitio generalis, 789
   religious reform 42-44
Aelfric
   and catechetical goal of
      preaching 61-70
   Ascension homilies and Enoch
      13-14, 17-19, 21-22
   catechetical intent in works
      other than Lenten homilies
      61-62, 64-65, 69
   Eynsham Customary 16-17
   Lenten homilies 13-14, 17-19,
      21-22, 61-63, 65-70
Alain of Lille
   definition of preaching 5
Alexander III
   inscribed Thomas Becket in
      catalogue of saints (1173) 78
Alphege, St. 85
Amalarius of Metz
   and *Liber officialis* 50
Ambrose
   and Bede's exegesis 34
Antichrist
   and Enoch and Elias 14-15,
      18, 20-22
Antonino of Florence 211,
   220-22
Arno of Salzburg
   and *Instructio pastoralis* 45
Artes praedicandi
   and Humbert of Romans's *De
      eruditione praedictorum* as 106

   and Llull's *Rethorica nova*
      119-37
   and thematic sermon structure 8-9
   content 8-9
   influence on exegetical prac-
      tice 9
   methods in Langton's sermons
      78, 83-84
   use and production in scholas-
      tic period 7-9
Ascension
   and Enoch 13-14, 17-22
   Hélinand's Sermon Fourteen
      98-99
   Hereford's sermon 177
   iconography 19-22
   Repyngdon's sermon 173-74
Audience
   experience of listeners and
      Bede 27-36
   in public squares for friars 6
   in Llull's *Rethorica nova* 121,
      124-25, 134-37
   lay persons 120-21, 135-37,
      211-26
   listener's preparation of heart
      94, 96-97, 99
   mixed--lay and ecclesiastic--
      for Langton's sermon 77
   mixed of Christians and Jews
      in Siena 235
   monastic, for Langton's ser-
      mons 77, 83

Index

of earlier medieval sermons 4, 44-46
Augustine of Hippo
   and Carolingian sermonaries 48
   and Llull's *Rethorica nova* 124, 129, 132-33
   De doctrina christiana and medieval preaching 8
   influence of catechizing interests 4, 64
   influence on Bede's style 35
   influence on earlier stage of medieval preaching 3
   recommendation for catechetical *narratio* and influence on the works of Aelfric 64-65, 67
   source for Hélinand 97
Augustinians 235-51
   See also Egidio of Viterbo.

Bede
   Gospel Homilies 27-28, 36
   and listener's experience, *see* Audience
   little reference to social reality 28
   on Enoch and Elias 15
   popularity and accessibility 28, 36
   stylistic figures 35-36
   typological exegesis 27-36
Bernard of Clairvaux
   and tradition of meditations on the life of Christ 149
Bernardino of Siena
   and comparison of vernacular and Latin texts 9, 215-16
   and Egidio of Viterbo 247-48
   preaching against vanity of women 211-26

Bible
   Bede's exegesis, *see* Bede
   Langton's biblical scholarship 76-80
   scholarship in later Middle Ages 169
   See also Elias, Enoch.
Birds
   images in Hélinand's sermons 94, 98-100, 102nn 9, 11, 103nn 12, 13
Bishops
   role in medieval preaching 5, 6, 212
Blickling Homilist
   and Ascension 20
   First Lenten Sunday homily compared to Aelfric's 68-70
Boncompagno
   and rhetoric 123
Boniface
   and sermon collection in *PL*, (Pseudo-Boniface) 48
   beginnings of religious reform in Frankish Kingdom 43
Bury St. Edmunds Psalter 19-20

Caesarius of Arles
   and Carolingian sermonaries 48
   and references to social reality in sermons 28
Canon law on "vanities" 219-22
Canterbury 75-83, 85-86
Capitularies
   issued to Charlemagne's *missi* 44
Carthusians
   Nicholas Hereford 178
   spirituality and *Vita Jesu Christi* of Ludolf of Saxony 148-50, 155-63

Index

Catechesis
  adapted for an urban environment 195-97
  and preaching in fifteenth-century Germany 186-87
  catechetical *narratio, see* Augustine of Hippo
  catechumenate of first six Christian centuries 61, 63-64, 66, 69
  preaching as religious education 43-46, 64, 71n 10
  state in tenth-century England 63-64
Centonization 35
Charlemagne
  Admonitio generalis 43-44
  religious reform and program for preaching 43-46
Chigi, Agostino 240-43, 250-51
Christ
  Lives of Christ 147-63
  Passion and Carthusian spirituality in *Vita Jesu Christi, see* Carthusians
  Passion and Franciscan spirituality in *Meditationes vitae Christi, see* Franciscan(s)
Christmas
  Bede's sermon 31-32, 34
  Langton's sermon in 1220 83-84
Church
  and State 76
  liberties, Becket defender of 76-78, 82, 86
Cistercians
  devotion to Mary 94-95
  Langton in exile at Pontigny (1207-13) 77

  writings
    exegesis 4
    poetic interpretation 4, 100
    preference for sapiential literature 4
    use of maternal imagery 93, 94, 101n 4, 102nn 8-10, 103n 13
Cluny
  displacement of preaching by other forms of liturgy 5
Concordia canonum
  and legislation on preaching 45
Councils
  Carolingian era reform councils and preaching 45-46
  Arles, Council of (813) 45
  Friuli (797) 45
    religious reform and relation to *Admonitio generalis* 45-46
  Lateran IV (1215)
    Langton's efforts to effect its reforms in England 77
  Riesbach (798)
    and religious reform 45
  Tours (813)
    and legislation on preaching 46
  Trent
    decree on preaching 6-7
Cynewulf
  and Ascension 18

Direct address
  in Bede's homilies 27, 29-30, 32
Distinctiones
  in later medieval literature 120
  in Llull's *Rethorica Nova* 119, 125-28, 130-34, 136-37
  in transitional sermon 5

Index

Dominicans
  Humbert of Romans 105-06, 108-11
    and Dominican preachers 105-06
  in later medieval preaching 212
  Johannes Herolt and practical theology in fifteenth-century Germany 185-87, 199

Easter
  sermon of Bede 29-30
Edmund the Martyr, St. 85, 92n 48
Egidio of Viterbo
  career and preaching 235-40, 243-51
Elias
  and Enoch 13-15, 17-20
Eligius
  sermon collection in *PL* (Pseudo-Eligius) 48
Enoch 13-15, 17-22
Erasmus
  admiration for Origen's style 11
  and *Ecclesiastes sive De arte concionandi* 11
Exegesis
  in later Middle Ages 10-11
  influence of thematic sermon and *artes praedicandi* 9
  typological and historical character of biblical texts 4
  typological in Bede's homilies, *see* Bede
  See also Elias, Enoch.
Exemplum
  collections in *Rethorica Nova* 122, 129-30, 134
  in Hélinand's sermons 93
  in Humbert of Romans's *De Eruditione Praedicatorum* 109-10
  in Langton's sermons 81, 83
  in popular preaching 9
Eynsham Customary, *see* Aelfric
Eyton, John
  career and sermons 169, 177-79

Figura
  in typological exegesis 29-30
Francis
  and itinerant preaching 6
  Rule and instruction to preachers 6-7
Franciscan(s)
  and preaching against vanity, *see* Bernardino of Siena
  order and preaching 5-7, 212, 223
  preachers
    Bernardino of Siena, *see* Bernardino of Siena
    Jacques Vitrier 11
  Rule of Francis and preaching 6-7
  sermon style and vernacular literature 120
  spirituality in *Meditationes Vitae Christi* 148-55, 158-63
Friars
  and itinerant preaching 6
  and urban ministry 6, 195-97, 235; *see also* Bernardino of Siena.
  enthusiasm for *vita apostolica* 6
  in later medieval preaching 10, 185-87, 199, 212, 223

Gervase of Chichester 85-86

Index

Gilbert of Hoyland 86
Gregorian Reform
  influence on preaching and sermon form 5
Gregory I, the Great
  and Carolingian Sermonaries 48
  and references to social reality in sermons 28
  catechetical *narratio* in Aelfric 65
  Forty Homilies on the Gospels and Carolingian preaching 48-49
  influence on earlier stage of medieval preaching 3
  Pastoral Rule and Carolingian preaching 44
  source for Aelfric 14, 17-19, 21, 65, 68-70

Haistulf of Mainz
  and homiliary written by Rabanus Maurus 48
Haymo of Auxerre
  catechetical *narratio* in Aelfric 65
Hélinand of Froidmont
  conversion 93-94
  devotion to Mary 93-95
  sermons 93-101
  style 93, 95, 100-01
  use of maternal imagery 93-101, 102nn 8-10
Henry II of England 78, 82, 86
Henry III of England 78, 82
Henry VIII of England
  destruction of Becket's shrine 86
Hereford, Nicholas
  career and sermons 169, 177-79
Hereford Troper 20

Herolt, Johannes
  life and works 185-87
  sermons and treatises compared 185-99
Holy Week
  homilies of Bede 32-34, 36
Homiliary
  of Rabanus Maurus 48
  of School of Auxerre 47
Homily
  admiration for in Renaissance 11
  at end of Middle Ages 10
  form described 3-4, 93, 100
  question of difference from sermon 47
Honorius III 78-79, 83
Hubert de Burgh
  attended translation of Becket's relics 79
Humbert of Romans
  and Llull's *Rethorica nova* 122, 133
  De eruditione praedicatorum 105-06, 110
  other works 105
  sermon text 111-14
  See also Dominicans.

Imagery
  and twelfth-century symbolism 100, 102nn 6, 8-11
  maternal
    in Hélinand, *see* Hélinand
    in other Cistercian writers, *see* Cistercians
  nature-based 98-101, 102-03n 11, 103n 12
Imagination
  and meditation in *Meditationes Vita Christi*, *see* Franciscan(s)

Index

Innocent III
  visit to Canterbury 78

Jesuits
  and "ministry of the Word of God" 4
John of England
  struggle with Langton 77-78
John of Garland
  on word-order and ornament 125
John XXII
  and decree *Cupientes* 219
Jubilee
  theme of Langton's sermons 80
Julius II 237-43, 250-51
Junius Manuscript 19

Kingship
  Carolingian concept 43

Lent
  Aelfric's Homilies, *see* Aelfric
  Bernardino of Siena's sermons against the vanity of women, *see* Bernardino of Siena
  Lenten preaching in the later Middle Ages 211-13
Leo the Great
  model for Renaissance preaching 11
Listener. *See* Audience
Lives of Christ, *see* Christ
Llull, Ramon
  and popular preaching 119-21, 135-37
  and scholastic culture 119-22, 124-27, 129, 132, 134, 136-37
  Great Universal Art of Finding Truth 119-24, 126, 131, 135-36
  Rethorica nova 119-37

Lothar of Segni, *see* Innocent III
Louis the Pious
  religious reform 43
Louis VII
  visit to Canterbury 78
Ludolf of Saxony
  and *Vita Christi*, *see* Carthusians

Martyrdom
  of Thomas Becket 75-86
Maximus of Turin
  and Carolingian sermonaries 48-49
Missi dominici
  and religious reform 44
Moralizing
  in Lenten sermons 211-13
  in popular spirituality and Llull's *Rethorica nova*, *see* Llull
Moses
  as type of Christ 14, 17-18
Motif
  altar-shaped manger 32
  banqueting house 84-85
  martyrdom 84

Old English Genesis 19
Origen
  homiletic style admired by Erasmus 11
Oxford
  and theological study in late fourteenth century 170, 178

Palm Sunday
  Aelfric's homilies 67
  Bede's homily 36
Paris
  Langton there as student and master 77, 80

266

Index

Passion
  in fourteenth-century Lives of Christ, *see* Christ
Paul
  and sermon material in Humbert of Romans 110-16
  model for friars 6
Paul the Deacon 14, 27
Paulinus of Aquilea
  presider at Council of Friuli 45
Penitence
  sermon theme 77, 80, 158, 162, 211-13
Peyraud, Guillaume
  as source for Philip Repyngdon 171-72
Pilgrimage
  to Canterbury 78, 86
Plato
  Seventh Letter and Egidio of Viterbo's preaching 245-47
Pontigny
  Langton in exile (1207-13) 77
Preacher
  conceiver and begetter of the word 96-97, 99, 102n 8
  four types according to Hélinand 96
  self-preparation 94-96, 99
  spiritual mother of the word 94-95, 99, 101-02n 4
Preaching
  aids
    De eruditione praedicatorum, *see* Humbert of Romans
    development 7
    distinctiones, *see* Distinctiones
  as religious education 43-46; *see also* Catechesis
  by women religious and lay persons in later Middle Ages 6
  definition by Alain of Lille 5
  duty of scholastic masters 7
  four types according to Hélinand 96
  in late fifteenth-century Italy 10-11
  in Reformation 11
  influence of classical rhetoric 10
  instruction for in Rule of St. Francis 6-7
  popular and penitential in later Middle Ages 9-10; *see also* Ramon Llull, Bernardino of Siena, Egidio of Viterbo
  popular characteristics in Llull's *Rethorica nova*, *see* Llull
  requirements for Carolingian clergy 46
  three styles at end of Middle Ages 10
Prone
  existence in Carolingian era unlikely 50

Rabanus Maurus
  homiliary for Haistulf of Mainz 48
  on Enoch and Elias 15
Repyngdon, Philip
  career and sermons 169-79
Rhetoric
  and *De doctrina christiana* 8
  and Llull's *Rethorica nova*, *see* Llull
  influence of classical rhetoric in fifteenth century 10
Richard of Dover
  Archbishop, death 78

Index

Richard the Lion Heart
  visit to Canterbury 78
Richard of Salisbury
  suffragan of Langton 79
Rogation
  thematic similarities with early English Lenten homilies 62, 65, 69

Sacraments
  and validity of in Repyngdon's sermons 172, 174-75
Sainthood
  as sermon theme 81
Saints
  feasts
    conversion of Paul, *see* Paul
    Mary 95, 102n 5
    See also Thomas Becket
Savonarola, Girolamo
  and burning of vanities 217-18
Scholasticism
  and *artes praedicandi*, *see* Artes praedicandi
  and preaching aids 7
  and Ramon Llull, *see* Llull
  duty of masters 7
Schools
  evidence of influence on sermon 93, 100, 103n 15
  influence on change in the sermon 5
  theology and sermons at Oxford, *see* Oxford
Sermon
  and references to social reality 28
  as literary form intended to be read 169, 175, 178
  catechetical purpose in Aelfric's homilies, *see* Aelfric
  catechetical role in Carolingian era 43-46
  detachment from Eucharistic setting by friars 6
  development of form 3-5, 8-10
  homily 3-4
  transitional phase 5, 93, 100
  thematic sermon and *artes praedicandi* 8-9
  distinction from homily 47
  form compared to tractatus 185, 197-99
  forms used by fourteenth-century English preachers 169, 171-72, 175, 178
  Hélinand's advice on delivery 96
  monastic use in night office 50
  part of the Mass in Carolingian era 49
  source for historians 53, 76
  vernacular in Carolingian era 51-52
Sermonaries
  use by Carolingians 48-49
Sermon studies
  methodology 1-2, 76, 169-71
Shaftesbury Psalter 20
Siena
  and Bernardino of, *see* Bernardino of Siena
  and Sigismondo Tizio, *see* Egidio of Viterbo
Sins
  nine accessary sins 185-99
Spiritual motherhood
  preacher and word, *see* Preacher
Sumptuary laws
  in fifteenth-century Italy 211, 222, 224-26

Index

Thema
  in *De eruditione praedicatorum* 109
Theme
  of ancient catechumenate in Aelfric's homilies, *see* Catechesis
  of Langton's sermons 77, 80, 83-84
Theodulph of Orléans
  and Carolingian themes 45
  and synod of 797 45
Thomas Becket
  fiftieth anniversary of martyrdom in 1220 75, 77-78, 82-86
  Langton's preaching on 75-86
  translation of relics in 1220 75, 77-82, 86
Tithes
  in Repyngdon's sermons 175
Tizio, Sigismondo
  and *Historia Senensium*, *see* Egidio of Viterbo
Typology 4
  in Aelfric's Palm Sunday homily (First Series) 67
  typological exegesis in Bede's homilies, *see* Bede

University
  and sermon form in scholastic period 9
  sermon form 9-10, 171-72
  theology and sermons of Oxford masters, *see* Oxford

Vergerio, Pier Paolo
  application of classical rhetoric to preaching 10-11
Veritas
  in typological exegesis 29

Vernacular
  comparison with existing Latin sermon text 9
  in later medieval preaching 9
  preaching in Germany 188
  preaching in Italy 212
  sermons in Carolingian era 51-52
  use in Aelfric's homilies 61, 63
Vita apostolica
  and friars 6
  influence on change in sermons at transitional period, 5
Vitrier, Jacques
  and Erasmus 11
Walter of Coventry 82, 83
Walter of Saint Victor
  on symbols 126
Woman
  vanity of dress denounced by Bernardino of Siena, *see* Bernardino of Siena
    Cupientes 219
    De ornatu mulierum 220-22
    medieval background 217
Word association
  in Llull's *Rethorica nova* 128, 133
  in transitional sermon 5
Word order
  in John of Garland, *see* John of Garland
  in Llull's *Rethorica nova*, *see* Llull
Wulfstan
  First Lenten Sunday sermon compared to Aelfric's 68, 70
Wycliffism
  and influence beyond the schools 169, 170
  ideas in sermons, *see* Eyton, Hereford, and Repyndon